JUDAISM
BELIEF & PRACTICE

JUDAISM
BELIEF & PRACTICE

AN INTRODUCTION TO THE JEWISH RELIGION, FAITH AND
TRADITIONS, INCLUDING 300 PAINTINGS AND PHOTOGRAPHS

PROFESSOR DAN COHN-SHERBOK

southwater

This edition is published by Southwater,
an imprint of Anness Publishing Ltd,
108 Great Russell Street,
London WC1B 3NA;
info@anness.com

www.southwaterbooks.com;
www.annesspublishing.com;
twitter: @Anness_Books

Anness Publishing has a new picture agency outlet for images
for publishing, promotions or advertising. Please visit our
website www.practicalpictures.com for more information.

© Anness Publishing Ltd 2016

A CIP catalogue record for this book
is available from the British Library.

Publisher: Joanna Lorenz
Senior Editor: Felicity Forster
Maps: Anthony Duke
Designer: Nigel Partridge
Production Controller: Pirong Wang

Previously published as part of a larger volume,
The Illustrated Guide to Judaism

PUBLISHER'S NOTE
Although the information in this book is believed to be accurate
and true at the time of going to press, neither the authors nor the
publisher can accept any legal responsibility or liability for any
errors or omissions that may have been made.

p1 Moses with the Ten Commandments *by Rembrandt, 1659.*
p2 Rabbi's Blessing *by Moritz Daniel Oppenheim, 1871.*
p3 Menorah window, Great Synagogue, Jerusalem, Israel.

CONTENTS

Below Seder plate with Passover foods.

Below Silver goblet used for Kiddush.

Below Jewish teacher and pupil, 1395.

Above A Theological Debate, *1888.*   *Above Writing a Torah scroll by hand.*   *Above Girls celebrating bat mitzvah.*

INTRODUCTION

FOR NEARLY 4,000 YEARS, JEWS HAVE WORSHIPPED THE GOD OF ISRAEL. DESPITE CENTURIES OF PERSECUTION AND EXILE, THEY HAVE REMAINED FAITHFUL TO THE TRADITION. TODAY, BOTH IN ISRAEL AND THE DIASPORA, JEWS CONTINUE TO CARRY ON THEIR ANCIENT HERITAGE. BUT WHO ARE THE JEWISH PEOPLE, WHAT DO THEY BELIEVE, AND WHAT DO THEY PRACTISE?

These are the central questions that this volume seeks to explore. Divided into two major parts – Belief and Practice – the book focuses on the nature of God, God and Israel, the spiritual path, the concept of the Messiah, the forms of Jewish worship, Jewish festivals, home ceremonies and life cycle events. Throughout, it draws heavily on images of the Jew as portrayed in the Western artistic tradition.

JEWISH BELIEF

In the first part of the book, the extensive outline of Jewish belief begins with a discussion of the primary religious doctrines of the faith. Each section highlights biblical teaching and traces its development

Below A rabbinical disputation about Jewish law; a 17th-century Dutch painting by Jacob Toorenvliet.

from rabbinic times to the present day. Following a survey of Jewish belief about God's unity, this part of the book examines traditional doctrines about the nature of God, including concepts such as divine transcendence, eternal existence, omnipotence, omniscience and divine goodness. Turning to a consideration of God's action in the world, the subsequent sections focus on subjects such as providence, revelation, Torah and mitzvot, and the promised land. There then follows an examination of ideas specifically connected with the Jewish spiritual path. Here, topics such as the Bible, Talmud, midrash, sin, repentance, forgiveness, and reward and punishment are examined in detail. The discussion concludes with sections exploring the nature of Jewish eschatology, including death and the afterlife.

Above A Jew wearing phylacteries and a prayer shawl, and holding a Torah. By Marc Chagall, c. 1930, a pioneer of modernism and leading Jewish artist.

JEWISH PRACTICE

The second part of the book opens with an outline of the Jewish calendar and Jewish worship embracing such institutions as the sanctuary, Temple and synagogue. This is followed by an examination of the major festivals in the yearly cycle, including Sabbath, Pilgrim Festivals, New Year, Day of Atonement, Days of Joy and Fast Days. The next sections discuss home ceremonies and personal piety, as well as major life cycle

Below A Sabbath Afternoon by Moritz Daniel Oppenheim, often regarded as the first Jewish artist of the modern era.

Above Jews praying at the Western Wall in Jerusalem. A 19th-century German painting by Gustav Bauernfeind.

events, from birth through circumcision to marriage, divorce, death and mourning. Throughout the book, readers are encouraged to engage with the material and to reflect on the issues that emerge.

MODERN JUDAISM

As this volume seeks to illustrate, in the past the Jewish community was united by belief and practice. Yet, all this has changed in the modern world. Prior to the Enlightenment in the 18th century, Jews did not have full citizenship rights of the countries in which they lived. Nevertheless, they were able to regulate the own affairs through an organized structure of self-government. Within such a context, Jewish law served as the basis of communal life, and rabbis were able to exert power and authority in the community.

However, as a result of political emancipation, Jews entered the mainstream of modern society, taking on all the responsibilities of citizenship. In the process, the rabbinical establishment lost its status and control, and the Jewish

legal system become voluntary. In addition, Jews took advantage of widening social advantages: they were free to choose where to live, whom to marry, and what career to follow. By gaining access to secular educational institutions, the influence of the surrounding culture also pervaded all aspects of Jewish life.

As a consequence of these changes, Jewry in modern times has become fragmented, secularized and assimilated. In addition, intermarriage is on the increase. Traditional Jewish belief and practice thus no longer have the same significance

they once had, and Jewish life has become essentially different from any time in the past. What is now needed is a fundamental shift in orientation: arguably, Jews today should be encouraged to find their own path through the Jewish heritage. Such an approach would be attuned to the realities of everyday Jewish existence in which Jews are free to choose those aspects of the tradition which they wish to observe.

Such a modernized vision of Judaism would celebrate the plurality of Jewish observance in the modern age. Respectful of the differences in the community, this concept of the Jewish faith – based on a recognition of the inevitable subjective quality of religious belief – would furnish an overarching ideological basis for Jewish life in a pluralistic age. As a remedy for the bitter divisions that beset the community today, such an approach to the Jewish heritage offers the hope of unity beyond diversity for the next millennium.

Below A boy reads the Torah during his bar mitzvah, a major life cycle event, with his rabbi and parents, at the Progressive Jewish community synagogue in Amsterdam.

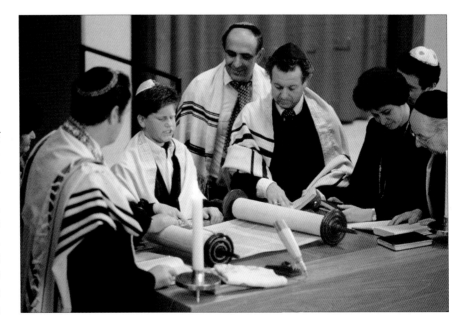

PART I

JEWISH BELIEF

The Jewish religion is grounded in belief about the nature of God and his relation to the world. The God of the Jewish people has no beginning nor end; he is the eternal deity who lives forever. In this respect there is an unbridgeable gap between God and humanity: God outlasts all that he has created and continues eternally. He does not dwell in time – time itself is part of creation. Consequently God is in the Eternal Now.

According to tradition, the Bible traces God's providential care for his chosen people from their origins in the 2nd millennium BCE through the Second Temple period. For the Jews, Scripture serves as the foundation of the faith. Later rabbinic sources amplify biblical doctrines about creation, revelation, Torah and mitzvah, sin and repentance, the Promised Land, the Messiah and the afterlife.

Despite the diversity of a multitude of Jewish movements in the contemporary world, Jews today can continue to look back to their sources for an understanding of God's nature and the spiritual life.

Opposite: A 12th-century Spanish illustration of the Temple of Solomon showing the menorah, the Ark of the Covenant and other traditional symbols.

Above Jew praying at the Western Wall in Jerusalem, the only structure still standing from the Temple Mount destroyed by the Romans in 70CE.

CHAPTER 1

GOD

According to the Bible, the struggle against Canaanite belief and practice was a constant concern. Later in the rabbinic period, scholars cautioned against worshipping two gods in heaven. Worship of one God was of paramount importance. With the rise of Christianity, Jews were admonished to remain faithful to monotheism, and Jewish theologians insisted on God's unity. For the Jewish people, God is both imminent and transcendent. He created the universe, yet is in no sense remote from his creation. In the rabbinic period, Jewish sages formulated the concept of the *Shekhinah* to denote God's abiding presence. It is the Shekhinah that serves as an intermediary between God and human beings.

For God there is no past, present, nor future. In rabbinic literature, the word *emet*, or truth, one of the names of God, is interpreted as having the first, middle and final letters of the Hebrew alphabet. According to Jewish thinkers, God is both omnipotent and omniscient. His power is unlimited as is his knowledge. Past, present and future lie unrolled before his eyes, and nothing is hidden from him. It is he who has created all things in his infinite goodness. From him benevolence and compassion flow as a mighty stream.

Opposite Abraham smashing idols. From the Leipnik Haggadah (1740) by Joseph of Leipnik, the most influential scribe of the Hamburg-Altona school of Hebrew illuminated manuscripts.

Above The Creation of Adam, in the Sistine Chapel, Rome, is one of the most famous paintings by the 16th-century artist Michelangelo.

THE GOD OF THE JEWS

THE STORY OF THE JEWISH PEOPLE BEGAN IN MESOPOTAMIA. IT WAS
HERE THAT SUCCESSIVE EMPIRES ROSE AND FELL BEFORE THE JEWS
EMERGED AS A SEPARATE PEOPLE, BELIEVING IN ONE INVISIBLE GOD.

According to the Bible, Abraham was the father of the Jewish nation. Living in Ur of the Chaldeans, a Sumerian city near the head of the Persian Gulf, he was called by God to go to Canaan. As Genesis 12:1–2 records, God proclaimed: 'Go from your country and your kindred and your father's house to the land I will show you. And I will make of you a great nation.'

ANCIENT MESOPOTAMIAN RELIGION

The rise of ancient Mesopotamian civilization occurred at the end of the 4th century BCE in southern Mesopotamia, where the Sumerians created city states, each with its local

Right A vision of the prophet Jeremiah showing Greek fire, an incendiary weapon, being poured over Jerusalem. From the 12th-century Souvigny Bible.

gods. During the 3rd millennium BCE, waves of Semitic peoples settled amid the Sumerians, adopting their writing and culture. These Semites identified some of their gods with the Sumerian ones. In their view, life was under the control of the gods. To obtain happiness, it was essential to keep them in a good humour through worship and sacrifice – yet the gods were unpredictable. It was here in the 2nd century BCE that God called the Jewish nation to be his chosen people.

EARLY MONOTHEISM

According to some scholars, the origins of Israelite monotheism stemmed from Abraham's disillusionment with Mesopotamian religion. These scholars attribute this radical break to Abraham's discovery that the concept of universal justice must rest on the belief in one supreme God. Other scholars see Moses as the principal architect of Israelite monotheism. Such scholars point out that before Moses there was evidence of monotheistic belief in the religious reforms of the Egyptian Pharaoh Akhenaton in the 14th century BCE. In this light, Moses is seen as following the path of this Egyptian revolutionary figure.

MONOLATRY

There are other scholars, however, who contend that it is unlikely that monotheism can be attributed to Abraham or Moses. Such a view, they believe, conflicts with the biblical narratives of the tribal and monarchial periods that give evidence of a struggle on the part of some Israelites to remain faithful to God in the face of competing deities. For these writers, monotheism

Left Daily life in Mesopotamia, showing weaving and farming, from a wall painting in the Museum of the Jewish Diaspora in Tel Aviv, Israel.

Above The Hospitality of Abraham. *A Russian icon by Andrei Rublev, painted around 1410.*

THE PSALMIST

According to some scholars, Psalm 82 gives evidence of the transition from monolatry to monotheism: in it God rebukes the other gods for their injustice and deprives them of divine status and immortality:

God has taken his place in the
  divine council;
In the midst of the gods he holds
  judgement;
How long will you judge unjustly,
and show partiality to the wicked?
  Selah.
Give justice to the weak and the
  fatherless;

maintain the right of the afflicted
  and the destitute.
Rescue the weak and the needy;
deliver them from the hand of the
  wicked –
They have neither knowledge, nor
  understanding,
they walk about in darkness;
all the foundations of the earth are
  shaken –
I say, 'You are gods,
sons of the Most High, all of you;
nevertheless you shall die like men,
and fall like any prince.'
Arise, O God, judge the earth,
for to thee belong all the nations!

should be understood as the result of a clash of cults and religious concepts over the centuries.

According to this latter view, ancient Israelite religion was not monotheism but monolatry: the worship of one God despite the admitted existence of other gods. Arguably, this may have been the meaning of Deuteronomy 6:4: 'Hear, O Israel: the Lord our God is one

Below The Sacrifice of Isaac, *a 6th-century floor mosaic from the Bet Alpha synagogue, Israel.*

Lord.' With this view, the God of Israel was understood as the Divine Being who revealed his will to Israel, inspired its leaders, protected the Israelites in their wanderings, and led them to the Promised Land. The worship of any other deity was, according to Exodus 20:3, betrayal and blasphemy: 'You shall have no other gods before me.'

The God of Israel was not like any other gods of Mesopotamia, Egypt or Canaan, and it was forbidden to make an image of him. It was this God, not the Canaanite El, who was the creator of heaven and earth; he, not Baal, was the source of rain and agricultural fertility; it was through his action, rather than that of any of the gods of Mesopotamia, that the Assyrian and Babylonian conquest took place.

Monotheism is thus understood as a later development in the history of Israel; it took place when foreign gods were seen as simply the work of human hands. Possibly this was the view of Elijah in the 9th century BCE when, confronting the prophets of Baal, he declared: 'The Lord He is God; the Lord He is God' (1 Kings 18:39). But certainly by the time of Jeremiah (several decades before the

Babylonian exile in the 6th century BCE), monotheism appears to have taken a firm hold on the Israelite community. In the words of Jeremiah: 'Their idols are like scarecrows, in a cucumber field, and they cannot speak; they have to be carried for they cannot walk. Be not afraid of them, for they cannot do evil, neither is it in them to do good' (Jeremiah 10:5).

Below The Assyrian goddess of abundance, a stylised marble idol dating from around 1950–1700BCE.

UNITY OF GOD

THE MOST UNCOMPROMISING EXPRESSION OF GOD'S UNITY IS THE PRAYER IN DEUTERONOMY: 'HEAR, O ISRAEL, THE LORD OUR GOD IS ONE LORD.' THIS BELIEF HAS SERVED AS THE FOUNDATION OF THE FAITH.

THE REJECTION OF DUALISM

According to Scripture, the universe owes its existence to the one God, the creator of heaven and earth, and since all human beings are created in his image, all men and women are brothers and sisters. Thus the belief in one God implies that there is one humanity and one world.

At the heart of Jewish biblical teaching is an emphasis that God alone is to be worshipped. As the prophet Isaiah declared:

I am the Lord, and there is no other,
besides me there is no God; ...
I form light and create darkness,
I make weal and create woe,
I am the Lord,
   who do all these things.
   (Isaiah 45:5,7)

Within the Bible, the struggle against polytheism became a dominant motif, continuing into the rabbinic period. Combating the dualistic doctrine that there are two gods in heaven, the rabbis commented on Deuteronomy 32:39 ('See now that I, even I, am he, and there is no god beside me'): 'If anyone says that there are two powers in heaven, the retort is given to him: "There is no god with me".'

In a passage in the *Mekhilta* (midrash on Exodus), the dualistic doctrine is rejected since when God said, 'I am the Lord your God' (Exodus 20:2) no one protested. Again the Mishnah states that if a person says in his prayers, 'We acknowledge Thee, we acknowledge Thee', implying belief in two gods, he is to be silenced.

Above William Blake's vision of God writing on the Tablets of the Covenant, the laws given to Moses on Mt Sinai. For Jews, God is transcendent, yet directly involved in their history.

JUDAISM AND CHRISTIANITY

In the early rabbinic period Jewish sages were troubled by the Christian doctrine of the incarnation, which they viewed as dualistic in character. In 3rd-century CE Caesarea, for example, Abahu commented on the verse: 'God is not man, that he should lie, or a son of man, that he should repent. Has he said, and will he not do it? Or has he spoken, and will he not fulfil it?' (Numbers 23:19). According to Abahu, the last part of this verse refers to man rather than God. Thus he declared: 'If a man says to you, "I am a god", he is lying; "I am the Son of Man", he will not end by being sorry for it; "I am going up to heaven", he will not fulfil what he has said.'

In the Middle Ages the Christian doctrine of the Trinity was frequently attacked by Jewish scholars since it appeared to undermine pure monotheism. In contrast to Christian exegetes who interpreted the Shema with its three references to God as denoting the Trinity, Jewish scholars maintained that the Shema implies that there is only one God, rather

THE KABBALAH

In the Middle Ages. Kabbalistic belief in divine unity was also of major importance. The early Kabbalists of Provence and Spain referred to the Divine Infinite as En Sof – the absolute perfection in which there is no distinction or plurality. The En Sof does not reveal itself; it is beyond all thought. In Kabbalistic thought, creation is bound up with the manifestation of the hidden God and his outward movement. According to the Zohar, a mystical work of the time, the *sefirot*, or 'divine emanations', come successively from above to below, each one revealing a stage in the process. The ten sefirot together demonstrate how an infinite, undivided and unknowable God is the cause of all the modes of existence in the finite plane.

Left A 17th-century Greek codex showing the Moon surrounded by Kabbalistic symbols.

***Above** Torah scroll from the 16th-century Ha'ari synagogue in Safed, Israel, one of the homes of Kabbalah.*

than Three Persons of the Godhead. For medieval Jewish theology, the belief in divine unity was a fundamental principle of Judaism. For a number of Jewish theologians the concept of God's unity implies that there can be no multiplicity in his being. Thus the 12th-century philosopher Moses Maimonides argued in *The Guide for the Perplexed* that no positive attributes can be predicated of God since the divine is an absolute unity. The only true attributes are negative ones; they lead to a knowledge of God because in negation no plurality is involved.

LURIANIC KABBALAH

The elaboration of early mystical ideas took place in the 16th century through the teachings of Isaac Luria. Of primary importance in the Lurianic system is the mystery of creation. In the literature of early Kabbalists, creation was understood as a positive act; the will to create

***Right** Prayer at the tomb in Meron, Israel, of Rabbi Simeon ben Yohai, traditionally the author of the Zohar, the most important medieval text of Kabbalistic Judaism.*

was awakened within the Godhead and this resulted in a long process of emanation. For Luria, however, creation was a negative event: the En Sof had to bring into being an empty space in which creation could occur since divine light was everywhere, leaving no room for creation to take place. This was accomplished by the process of *zimzum* – the contraction of the Godhead into itself.

After this act of withdrawal a line of light flowed from the Godhead into empty space and took on the shape of the sefirot in the form of Adam Kadmon (primeval man). In this process divine lights created the vessels – the external shapes of the sefirot – which gave specific characteristics to each emanation. Yet these vessels were not strong enough to contain such pure light and they shattered. This breaking of the vessels brought disaster and upheaval to the emerging emanations: the lower vessels broke down and fell, the three highest emanations were damaged and the empty space was divided

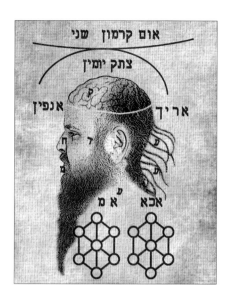

***Above** In Kabbalah, the term Adam Kadmon means Primeval Man. Copy of an illustration from* Kabbala Denudata *(1684) by Knorr von Rosenroth.*

into two parts. Despite the complexity of this Kabbalistic theory of creation, Jewish mystics affirmed their belief in the unity of the Godhead. The sefirot were ten in number, yet God himself is one.

TRANSCENDENCE AND IMMANENCE

ACCORDING TO TRADITIONAL JUDAISM, GOD TRANSCENDS THE UNI-
VERSE YET IS MANIFEST IN HIS CREATION. THROUGHOUT SCRIPTURE
GOD IS DEPICTED AS ACTIVE IN HUMAN HISTORY.

Transcendence is the concept of being entirely beyond the universe. For Jews, God is conceived as the transcendent creator of the universe. It is he who created the heavens and the earth; he reigns supreme over all creation. Yet, he does not remain remote from the cosmos. Repeatedly he is described as actively involved in the natural world and human affairs.

DIVINE TRANSCENDENCE
Throughout Scripture the theme of transcendence is repeatedly affirmed. Thus the prophet Isaiah proclaimed:

Have you not known?
Have you not heard?
Has it not been told you
   from the beginning?
Have you not understood from
   the foundations of the earth?
It is he who sits above the circle
   of the earth,

and its inhabitants are like
   grasshoppers;
who stretches out the heavens
   like a curtain
and spreads them like a tent
   to dwell in.
   (Isaiah 40:21–22)

Later in the same book, Isaiah declared that God is beyond human understanding:

For my thoughts are not
   your thoughts
neither are your ways my ways,
   says the Lord.
For as the heavens are higher than
   the earth,
so are my ways higher than
   your ways
and my thoughts than
   your thought.s
   (Isaiah 55:8–9)

In the Book of Job the same idea is repeated – God's purposes transcend human understanding:

Can you find out the deep things
   of God?
Can you find out the limit of the
   Almighty?
It is higher than heaven – what
   can you do?
Deeper than Sheol – what can
   you know?
Its measure is longer than the earth,
and broader than the sea.
   (Job 11:7–9)

Left A 12th-century miniature of the prophet Job afflicted by boils. The book of Job considers the dual themes of God's justice and human suffering.

Above North and South America from space. For Jews, God is seen as the transcendent creator of the universe.

IMMANENCE
Despite this view of God's remoteness from his creation, he is also viewed as actively involved in the created order. In the Bible his omnipresence is continually stressed.

Whither shall I go from thy Spirit?
Or whither shall I flee from thy
   presence?
If I ascend to heaven, thou art there!
If I take the wings of the morning
and dwell in the uttermost parts of
   the sea,
even there thy hand shall lead me.
   (Psalm 139:7–12)

In the rabbinic period, Jewish scholars formulated the doctrine of the *Shekhinah*, or 'divine presence', to denote God's presence in the world. The Shekhinah is compared to light. Thus the midrash paraphrases Numbers 6:25 ('The Lord make his face to shine upon you, and be gracious to you'): 'May He give thee of the light of the Shekhinah'. In another midrash, the 'shining' of the Shekhinah in the Tent of Meeting is compared to a cave by the sea. When the sea rushes in to fill the cave, it suffers no diminution of its waters. Likewise, the divine presence filled the Tent of Meeting, but simultaneously filled the world.

In the Middle Ages, the doctrine of the Shekhinah was further elaborated by Jewish scholars. According to the Jewish philosopher Saadia Gaon (9th to 10th century), the Shekhinah is identical with the glory of God, which serves as an intermediary between God and man during the prophetic encounter. For Saadia the 'Glory of God' is a biblical term whereas the Shekhinah is a rabbinic concept that refers to the created splendour of light that acts as an intermediary between God and human beings. At times this manifestation takes on human form. Thus when Moses asked to see God's glory, he was shown the Shekhinah. Similarly when the prophets in their vision saw God in human form, what they actually perceived was the Shekhinah.

In his *Guide for the Perplexed*, the 12th-century philosopher Moses Maimonides embraced Saadia's belief that the Shekhinah is a created light, identified with glory. In addition, he associated the Shekhinah with prophecy. According to Maimonides, prophecy is an overflow from God, which passes through the mediation of the active intellect and then to the faculty of imagination. It requires perfection in theoretical wisdom, morality and development of the imagination. On the basis of this conception, Maimonides asserted that human beings can be divided

Below The tide turns, and the sea floods into the cave. God is seen as actively present in his creation.

Above A vision of glory. Moses before the Burning Bush by Dieric Bouls the Elder, c. 1465–70. According to Scripture, God was present in the Burning Bush.

into three classes according to the development of their reasoning capabilities. First there are those whose rational faculties are highly developed and receive influences from the active intellect, but whose imagination is defective – these are wise men and philosophers. The second group consists of those where the imagination alone is in good condition, but the intellect is defective – these are statesmen, lawgivers and politicians. Thirdly there are prophets – those whose imagination is consistently perfect and whose active intellect is all developed.

In Kabbalistic teaching, the Shekhinah also played an important role. In early Kabbalistic thought it is identified as the feminine principle in the world of the *sefirot*, or 'divine emanations'. Later the Shekhinah was understood as the last in the hierarchy of the sefirot, representing the feminine principle. Like the moon, this sefirah has no light of her own, but instead receives the divine light from the other sefirot. As the divine power closest to the created world, she is the medium through which the divine light passes. Further, in Kabbalistic thought the Shekhinah is the divine principle of the Jewish people. Everything that happens to Israel is reflected upon the Shekhinah, which grows stronger or is weakened with every meritorious or sinful act of each Jew and of the people as a whole. Finally, the Shekhinah is viewed as the goal of the mystic who attempts to achieve communion with the divine powers.

ETERNITY

THROUGHOUT SCRIPTURE, GOD IS DESCRIBED AS HAVING NEITHER BEGINNING NOR END. UNLIKE THE REST OF CREATION, WHICH MAY SEE ETERNITY AS ENDLESS TIME, HE WAS, IS AND FOREVER WILL BE.

Many people have tried to define the concept of God and eternity. As the Psalmist declared:

Before the mountains were
  brought forth,
or ever thou hadst formed the
  earth and the world,
from everlasting to everlasting
  thou art God.
  (Psalm 90:2)

ETERNAL EXISTENCE
In the Bible the term *olam* is most frequently used to denote the concept of God's eternity. In Genesis 21:33 he is described as the Eternal God; he lives for ever (Deuteronomy 32:40), and reigns for ever (Exodus 15:18; Psalm 10:16). He is the living God and everlasting King (Jeremiah

Below Moses and Aaron show God's power before Pharaoh by James Tissot. For Jews, God is present in history, having neither beginning nor end.

10:10); his counsel endures for ever (Psalm 33:11), as does his mercy (Psalm 106:1). For the biblical writers, God's eternal existence is different from the rest of creation – he exists permanently without beginning or end.

THE RABBIS
This biblical teaching was elaborated by the rabbis. According to the Talmud, there is an unbridgeable gap between God and human beings. In midrashic literature God's eternal reign is similarly affirmed. Thus, according to a midrash, when Pharaoh was ordered by Moses and Aaron in the name of God to let the people go, Pharaoh declared that God's name is not found in his list of gods. In reply Moses and Aaron declared: 'O fool! The dead can be sought among the living but how can the living be sought among the dead. Our God lives, but those you mention are dead. Our God is "the

Above Some Jewish theologians think that God is outside time altogether in the way that sand dunes appear to stretch on for ever.

living God, and everlasting King"' (Jeremiah 10:10). In response Pharaoh asked whether this God is young or old, how old he is, how many cities he has conquered, how many provinces he has subdued, and how long he has been king. In reply they proclaimed: 'The power and might of our God fill the world. He was before the world was created and he will be when all the world comes to an end and he has created thee and gave thee the spirit of life.'

THEOLOGICAL SPECULATION
Although the rabbis were convinced that God would endure for ever, they discouraged speculation about the nature of eternity. Such reluctance is reflected in the Mishnah's dictum: 'Whoever reflects on four things, it were better for him that he had not come into the world: What is above? What is beneath? What is before? What is after?'

In the Middle Ages, Jewish theologians debated this issue. In the *Guide for the Perplexed*, the 12th-century Jewish philosopher Moses Maimonides argued that time itself was part of creation. Therefore, when God is described as existing before the creation of the universe, the notion of time should not be understood in its normal sense.

Above Maimonides argued that time was part of creation in his Guide for the Perplexed, *shown here in a 14th-century Italian illumination.*

This concept of time as part of creation was later developed by the 15th-century Jewish philosopher Joseph Albo. In his *Ikkarim* he maintained that the concepts of priority and perpetuity can only be applied to God in a negative sense. That is, when God is described as being 'before' or 'after' some period, this only means he was not non-existent before or after that time. However, these terms indicating a time span cannot be applied to God himself. Following Maimonides, Albo asserted that there are two types of time: measured time, which depends on motion, and time in the abstract. This second type of time has no origin – this is the infinite space of time before the universe was created.

ETERNAL NOW

According to other Jewish thinkers, God is outside time altogether – he is in the 'Eternal Now'. Thus the 13th-century theologian Bahya ibn Asher ibn Halawa, in his commentary on the Pentateuch, discussed the verse, 'The Lord will reign for ever and ever' (Exodus 15:18): 'All times, past and future, are in present so far as God is concerned, for he was before time and is not encompassed by it.' In the same way, the 16th-century scholar Moses Almosnino commented on the statement 'For now I know' (Genesis 22:12). According to Almosnino, God is in the 'Eternal Now', and he uses this notion to explain how God's foreknowledge is not incompatible with human free will.

According to these writers, God is outside time – he does not live in the present, have a past, or look forward to the future. On this view, God is experiencing every moment in the past and future history of the created world simultaneously and eternally. What for us are fleeting moments rushing by, bringing one experience after another, are for God a huge static tapestry, of which he sees every part continually. This conception of God's eternity – that he is outside time – and the alternative view that God exists in infinite duration before creation constitute the two central Jewish interpretations of the deity's relation to time. Yet for most Jews God's eternal existence is an impenetrable mystery.

None the less, the doctrine of God's eternity is a major feature of the Jewish faith. Through the centuries, Jews have been convinced that God was, is, and forever will be. Hence in Maimonides' formulation of the 13 central principles of the Jewish faith, the belief that God is eternal is the fourth tenet. In the Ani Maaimin prayer this principle is formulated as follows: 'I believe with perfect faith that the Creator, blessed be his name, is the first and the last.' And at the conclusion of synagogue services in all branches of Judaism, the faithful voice their commitment that God is eternal in time in the Adon Olam prayer:

He is the Lord of the universe,
Who reigned ere any creature yet
  was formed,
At the time when all things
  shall have had an end,
He alone, the dreaded one,
  shall reign:
Who was, who is, and who will
  be in glory.

Below Rain over the Golan Heights in Israel. Jewish thought suggests God sees every part of time continually – the time before, after and during the rain.

OMNIPOTENCE

AS LORD OF THE UNIVERSE, GOD IS CAPABLE OF ALL ACTIONS. IN GUIDING HIS CHOSEN PEOPLE, HE BROUGHT ABOUT THEIR DELIVERANCE AND REDEMPTION AND GUIDES THEM TO THEIR ULTIMATE DESTINY.

Above The prophet Elijah wrote that God's true spirit was not in the heart of the storm but in the still small voice. For Jews, God is the cause of all things.

From biblical times, the belief in God's omnipotence, that God is all powerful, has been a central doctrine.

GOD IN SCRIPTURE

According to the Book of Genesis, when Sarah expressed astonishment at the suggestion that she should have a child at the age of 90, she was criticized: 'The Lord said to Abraham, "Why did Sarah laugh, and say 'Shall I indeed bear a child now that I am old?' Is anything too hard for the Lord?"' Again, in the Book of Jeremiah, when the city was threatened by invaders, God declared: 'Behold I am the Lord the God of all flesh: is anything too hard for me?' (Jeremiah 32:27). Given such a view, there is nothing God cannot do. What appears impossible is within his power.

IMPOSSIBLE ACTIONS

Despite the conviction that God can do anything, in the Middle Ages Jewish theologians wrestled with the philosophical problems connected with this belief. Pre-eminent among their concerns was the question whether God could do absolutely everything. The 10th-century Jewish philosopher Saadia Gaon, for example, in his *Book of Beliefs and Opinions*, stated that the soul will not praise God for causing five to be more than ten without further addition, nor for being able to put the world through the hollow of a signet ring without making the world narrower and the ring wider, nor for bringing back the day that has passed in its original state. These, he argued, are absurd acts.

Later, the 15th-century Jewish philosopher Joseph Albo explored the same issue. In his opinion, there are two kinds of impossibility.

Some things are intrinsically impossible so that even God cannot make them possible. For example, we cannot imagine that God can make a part equal to the whole, a diagonal of a square equal to one of its sides, nor the angle of a triangle equal to more than two right angles. Further, it is impossible for God to make two contradictory propositions true at the same time, or the affirmative and negative true simultaneously. Likewise, it is impossible to believe that God could create another being like himself. In all these cases, the human intellect cannot conceive of such a state of affairs.

The other kind of impossibility is that which contradicts the law of nature, such as the resurrection of the dead. In such instances, it is possible to imagine such an occurrence. Thus Albo argued, God can bring about such events since they are not

Left The complex geometrical puzzles of 20th-century artist M.C. Escher reflect the complexity of the belief that God can do anything.

inherently impossible. Hence logical impossibilities are impossible for God, but not physical impossibilities.

LOGICAL IMPOSSIBILITIES

The 12th-century Jewish philosopher Maimonides argued along similar lines in his *Guide for the Perplexed*. There he explored the notion of God's omnipotence. In Maimonides' view, although God is all-powerful, there are certain actions that he cannot perform because they are logically impossible. That which is impossible, he wrote, has a permanent and constant property which is

Below Nothing is impossible with God. Sarah, Abraham's ageing wife, hears that she is to bear a son, and laughs. Painting by French artist James Tissot.

Above As the wave breaks on the shore and withdraws, so God allows humans space for the exercise of personal freedom.

not the result of some agent. It cannot in any way change, and thus it is a mistake to ascribe to God the power of doing what is impossible. It is impossible, he went on, for God to produce a square with a diagonal equal to one of its sides, or a solid angle that includes four right angles. Thus Maimonides concluded: 'We have thus shown that according to each one of the different theories there are things which are impossible, whose existence cannot be admitted, and whose creation is excluded from the power of God.'

THE HOLOCAUST

In addressing the religious perplexities connected with the Holocaust, a number of modern writers have advanced the concept of a limited God. In the view of these writers, God intentionally limited himself when he bestowed free will on human beings. Thus, the Orthodox rabbi and Jewish theologian Eliezer Berkovits (1908–92) argued in *Faith After the Holocaust* that if God did not respect human freedom, morality would be abolished and men and women would cease to be fully human. God, he

Right Jewish thought rules that God is all-powerful. The Creation of Adam by Michelangelo in the Sistine Chapel in Rome represents this idea.

insisted, did not intervene to save the Jewish nation because he had bestowed human free will on humanity at the time of creation.

In *God and Evil*, the Orthodox scholar David Birnbaum similarly argued that human beings must accept that God is 'Holy Potential', allowing through the process of divine contraction space for the exercise of personal freedom. In Birnbaum's view, men and women are able to attain spiritual maturity in the exercise of liberty, and thereby attain their fullest possible potential. This view serves as the basis for reconciling the tragedy of the Holocaust with the traditional understanding of God's nature.

RADICAL THEOLOGY

A more radical approach was adopted by the Reform rabbi Steven Jacobs in *Rethinking Jewish Faith*. Here he argued that the concept of God in the Bible and rabbinic Judaism must be reformulated in the post-Holocaust world. What is now needed, he wrote, is a notion of a deity compatible with the reality of radical evil at work and at play in our world. To continue to affirm the historically traditional notions of faith in God as omnipotent is a theological error. Similarly the feminist

Above Jewish quarter, Barcelona, Spain. Birthplace of Hasdai Crescas, author of Or Adonai, The Light of the Lord, *in which he wrestles with a range of theological issues.*

Jewish theologian Melissa Raphael argued in *When God Beheld God* that the patriarchal model of God should be set aside. Drawing on the records of women's experiences during the Nazi period, she offered a post-Holocaust theology of relation that affirms the redemptive presence of God at Auschwitz.

OMNISCIENCE

ACCORDING TO THE JEWISH TRADITION, GOD KNOWS ALL. YET THIS CONCEPT GAVE RISE TO THEOLOGICAL SPECULATION ABOUT GOD'S KNOWLEDGE OF THE FUTURE.

According to the Jewish tradition, God knows everything: past, present and future. Nothing is hidden from his sight. As an all-knowing deity, he looks down from heaven on all his creation. This does not imply that human beings lack free will since God knows in advance what their actions will be. Rather, Judaism asserts that God knows all, yet men and women possess freedom of the will.

FOREKNOWLEDGE AND FREE WILL

In line with this biblical view, rabbinic Judaism asserted that God's knowledge is not limited by space and time. Instead, nothing is hidden from him. Moreover, the rabbis

stated that God's knowledge of events does not deprive human beings of free will. Thus in the Mishnah, the 2nd-century CE sage Akiva declared: 'All is foreseen but freedom of choice is given.'

In the *Guide for the Perplexed* Maimonides argued that God knows all things before they occur. None the less, human beings are unable to understand the nature of God's knowledge because it is of a different order from that of human beings. On this account, it is not possible to comprehend how divine foreknowledge is compatible with human freedom. Other medieval writers, however, were unconvinced by such an explanation. In *The Wars*

Above The Middle East and the Red Sea from the air. God's knowledge is not limited by time or space.

Below 15th-century painting of God as the divine architect. The act of creation is part of the tapestry of God's knowledge.

THE BIBLICAL VIEW
According to the Hebrew Bible, God is aware of all human action. As the psalmist proclaimed:

The Lord looks down from
  heaven,
He sees all the sons of men...
He who fashions the hearts of
  them all,
and observes their deeds.
  (Psalm 33:13,15)

Again, in Psalm 139:2–3, the psalmist declared:

Thou knowest when I sit down
  and when I rise up;
thou discernest my thoughts
  from afar.
Thou searchest out my path
  and my lying down,
and art acquainted
  with my ways.

of the Lord, the 14th-century theologian Gersonides argued that only God knows things in general. Hence the world is constituted so that a range of possibilities is open to human beings. Since men and women are able to exercise free will, these are possibilities rather than certainties, which they would be if God knew them in advance.

Thus, although God knows all it is possible to know, his knowledge is not exhaustive. He does not know how individuals will respond to the possibilities open to them since they are only possibilities. For Gersonides, such a view does not undermine God's providential plan. Although God does not know all future events, he is aware of the outcome of the whole process. In the same century, however, the Jewish theologian Hasdai Crescas (1340–1410) held a different view in *The Light of the Lord*. According to Crescas, human beings only appear to be free, but in reality all their deeds are determined by virtue of God's foreknowledge. Therefore, rather than attempting to reconcile free will and omniscience, he asserted that God's knowledge is absolute and free will is an illusion.

MODERN JUDAISM

In recent times the devout have been less concerned about such philosophical perplexities. Jewish scholar Michael Friedländer was best known for his English translation of Maimonides' *Guide for the Perplexed*. In 1890 he considered the subject of divine foreknowledge in *The Jewish Religion*: 'His knowledge is not limited, like the knowledge of mortal beings, by space and time. The entire past and future lies unrolled before his eyes, and nothing is hidden from

Above An omniscient eye on the Cao Dai temple in the Mekong Delta, Vietnam, portrays the idea of God's all-encompassing knowledge.

him. Although we may form a faint idea of the knowledge of God by considering that faculty of man that enables him within a limited space and time, to look backward and forward, and to unroll before him the past and the future, as if the events that have happened and those that will come to pass were going on in the present moment, yet the true nature of God's knowledge no man can conceive. ... It is the will of God that man should have free will and should be responsible for his actions; and his foresight does not necessarily include predetermination.'

In the modern period, there has been a universal reaffirmation of the traditional belief that God knows past, present and future and that men and women have freedom of choice.

Left The Creation from the Sarajevo Haggadah, c. 1350, one of the oldest Sephardic Haggadahs. Images include the separation of light from darkness, and the spirit of God hovering over the waters of chaos. According to Judaism, God knows and does all things.

CREATION

THE DOCTRINE OF CREATION IS A CENTRAL ELEMENT OF THE JEWISH
FAITH. YET AMONG JEWISH THEOLOGIANS THIS BELIEF GAVE RISE TO
SPECULATION ABOUT THE CREATIVE PROCESS.

According to the Bible, God created the cosmos. This belief became a central feature of the synagogue liturgy. Repeatedly, Jews praise God for his creative works and extol his providential concern for all that he has formed. The doctrine of divine creation also became a central doctrine of Jewish philosophy and mysticism.

THE BIBLE
According to Genesis 1:1–4 God created the universe:

In the beginning God created
  the heaven and the earth.
The earth was without form
  and void,
and darkness was upon the face
  of the deep;
and the Spirit of God was moving
  over the face of the waters.
And God said,

*Below This early 13th-century mosaic
for Monreale Cathedral, Sicily, shows
God creating Heaven and Earth.*

*Right According to the Bible God
created the cosmos and everything in it.
Animals in the* Rothschild Miscellany,
a 15th-century Italian illumination.

'Let there be light':
  and there was light.
And God saw that the light was good.
Based on the Psalms, synagogue liturgy depicts God as the creator of all:

Blessed be He who spake, and the
  world existed:
Blessed be He;
Blessed be He who was the Master
  of the world in the beginning.

In the Ani Maamin prayer, the first principle of the Jewish faith concerns creation:

I believe with perfect faith that
the creator, blessed be his name, is
the author and guide of everything
that has been created, and that He
  alone
has made, does make, and will
  make all things.

RABBINIC LITERATURE
In rabbinic sources, scholars speculated about the creative process. In Genesis Rabbah (midrash on Genesis), for example, the concept of the world as a pattern in the mind of God is expressed in relation to the belief that God looked into the Torah and then created the universe. Here the Torah is conceived as a primordial blueprint. Regarding the order of creation, the School of Shammai stated that the heavens were created

---

EXTRATERRESTRIAL CREATION

Regarding the question whether in the process of creating the cosmos, God also formed intelligent beings on other planets, the Bible provides no information. Even though rabbinic sources attest to the creation of other worlds, they similarly contain no reference to the existence of other sentient creatures. However, in the 19th century Phineas Elijah ben Meir Hurwitz of Vilna discussed this topic. On the basis of Isaiah 45:18 ('For thus says the Lord who created the heavens, who formed the earth and made it, he established it; he did not create it a chaos; he formed it to be inhabited: "I am the Lord; and there is no other."'), he stressed that there are creatures on other planets than the earth. He went on to say that creatures on other planets may have intelligence, yet he did not think that they would have free will since only human beings have this ability. Consequently, he wrote, there is only room for Torah and worship in this world, for neither Torah nor worship has any meaning where there is no free will.

Kabbalah, the notion of God creating and destroying worlds before the creation of this world is viewed as referring to spiritual worlds. Thus *tohu*, or 'void', in Genesis denotes the stage of God's self-revelation known as world of the void that precedes the world of perfection. In later Kabbalistic thought, the 14th-century Kalonymus Kalman of Cracow in his *Maor Va-Shemsh* maintained that the void in Genesis is the primordial void remaining after God's withdrawal to make room for the universe. On this reading, God's decree 'Let there be light' (Genesis 1:3) means that God caused his light to be emanated into the void in order to provide sustaining power required for the worlds that were later to be formed.

Below Map showing the Earth, planets and zodiac circling the Sun, by Nicolaus Copernicus, c. 1543.

first and then the earth. The School of Hillel, however, maintained that the heaven and the earth were created simultaneously. According to one rabbinic source, all things were formed at the same time on the first day of creation, but appeared on the other six days just as figs are gathered simultaneously in one basket but each selected individually.

Again, in the Genesis Rabbah midrash, scholars stressed that God created several worlds but destroyed them before creating this one. The goal of creation is summed up in the rabbinic claim that God created the world for his glory.

THE MEDIEVAL PERIOD

In the Middle Ages, a number of Jewish philosophers argued that God created the cosmos *ex nihilo*. The Kabbalists, however, interpreted the doctrine of *ex nihilo* in a special sense. In their view, God should be understood as the Divine Nothing because as he is in and of himself nothing can be predicated. This is because the divine is beyond human comprehension. Creation *ex nihilo* therefore refers to the creation of the universe out of God, the Divine Nothing. This took place, they stated, through a series of divine emanations.

For the Kabbalists the first verses of Genesis allude to the process within the Godhead prior to the creation of the universe. In Lurianic

GOODNESS

BIBLICAL AND RABBINIC SOURCES EXTOL GOD'S GOODNESS. TRADITION
SAYS HE IS BENEVOLENT, MERCIFUL AND COMPASSIONATE. YET SUCH A
BELIEF GAVE RISE TO SPECULATION ABOUT THE ORIGIN OF EVIL.

As the supreme ruler of the universe, God is depicted in biblical and rabbinic sources as all-good. He is the beneficent creator who watches over all he has formed and extends mercy to his chosen people. As the Psalmist declared, he is good and ready to forgive (Psalm 86:5).

THE RABBIS

According to rabbinic literature, God is the supremely beneficent deity who guides all things to their ultimate origin. In the unfolding of his plan, God has chosen Israel as his messenger to all peoples – as creator and redeemer, he is the father of all. Such affirmations about God's goodness have given rise to speculation about the existence of evil. In the Bible, the authors of Job and Ecclesiastes explore the

*Below According to the Bible, Adam
and Eve were expelled from the Garden
of Eden because of their disobedience.
12th-century Spanish painting.*

question why the righteous suffer, and this quest extended into the rabbinic period. However, it was not until the Middle Ages that Jewish theologians began to explore the philosophical perplexities connected with the origin of evil.

THE SOURCE OF EVIL

In the 12th century, the Jewish philosopher Abraham Ibn Daud argued that both human reason and the Jewish tradition teach that God cannot be the cause of evil. Reason demonstrates that this is the case because God is all-good; it would be self-contradictory for him to be the source of evil. Since God does not have a composite nature, it is logically impossible for him to bring about both good and evil. Why then does evil exist? Poverty, he argued, is in fact the absence of wealth; darkness the absence of light; folly the absence of understanding. It is an error to believe that God creates any of these

*Above The Rabbi by Martin Archer-
Shee, 1837, shows its subject as wise,
knowing and benevolent.*

things just as it would be an error to assume that God made no elephants in Spain. Such a lack of elephants is not divinely willed. Likewise, evil is not created by God. It occurs when goodness is not present. The absence of good is not an inherent evil. Rather, imperfections in the world exist so that God can benefit a multitude of creatures in different forms.

THE KABBALISTS

According to Jewish Kabbalists, the existence of evil constitutes a central problem for the Jewish faith. One tradition asserts that evil has no objective reality. Men and women are unable to receive all of the influx from the *sefirot*, or 'divine emanations'; it is this inability that is the origin of evil. Created beings are estranged from the source of emanation and this results in the illusion that evil exists. Another view depicts the sefirah of power as an attribute whose name is evil. On the basis of such teaching, Isaac the Blind (*c.* 1160-1235) concluded that there must be a positive root of evil and death. During the process of differentiation of forces below the sefirot, evil became

concretized. This interpretation led to the doctrine that the source of evil is the supra-abundant growth of judgement – this was due to the separation and substitution of the attribute of judgement from its union with compassion. Pure judgement produced from within itself the Sitra Ahra, or 'the other side'. The Sitra Ahra consists of the domain of emanations and demonic powers. Though it originated from one of God's attributes, it is not part of the divine realm.

THE ZOHAR

According to the Zohar, the major Kabbalistic source of the Middle Ages, evil is like the bark of a tree of emanation – it is a husk or shell in which lower dimensions of existing things are encased. Evil is perceived as a waste product of an organic process. It is compared to bad blood, foul water, dross after gold has been refined and the dregs of wine. Yet despite this depiction, the Zohar asserts that there is holiness even in the Sitra Ahra, whether it is understood as a result of

Below Evil can triumph when good men do nothing. The Holocaust Memorial at Mauthausen Concentration Camp is in the shape of a menorah.

the emanation of the last sefirah or a consequence of human sin. The domains of good and evil are intermingled, and it is a person's duty to separate them.

MODERN JEWISH THOUGHT

In modern times philosophical theories about the existence of evil have ceased to attract attention within Judaism, and most Jews have ignored the mystical theories in early and medieval Jewish literature. Instead, writers have wrestled with the question whether it is possible to believe in God's goodness after the Holocaust.

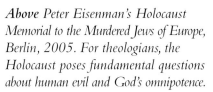

Above Peter Eisenman's Holocaust Memorial to the Murdered Jews of Europe, Berlin, 2005. For theologians, the Holocaust poses fundamental questions about human evil and God's omnipotence.

In *The Face of God after Auschwitz* (1965) Reform Jewish theologian Ignaz Maybaum contended Jews died in the concentration camps for the sins of humanity as God's suffering servant. For Maybaum, Jews suffer in order to bring about the rule of God over the world and its peoples – their God-appointed role is to serve the course of historical progress and bring human beings into a new era.

An alternative approach to the Holocaust is to see in the death camps a manifestation of God's will that his chosen people survive. Such a view was expressed by the Reform Jewish philosopher Emil Fackenheim (1916–2003), who asserted that God revealed himself to the Jewish people out of the furnaces and through the ashes of the victims of the death camps. Through the Holocaust, he argued, God issued an additional 614th commandment to the 613 commandments found in Scripture: 'Jews are forbidden to hand Hitler posthumous victories.' In this way, God commanded his people to survive as Jews, lest the Jewish people perish.

CHAPTER 2

GOD AND ISRAEL

According to traditional Judaism, God is understood as the providential Lord of all creation. In the Hebrew Bible, God is depicted as ever-present, directing the course of human affairs. In rabbinic sources, he is intimately involved with his people, continually leading them to their ultimate redemption. The revelation to Moses on Mount Sinai is the basis of the 613 commandments in the Torah, which were later interpreted by rabbinic scholars. According to tradition, God's eternal covenant with Israel means both the Written and the Oral Law are binding for all time.

As the all-good ruler of the universe, God chose the Jews as his special people. Israel was to be a messenger to all nations in the unfolding of God's divine plan for humanity. In acceptance of God's love, the Jewish people were to worship God and keep his commandments. In biblical times, worship and sacrifice were carried out in the Temple. Sacrifices were offered to God to obtain his favour and atone for sin. With the destruction of the Temple, the synagogue became the focus for divine worship. Prayers replaced sacrifices, which could no longer be offered. A new ritual, referred to as 'service of the heart', became a central focus of Jewish life.

Opposite This magnificent illustration from the Golden Haggadah of 1320 shows, anti clockwise from top right, Pharaoh letting the people of Israel go, the strangling of the firstborn, the Egyptians pursuing the people of Israel, and the drowning of the Egyptians in the Red Sea.

Above This 6th-century Byzantine mosaic from Madaba, Jordan, is the oldest extant map of Palestine.

PROVIDENCE

FOR THE JEWISH PEOPLE, GOD IS THE TRANSCENDENT CREATOR OF THE UNIVERSE AND ACTIVELY INVOLVED IN HISTORY. PROVIDENTIALLY, HE INTERVENES IN EVERYDAY LIFE, SUSTAINING AND GUIDING HIS CREATURES.

In Scripture, God is continually presented as controlling and guiding his creation. The Hebrew term for such divine intervention is *hashgahah*, derived from Psalm 33:14: 'From where he sits enthroned he looks forth [*hisgiah*] on all the inhabitants of the earth.' This view implies that the dispensation of a wise and benevolent providence is manifest everywhere.

THE BIBLE
According to the Hebrew Bible, there are two types of providence: general providence (God's provision for the world in general) and special providence (God's care for each person). In the Bible, God's general providence was manifest in his freeing the ancient Israelites from bondage; special providence relates to God's care for each individual. In the words

Below When God told Abraham to send Hagar and Ishmael into the desert, was this general or special providence? By Italian painter Veronese, 1580.

of Jeremiah: 'I know, O Lord, that the way of man is not in himself, that it is not in man who walks to direct his steps' (Jeremiah 10:23).

THE RABBINIC TRADITION
The doctrine of divine providence was developed in rabbinic sources. According to the Mishnah, 'everything is foreseen'. Developing this concept, the Talmud states: 'No man suffers so much as the injury of a finger when it has been decreed in heaven.' This belief became a major feature of the Rosh Hashanah, or New Year, liturgy where God, the judge of the world, provides for the destiny of individuals as well as nations on the basis of their actions.

THE MIDDLE AGES
Jewish medieval theologians were preoccupied with the problem of divine causality. In the *Guide for the Perplexed*, the 12th-century Jewish philosopher Moses Maimonides defended both general and special

Above 14th-century Spanish drawing of the ancient Hebrews as slaves in Egypt. For Jews, the Exodus from Egypt was an act of divine deliverance.

providence. Special providence, he argued, extends only to human beings and is in proportion to a person's intellect and moral character. This view implies God is concerned about non-human species, but not with every individual. Only men and women come under divine care as they rise in intellectual and moral stature.

However, in the 15th century, the Jewish theologian Hasdai Crescas (1340–1410) maintained that God created human beings out of his love for them. Therefore, his providential care is not related to their personal characteristics. Instead, all persons enjoy God's special providence.

THE KABBALISTS
Jewish Kabbalists were also concerned about providence. In his *Shomer Emunim*, the 18th-century scholar Joseph Ergas explained there are various types of providence. 'Nothing', he wrote, 'occurs by accident, without intention and divine providence, as it is written: "Then will I also walk with you in chance." (Leviticus 21:24). You see that even the state of chance is attributed to God, for all proceeds from him by reason of

HASIDIC TEACHERS

Such a restriction of special providence was rejected by a number of Hasidic thinkers. Divine providence, they insisted, is exercised over all things. In the 18th century, for example, Phineas of Koretz (1726–91) wrote in his *Peer La-Yesharim* that 'a man should believe that even a piece of straw that lies on the ground does so at the decree of God.' Hayim of Sanz (1793–1876), the founder of the Sanz Hasidic dynasty, stated: 'It is impossible for any creature to enjoy existence without the creator of all worlds sustaining it and keeping it in being, and it is all through divine providence.'

special providence.' None the less, Ergas limited special providence to human beings. 'The guardian angel', he continued, 'has no power to provide for the special providence of non-human species. For example, whether this ox will live or die, whether this ant will be trodden on or saved, whether this spider will catch this fly …There is no special providence for this kind of animals, to say nothing of plants and minerals.'

Below Cosmographical Diagram from the Catalan Atlas by Abraham Cresques, 1375. For Jews, God is both transcendent and immanent in human history.

Above The destruction of the Temple of Jerusalem can be seen as providentially willed or as the result of human action. Painting by Francesco Hayez, 1867.

MODERN JUDAISM

In the contemporary world, such theological issues have not been at the forefront of Jewish thought. Rather, the rise of science has challenged the traditional understanding of God's providential activity. In place of the religious interpretation of the universe as controlled by God, scientific investigation has revealed that nature is governed by complex natural laws. Thus it is no longer possible for most Jews to accept the biblical and rabbinic concept of divine providential activity. As a result, many Jews have simply abandoned the belief in providence.

Others envisage God as working through natural causes. As creator of all, he established the laws that regulate the natural order. Regarding special providence, many Jews would want to say that God is concerned with each individual, even though he does not miraculously intervene in the course of human affairs. Divine providential concern should thus be understood as a mode of interaction in which God affects the consciousness of individuals without curtailing their free will. Knowing the innermost secrets of the human heart, he introduces into the conscious awareness of individuals aims consonant with his will.

REVELATION

TRADITION IS THAT GOD REVEALED HIMSELF TO THE JEWISH NATION.
THIS BELIEF SERVES AS THE FOUNDATION OF THE LEGAL SYSTEM AND
THE AUTHORITATIVE BASIS OF JEWISH THEOLOGY.

According to the Jewish tradition, God revealed the Torah to Moses on Mount Sinai and, therefore, 613 commandments in the Five Books of Moses are binding for all time. In addition, God's revelation on Mount Sinai serves as basis for the conviction that the descriptions of God's nature and activity found in Scripture are authoritative and unchanging.

THE RABBIS

In rabbinic sources a distinction is drawn between the revelation of the Torah and the prophetic writings. This is frequently expressed by saying that the Torah was given directly by God, whereas the prophetic books were given by means of prophecy. The other books of the Bible, however, were conveyed by means of the holy spirit. Yet despite these distinctions, all the writings in the Hebrew Bible constitute the canon of Scripture. The Hebrew term referring to the Bible as a whole is Tanakh. This word is made of the first letters of the three divisions of Scripture: Torah, Neviim (Prophets), and Ketuvim (Writings).

THE ORAL TORAH

For the rabbis, the expositions and elaborations of the Written Law were revealed on Mount Sinai and passed down from generation to generation. This process is referred to as the Oral Torah. Hence, traditional Judaism affirms that God's revelation is two-fold and binding. Committed to this belief, Jews pray in the synagogue liturgy that God will guide them to do his will.

THE MEDIEVAL PERIOD

In the Middle Ages, the traditional belief in the Written and Oral Torah was repeatedly affirmed. The Jewish writer Nahmanides (1194–1270) stated in his *Commentary to the Pentateuch* that Moses wrote the Five Books of Moses at God's dictation. It is likely, he observed, that Moses

Above Revelation at Sinai as Moses receives the Ten Commandments. From the mid 9th-century Moutier-Grandval Hebrew Bible.

wrote Genesis and part of Exodus when he came down from Mount Sinai. After 40 years in the wilderness, he completed the rest of the Torah.

Nahmanides stated that this view follows the rabbinic tradition that the Torah was given scroll by scroll. For Nahmanides, Moses was like a scribe who copied an older work. Underlying this conception is the mystical idea of a primordial Torah, which contains the words describing events long before they occurred. This entire record was in heaven before the creation of the world. Further, Nahmanides maintained that the secrets of the Torah were revealed to Moses and are referred to in the Torah by the use of special letters, and by the adornment of Hebrew characters.

KABBALAH

Parallelling Nahmanides' mystical interpretation of the Torah, the medieval mystical work the Zohar

Left The first Great Sanhedrin of French Jews in Paris, 1807. The Jewish legal system is based on God's revelation of Mount Sinai, as interpreted by rabbinic sages through the centuries.

asserts that the Torah contains mysteries beyond human comprehension. As Rabbi Simeon ben Yohai, traditionally thought to be the author of the Zohar, explained, 'Alas for the man who regards the Torah as a book of mere tales and everyday matters! If that were so, even we could compose a Torah dealing with everyday affairs, and of even greater excellence. Nay, even the princes of the world possess books of greater worth which we could use as a model for composing such Torah. The Torah, however, contains in all its words supernal truths and sublime mysteries.'

BIBLICAL SCHOLARSHIP
In the modern period it has become increasingly difficult to sustain the concept of divine revelation in the light of scholarly investigation and discovery. According to biblical scholars, the Torah is composed of various sources from different periods in the history of ancient Israel.

Below Tradition teaches that God revealed the Torah to Moses. This new Torah scroll is being completed before it is paraded in procession to an Ashkenazi synagogue in Stamford Hill, London.

Some scholars stress that these sources themselves contain early material; thus it is a mistake to think they originated in their entirety at particular periods. Other scholars reject the theory of separate written sources; instead, they argue that oral traditions were modified throughout the history of ancient Israel and only eventually were compiled into a single narrative. Yet, despite these rival claims, there is a general recognition that the Torah was not written by Moses; rather, it is seen as a collection of traditions originating at different times.

Above 1350 Passover Haggadah. In following such liturgy, Jews pray God will guide them to do his will.

MODERN JUDAISM
Orthodox Jews remain committed to the view that the Written and the Oral Torah were imparted by God to Moses on Mount Sinai. This is the basis of the legal system and doctrinal beliefs about God. Non-Orthodox Jews have a general acceptance of the findings of biblical scholarship. The Five Books of Moses are perceived as divinely inspired, but at the same time the product of human reflection.

THE TORAH
According to the Jewish tradition, the Torah was given by God to the Jewish nation. Moses Maimonides explained: 'The Torah was revealed from heaven. This implies our belief that the whole of the Torah found in our hands this day is the Torah that was handed down by Moses, and that it is all of divine origin. By this I mean that the whole of the Torah came unto him from before God in a manner which is metaphorically called "speaking". But the real nature of that communication is unknown to everybody except Moses.'

TORAH AND COMMANDMENTS

JEWISH OBSERVANCE IS BASED ON THE BELIEF THAT GOD REVEALED 613 COMMANDMENTS TO MOSES ON MOUNT SINAI – THESE ARE RECORDED IN THE TORAH AND SERVE AS THE BASIS OF JEWISH LAW.

Traditional Judaism affirms that Moses received the Oral Torah in addition to the Written Law. These commandments were passed down from generation to generation and were the subject of rabbinic discussion and debate.

THE RABBINIC TRADITION
The first authoritative compilation of the Oral Law was the Mishnah, composed by Yehuda Ha-Nasi in the 2nd century CE. This work is the most important book of law after the Bible – its aim was to supply teachers and judges with a guide to the Jewish legal tradition.

In later centuries, sages continued to discuss the nature of Jewish law. Their deliberations and conclusions are recorded in the Palestinian and Babylonian Talmuds. Both Talmuds incorporate the Mishnah and later rabbinic debate known as the Gemara. The Gemara text preserves the proceedings of scholarly academies in both Palestine and Babylonia. The central purpose of these works was to elucidate the Mishnah text.

CODES OF LAW
After the compilation of the Talmuds in the 6th century CE, outstanding scholars continued the development of halakha, or 'Jewish law', by issuing answers to specific questions. These responsa, or 'responses', touched on all aspects of the Jewish tradition and insured a standardization of practice. In time, various scholars felt the need to produce codes of Jewish law so that all members of the community would have access to the legal tradition. Isaac Alfasi (1013–1103) produced a work in the 11th century that became the standard code for Sephardic Jewry. Two centuries later, Asher ben Jehiel (c.1250–1327) wrote a code for Ashkenazi Jews. In the 12th century Moses Maimonides wrote the Mishneh Torah, which had a wide influence, as did the code by Jacob ben Asher in the 14th century. In the 16th century, Joseph Caro (1488–1575) published the *Shulkhan Arukh*, which together with the glosses by Moses Isserles (c.1525–72) has served as the standard code of Jewish law for Orthodox Jews.

THE KABBALAH
In Kabbalistic sources the observance of the *mitzvot*, or 'commandments', takes on cosmic significance. For the Jewish mystic, deeds of *tikkun*, or 'cosmic repair', sustain the world, activate nature to praise God, and bring about the coupling of the 6th and 10th sefirot, or 'divine emanations'. Such repair is brought about

Above Brass hanging lamp in the shape of a Jewish 'Sabbath lamp', lit on the eve of Sabbath and festivals. Jews are commanded to rest and worship on the Sabbath.

Below Dutch artist Rembrandt's painting of Moses with the Ten Commandments, 1659.

Below The rabbi in his pulpit reading a Torah scroll to his congregation, from the Barcelona Haggadah, c.1350.

LURIANIC KABBALAH

According to the 16th-century Kabbalist Isaac Luria (1534–72), when the vessels were shattered the cosmos was divided into two parts: the kingdom of evil in the lower part and the realm of divine light in the upper part. God, he believed, chose Israel to vanquish evil and raise up the captive sparks. The Torah was given to symbolize the Jews' acceptance of this task. Luria and his disciples believed they were living in the final stages of the last attempt to overcome evil, in which the coming of the Messiah would signify the end of the struggle. For Lurianic mystics, the concept of tikkun refers to the mending of what was broken during the shattering of the vessels. By keeping God's commandments it is possible for the righteous to redeem the world.

Above Jews kissing the Torah scrolls, Nevatim, Israel. Tradition states that God revealed the words of the Torah to Moses.

by keeping the commandments, which were conceived as vessels for establishing contact with the Godhead and for enduring divine mercy. Such a religious life provided the Jewish mystic with a means of integrating into the divine hierarchy of creation.

MYSTICAL CLEAVING

The highest rank attainable by the soul at the end of its sojourn on earth is mystical cleaving to God. Early Kabbalists of Provence defined such cleaving as the ultimate goal.

According to the 13th-century mystic Isaac the Blind, the principal task of the mystics and of those who contemplate the divine name is to cleave to God. This, he argued, is a central principle of the Torah and of prayer. The aim should be to harmonize one's thoughts above, to conjoin God in his letters and to link the ten sefirot to him. For the 13th-century writer Nahmanides, such cleaving is a state of mind in which one constantly remembers God and his love.

MODERN JUDAISM

In the modern world, such traditional mystical ideas have lost their force except among the Hasidim. Today the majority of those who profess allegiance to Orthodox Judaism do not live by the code of Jewish law. Instead, each individual Jew feels free to write his or her own *Shulkhan Arukh*. This is also the case within the other branches of Judaism. For most Jews the legal tradition has simply lost its hold on Jewish consciousness. This means that there is a vast gulf fixed between the requirements of legal observance and the actual lifestyle of the majority of Jews, both in Israel and the Diaspora.

Below Hasidic life is regulated by Jewish law. A Hasidic couple walk through the Mea Shearim, one of the oldest Jewish neighbourhoods in Jerusalem.

Left Cover page of Leviticus, dated 1350, which covers laws about sacrifice, the sanctuary, impurity and holiness.

CHOSEN PEOPLE

ACCORDING TO TRADITION, GOD CHOSE THE JEWS FROM AMONG ALL PEOPLES. THEY ARE TO BE HIS SERVANTS AND DO HIS WILL. THIS BELIEF HAS ANIMATED JEWISH CONSCIOUSNESS THROUGH THE AGES.

According to Scripture, God chose the Jewish nation as his special people. As the Book of Deuteronomy proclaims: 'For you are a people holy to the Lord your God: The Lord your God has chosen you to be a people for his own possession out of all the peoples that are on the face of the earth' (Deuteronomy 7:6).

DIVINE LOVE

According to the Hebrew Bible, God's selection of Israel was motivated by divine love. The Book of Deuteronomy states: 'It was not because you were more in number than any other people that the Lord set his love but it is because the Lord loves you' (Deuteronomy 7:7–8). Such affection was later echoed in the synagogue liturgy, particularly in the prayer for holy days: 'Thou has chosen us from all peoples; thou has

Below The Book of Genesis from a 1472 Pentateuch, showing Adam, Eve and a unicorn, which in Jewish tradition stands for the final redemption of Israel.

loved us and found pleasure in us and hast exalted us above all tongues; thou hast sanctified us by thy commandments and brought us near unto thy service, O king, and hast called us by thy great and holy name.'

AN HISTORIC MISSION

By its election, Israel was given an historic mission to bear truth to all humanity. Hence, before God proclaimed the Ten Commandments on Mount Sinai, he admonished the people to carry out this role: 'You have seen what I did to the Egyptians, and how I bore you on eagles' wings, and brought you to myself. Now, therefore, if you will obey my voice, and keep my covenant, you shall be my own possession among all peoples; for all the earth is mine, and you shall be to me a kingdom of priests and a holy nation' (Exodus 19:4-6).

OBLIGATION AND RESPONSIBILITIES

Such a choice of Israel carries with it numerous responsibilities: 'For I have chosen him, that he may charge his children and his household after him to keep the way of the Lord by doing righteousness and justice' (Genesis 18:19). Divine choice therefore brings about reciprocal response: Israel is obliged to keep God's law. In doing so, the nation will be able to persuade other nations that there is only one universal God. Israel is to be a prophet to the nations in that it will bring them to salvation. However, despite such an obligation, the Bible asserts that God will not abandon his chosen people even if they go astray. The wayward will be punished, but God

Above The Ark of the Law, 6th-century CE mosaic at Beth Alpha synagogue, Israel. Tradition says God chose the Jews from all nations to be his special people and observe his commandments.

will not reject them: 'Yet for all that, when they are in the land of their enemies, I will not spurn them, neither will I abhor them so as to destroy them utterly and break my covenant with them: for I am the Lord their God' (Leviticus 26:44).

THE RABBINIC VIEW

In rabbinic literature the concept of the chosen people is a constant theme. While maintaining that God chose the Jews from all peoples, the rabbis argued their election was due to an acceptance of the Torah. This belief was based on Scripture: 'If you will hearken to my voice, indeed, and keep my covenant, then you shall be my own treasure from among all the peoples' (Exodus 19:5). For the rabbis, the Torah was offered first to other nations of the world, but they all rejected it because its precepts conflicted with their way of life. Only Israel was willing to keep his covenant.

THE MEDIEVAL PERIOD

In the Middle Ages, the Jewish claim to be God's chosen people was disputed by Church authorities who regarded the Church as the true Israel. In response, such Jewish philosophers as the 12th-century Spanish Jew Judah Halevi stressed that the entire Jewish people were endowed with a special religious sense. According to Halevi, this faculty was first bestowed on Adam, and then it was passed on through a line of Jewish representatives. As a result, the Jewish nation was able to enter into communion with God. Moreover, because of this divine influence, the election of Israel implies dependence on special providence, which sustains the people while the remainder of the human race is subject to the general workings of the laws of nature and general providence.

Below The Spanish philosopher Judah Halevi held that Jewish people had a special religious sense. Thus Moses could talk to God on Mount Sinai. A 14th-century Italian fresco by Bartolo di Fredi.

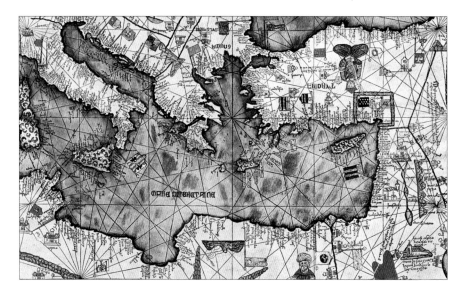

KABBALAH

The concept of Jewish chosenness is a central theme of medieval Kabbalistic thought. According to medieval Kabbalah, the Jewish people on earth has its counterpart in the Shekhinah, or 'divine presence', in the sefirotic realm – the sefirah, or 'divine emanation', *Malkhut* is known as 'the

Above Israel and the Mediterranean from the Catalan Atlas by Jewish cartographer Abraham Cresques, 1375. According to tradition, Israel was chosen to be a light to all nations.

community of Israel' which serves as the archetype of the Israelite people on earth. For the Kabbalists, Israel's exile mirrors the cosmic disharmony in which the Shekhinah is cast into exile from the Godhead. The dynamic of Israel's exile and its restoration reflects the dynamic of the upper worlds.

MODERN JUDAISM

In the contemporary Jewish world, the notion of Israel's chosenness remains an important doctrine. Yet within Reform Judaism the concept of Jewish mission was developed, stressing the special message of God that is to be passed on to all peoples. Within the various non-Orthodox branches of the faith a number of writers have expressed unease about the claim that the Jews constitute a divinely chosen people. The rejection of this traditional doctrine derives from universalistic and humanistic tendencies. Although the Jewish community has a unique history, the people of Israel are not perceived as divinely chosen. Instead, the God of Israel is also the Lord of history who loves all peoples and guides their destiny.

LOVE OF GOD

OF CENTRAL IMPORTANCE IN JUDAISM IS THE LOVE OF GOD.
THE OBLIGATION TO LOVE GOD INVOLVES BEING FAITHFUL, EVEN IF
THIS REQUIRES THE LOSS OF ONE'S WEALTH OR ONE'S LIFE.

At the heart of Judaism lies the love of God. According to Scripture: 'You shall love the Lord your God with all your heart and with all your soul and with all your might' (Deuteronomy 6:5). The Mishnah teaches that this biblical verse implies that human beings must love God not only for the good that befalls them, but for their sufferings as well. This explanation is based on an interpretation of three expressions in this verse: 'with all your heart' means with both the good and evil inclinations; 'with all your soul' means even if God takes away your soul through martyrdom; 'with all your might' means with all your wealth.

MIDRASHIC TEACHING

Alongside the Mishnah, the midrash also comments on this biblical verse. Concerning the phrase 'You shall love the Lord your God', the *Sifra* (midrash on Exodus) declares: 'Do it out of love. Scripture distinguishes between one who does it out of love

and one who does it out of fear. Out of love, his reward is doubled and gain doubled. Scripture says: "You shall fear the Lord your God: you shall serve him and cleave to him" (Deuteronomy 10:20). A man who fears his neighbour will leave him when his demands become too troublesome, but you do it out of love. For love and fear are never found together except in relation to God.'

THE MIDDLE AGES

Among medieval Jewish writers, stress was placed on mystical love. Thus the Jewish philosopher Saadia Gaon (882–942CE) in *Beliefs and Opinions* asked how it is possible to have knowledge of God, much less love him, since we have not perceived

Below This carving of 1420 from Roskilde, Denmark, depicts Job, a righteous man who is put to the test with illness and the loss of his wealth and family, but remains faithful to God.

Above I Will Worship toward Thy Temple. A 19th-century painting of Jerusalem by the French artist James Tissot shows the obligation to love God.

him with our senses. In response he asserted that certain statements are believed to be true even though they cannot be proved. For Saadia, it is possible to acquire knowledge of God through rational speculation and the miracle s afforded by Scripture. Hence, truth about God is able to mingle with the human spirit. For this reason the prophet Isaiah stated:

BAHYA IBN PAKUDAH

In the 11th century the Jewish philosopher Bahya Ibn Pakudah viewed the love of God as the final goal – this is the aim of all virtues. According to Bahya, the love of God is the soul's longing for the creator. When human beings contemplate God's power and greatness, they bow before his majesty until God stills whatever fear they might have. Individuals who love God in this fashion have no other interest than serving him. With complete faith they accept all their sufferings.

Above Paradise *by Lucas Cranach the Elder, 1530. Scripture says, Adam and Eve were driven out of Paradise for failing to observe God's commandments.*

'My soul yearns for thee in the night, my spirit within me earnestly seeks thee' (Isaiah 26:9). As a consequence, the soul is filled with love.

MOSES MAIMONIDES

In the Mishneh Torah, the 12th-century thinker Moses Maimonides discussed the love of God in relation to the nature of the universe. 'It is a religious obligation to love and fear this glorious and tremendous God,' he wrote. 'And it is said: "You shall love the Lord your God" (Deuteronomy 6:5). And it is said: "You shall fear the Lord your God" (Deuteronomy 6:13). How does a man come to love and fear God? No sooner does man reflect on his deeds and on his great and marvellous creatures, seeing in them his incomparable and limitless wisdom, than he is moved to love and to praise and to glorify and he has an intense desire to know the great Name.'

Right Jews praying before the Western Wall in Jerusalem. Such prayer should be based on love of God.*

According to Maimonides, one who truly loves God serves him disinterestedly rather than out of an ulterior motive. When a person loves God, he automatically carries out the divine commandments. This state is like being lovesick, unable to get the person he loves out of his mind, pining constantly when he stands, sits, eats or drinks. Yet Maimonides maintained that not everyone is able to attain such a state of pure love. God, he maintained, can only be loved in proportion to the knowledge one has of him.

KABBALAH

In Kabbalistic literature the love of God is highly important. Concerning the verse, 'You shall love the Lord your God', the Zohar states that human beings are here commanded to cleave unto God with selfless devotion: 'It is necessary for man to be attached to God with a most elevated love, that all man's worship of the Holy One, blessed be he, should be with love; for no form of worship can be compared to the love of the Holy One, blessed be he.'

LATER KABBALISTS

In the writings of later Kabbalists the theme of the love of God was further elaborated. According to the 16th-century writer Elijah de Vidas in his *Reshite Hokhmah*, it is impossible for human beings to love a disembodied spirit. Here the love of God must refer to something that is embodied. Since God as En Sof has no body, human love of the divine must be understood as love of the Shekhinah (God's presence). For de Vidas, the Shekhinah is in no way apart from God; rather God manifests himself through the Shekhinah in order to provide human beings with something tangible they are able to grasp so as to rise above worldly desires.

FEAR OF GOD

THE FEAR OF GOD IS TO BE COUPLED WITH THE LOVE OF GOD.
ACCORDING TO MEDIEVAL JEWISH THINKERS, SUCH FEAR SHOULD BE
UNDERSTOOD AS AWE BEFORE GOD'S GREATNESS.

In the Jewish tradition, there are numerous references to the fear of God. In the Book of Job, for example, Job is described as 'blameless and upright, one who feared God and turned away from evil' (Job 1:1). In rabbinic sources the Hebrew terminology for such awesome reverence is *yirat shamayim*, or 'the fear of heaven'. In the medieval period a distinction was drawn between fear of punishment and fear in the presence of the exalted majesty of God.

MEDIEVAL THEOLOGIANS
In the 12th century, the Jewish philosopher Abraham Ibn Daud (1040–1105) discussed the concept of the fear of God in *Emunah Ramah*. Referring to Deuteronomy

Below The reading of the Torah in a synagogue is interrupted by a crowd led by a Christian priest, 1868. Out of love and fear of God, Jews have revered the Torah and God's commandments.

10:20 ('You shall fear the Lord your God'), he argued that the reference is to the fear produced by God's greatness, not to the fear of harm. There is a fundamental difference between these two types of fear, he stated. A person may be afraid of an honourable prophet who would certainly not harm him, or he might be afraid of a hyena or a snake. The first type is fear at the greatness of the one feared and shame in his presence. Fear of God, he asserted should be of this kind, not of the kind of fear we have for kings whom we are afraid will do harm to us.

In *Duties of the Heart*, the 11th-century theologian Bahya Ibn Pakudah drew a similar distinction. Only fear in the presence of the exalted majesty of God can lead to pure love. A person who attains this degree of reverence will neither fear nor love anything other than the creator. In this regard Bahya referred to a saint who found a God-fearing man sleep-

Above Breaking waves at Monteray Bay, California. Accepting the power of the natural world may be seen as a way of interpreting the fear of God.

ing in the desert. He asked if he were afraid of lions sleeping in such a place. In reply, the God-fearer said: 'I am ashamed that God should see that I am afraid of anything apart from him.'

LATER PHILOSOPHERS
In the 15th century, Jewish philosopher Joseph Albo defined fear as the receding of the soul and the gathering of all her powers into herself, when she imagines some fear-inspiring thing. Yet there is another type of fear in which the soul is awe-struck not because of any fear of harm, but because of her unworthiness in the face of majesty. For Albo this higher fear is elevating. Fearing God in this way, a person will stand in awe before him and be ashamed to transgress his commandments.

In the following century, Elijah de Vidas maintained in *Reshite Hokhmah* that the fear of God is the gate through which every servant of the Lord must pass. It is a necessary condition for loving God and doing his will. Basing his views on Kabbalah, de Vidas stated that, since human beings are created after the pattern of the upper world, all acts have a cosmic effect. Good deeds cause the divine grace to flow through all worlds, whereas evil actions arrest this flow. The fear of sin thus has cosmic significance.

Right The fear of the Lord. Elijah curses the boys who have mocked his baldness, and they are eaten by bears. Painting by James Tissot (1836–1902).

HASIDIM

Among the Hasidim, the fear of God was also an important issue. In the 19th century, Zevi Elimelech Spira in *Bene Yisakhar* argued that effort is required to reach this state. He wrote: 'The disciples of the Ba'al Shem Tov wrote in the name of their master that human effort is only required in order to attain to the state of worship out of fear, whereas God himself sends man the love of him since the male pursues the female; and you know that fear is the category of the female and love that of the male.' In the 18th century Levi Isaac of Berdichev argued in *Kedushat Levi* that a distinction should be drawn between the lower fear of sin and the higher fear whereby one is over-awed by God's majesty. In this state a person has no self-awareness. Yet, this higher fear can only be attained as a product of the lower fear.

THE ZOHAR

According to the medieval mystical work the Zohar, there are three types of fear. Two of these have no proper foundation, but the third is the main source of fear. A person may fear God in order that his sons may live and not die, or because he is afraid of some punishment. Because of this he is in constant fear. Or there is a person who fears God because he is terrified of punishment in the next world. Both these types of fear do not belong to the main foundation of fear. The fear that does have a proper foundation is when a person fears his master because he is the great and mighty ruler. This is the highest type of fear.

MUSAR

This was a movement for ethical education in the spirit of the halakha or Jewish law. It emerged in the 19th century in Lithuania, where fear of punishment was viewed as essential for those struggling to reach perfection. According to Isaac Blazer (1837–1907), the highest fear is the ultimate aim, but it is impossible to attain it without serious reflection on the fear of punishment. Only serious contemplation of severe punishment can penetrate the human heart so that this deeper understanding can be gained.

Below Living with fear. An anti-Semitic riot outside a synagogue in 1750, by Daniel Chodowiecki.

41

PROMISED LAND

TRADITIONAL JUDAISM MAINTAINS THAT THE HOLY LAND WAS PROM-
ISED BY GOD TO ISRAEL. THROUGH THE CENTURIES, JEWS HAVE
LONGED TO RETURN TO THEIR ANCESTRAL HOME.

According to Scripture, God told Abraham to travel to Canaan: 'Go from your country and your kindred and your father's house to the land that I will show you. And I will make of you a great nation' (Genesis 12:1–2). This divine promise became the basis of the Jewish claim to the Holy Land, a conviction that animated Jewish aspirations in the Diaspora to return to the land of their ancestors.

ANCIENT ISRAEL

God's promise to Abraham was repeated to his grandson Jacob who was renamed Israel (meaning 'he who struggles with God'). After Jacob's son Joseph became a vizier in Egypt, the Israelite clan settled in Egypt for several hundred years.

Below The fall of the Temple in 70CE marked the loss of the Jews' homeland for nearly 2,000 years. From the Hours of Neville of Hornby, c. 1340.

Eventually they were freed from Egyptian bondage by Moses, who led them into the desert. Under Joshua's leadership, the Jewish nation conquered the Canaanites and settled in the land, establishing a monarchy. A sacred Temple was built in Jerusalem by King Solomon which became the central cult for the nation. This was followed by a rebellion by the Northern tribes and the establishment of two kingdoms: Israel in the north and Judah in the south. In 722BCE the Northern Kingdom was devastated by Assyrian invaders, and two centuries later the Southern Kingdom was conquered by the Babylonians. Although Jews were allowed to return to Judah by Cyrus of Persia in 538BCE, the Romans destroyed the Temple in 70CE.

Below Palestine and the Promised Land; a map of 1603 after Flemish Abraham Ortelius, generally recognized as the creator of the first modern atlas.

Above The sack of Antioch, 1098. Some Jews saw Jewish deaths in this crusade as a sign that the Messiah was on his way.

MESSIANIC REDEMPTION

Following these events, the Jews were bereft of a homeland. In their despair the Jewish people longed for a messianic deliverer who would lead them back to Zion. Basing their beliefs on biblical prophecy, they foresaw a period of redemption in which earthly life would be transformed and all nations would bow down to the one true God. This vision animated rabbinic reflection about God's plan for his people.

According to rabbinic sources, the process of divine deliverance involved the coming of a messianic

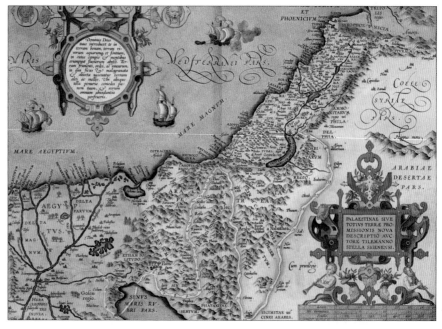

Above View of Jerusalem Seen From the Mount of Olives *by the Russian artist N.G. Chernezov, 1863.*

figure, Messiah ben Joseph, who would serve as the forerunner of the second Messiah, Messiah ben David. This second messiah would bring back all the exiles to Zion and usher in the messianic age. At the end of this period all human beings would be judged: the righteous would enter into heaven whereas the wicked would be condemned to eternal punishment. This vision served as a means of overcoming the nation's trauma at suffering the loss of the Holy Land.

FALSE MESSIAHS

In the early rabbinic period some Jews believed that Jesus was the long-awaited redeemer of Israel. Although mainstream Judaism rejected such claims, the Jewish community continued to long for deliverance. In 132CE the Palestinian military leader Simeon bar Kochba was acclaimed by many Jews as the Davidic Messiah. When his rebellion against Rome resulted in failure, Jews put forward the year of redemption until the 5th century CE, when another messianic pretender, Moses from Crete, declared he would lead Jewish inhabitants from the island back to their homeland.

After this plan failed, Jews continued to hope for a future return and their aspirations are recorded in various midrashic sources.

This longing continued into the early Middle Ages. The traveller Eldad Ha-Dani brought news from Africa of the ten lost tribes, which stimulated messianic longing. Many Jews viewed the year of the First Crusade (1096) as a year of deliverance: when Jews were slaughtered, their suffering was viewed as the birth pangs of the Messiah. In later years the same yearning for a return to Zion was expressed by Jews who continued to be persecuted by the Christian population. The early modern period witnessed this same aspiration for redemption. In 1665 the arrival of Shabbetai Tzvi electrified the Jewish world. Claiming to be the Messiah, he attracted a large circle of followers; however, his conversion to Islam evoked widespread despair.

THE ZIONIST MOVEMENT

With the apostasy of Shabbetai Tzvi, the Jewish preoccupation with messianic deliverance diminished. Many Jews became disillusioned with messianic anticipation. Yet despite this shift in orientation, a number of Jews continued to pray for the coming of the Messiah, and linked this yearning to an advocacy of Zionism. Paralleling

these religious aspirations to establish a Jewish settlement in the Holy Land prior to the coming of the Messiah, modern secular Zionists encouraged such a development in order to solve the problem of anti-Semitism.

As time passed, the Zionist cause gained increasing acceptance in the Jewish world. The first steps towards creating a Jewish homeland were taken at the end of the 19th century with the first Zionist Congress. Subsequently, Zionists attempted to persuade the British government to permit the creation of a Jewish home in Palestine. Although Britain eventually approved of such a plan, the British government insisted that the rights of the Arab population be protected. After World War II, the creation of a Jewish state was approved by the United Nations. Yet despite such an official endorsement, this plan was rejected by the Arabs. In subsequent years, Arabs and Jews have engaged in a series of conflicts, and this antagonism has continued until the present day.

Below The Zionist dream. This Israeli poster shows a Hebrew soldier removing a yellow Star of David armband from an old man, c. 1950.

PRAYER

THROUGHOUT THE AGES, JEWS HAVE TURNED TO GOD IN PRAYER. THROUGH PRAYERS OF PRAISE, THANKSGIVING AND PETITION, THEY HAVE EXPRESSED THEIR LONGINGS AND ASPIRATIONS.

Within the Jewish faith, worship is of fundamental importance. From the biblical period to the present, Jews have turned to God in times of distress. In the synagogue, prayers are addressed to God during daily and Sabbath services and during festivals. In the belief that God listens to the voices of those who turn to him, Jews have expressed their deepest longings and hopes in words of prayer.

THE BIBLE

The Hebrew Scriptures list more than 80 examples of formalized and impromptu worship. Initially no special prayers were required for regular prayer. It was only later that worship services became institutionalized through sacrifices and offerings. Sacrifices to God were made to obtain his favour or atone for sinful acts. Unlike the Canaanites, who sacrificed human beings, the ancient

Below A French postcard for Jewish New Year showing worshippers in prayer shawls, c. 1920.

Israelites slaughtered only animals. In biblical times there were three types of sacrifice offered in the Temple: animal sacrifice, made as a burnt offering for sin; meal offerings; and libations. The rituals and practices governing these acts were set down in Leviticus 2, 23 and Numbers 28, 29.

FIXED WORSHIP

According to the Mishnah, priests serving in the Temple participated in a short liturgy comprising the Shema (Deuteronomy 6:4), the Ten Commandments (Exodus 20:3–17), and the priestly blessing (Numbers 6:24–6). During this period the entire congregation began to pray at fixed times; later, an order of service was established by the men of the Great Assembly. Regular services were held four times daily by the delegations of representatives from the 24 districts of the country. These services consisted of *shaharit*, or 'morning', *musaf*, or 'additional', and *neilat shearim*, or 'evening'.

Above A 5th-century Roman mosaic of Daniel in the lions' den, from Bordj El Loudi, Tunisia. According to Scripture, God protected Daniel from harm.

RABBINIC TIMES

Several orders of prayers coexisted until Gamaliel II produced a regularized standard after the Temple was destroyed in 70 CE. Prayers officially replaced the sacrificial system since they could no longer be offered in the Temple. This new ritual – the service of the heart – was conducted in the synagogue. The core of the liturgy included the prayer formula 'Blessed are You, O God', the Shema, and the Amidah (known also as the tefillah), consisting of 19 benedictions. On special occasions, an additional Amidah was included.

Prayers were recited by a *minyan*, or 'quorum of ten men': if such a number could not be found, certain prayers had to be omitted (including the Kaddish, Kedushah and the reading of the Law). The Alenu prayer, originating from the New Year liturgy, and the Kaddish were the two concluding prayers of all services.

HEBREW BIBLE READINGS

During the worship service, portions of the Torah (Five Books of Moses) and the Prophets were recited, and this became a normal practice by the time of the Mishnah in the 2nd

Above Prayer ceremony from an illustrated Hebrew prayer book, Germany, 1471.

century CE. By the end of the talmudic period (6th century CE), the prayer service was supplemented by piyyutim, or 'liturgical hymns'. These compositions were produced in Palestine as well as Babylonia from geonic times until the 12th century.

The Palestine rite was distinguished by a triennial cycle of reading from the Torah, a recension of the benedictions of the Amidah, and an introductory blessing before the recitation of the Shema.

The Babylonian rite was first recorded by Amram Gaon in the 9th century CE. This work served as the official ordering of prayers with their legal requirements. This act of setting down liturgical arrangements led to the dissolution of the ban against committing prayers to writing. In the 10th century CE the first authoritative prayer book (*siddur*) was edited by Saadiah Gaon (882–942CE).

JEWISH MYSTICISM

For Jewish mystics, *devekut*, or 'cleaving to God in prayer', was of fundamental importance. For the early Kabbalists of Provence devekut was the goal of the mystic way. According to the 13th-century Jewish philosopher Nahmanides,

devekut is a state of mind in which one constantly remembers God and his love to the point that when a person speaks with someone else, his heart is not with them at all but is still before God. In Nahmanides' view, the true Hasid, or 'pious individual', is able to attain such a spiritual state – devekut does not completely eliminate the distance between God and human beings. Rather, it denotes a state of beatitude and intimate union between the soul and its source.

MYSTIC PRAYER

In ascending to the higher worlds, the path of prayer paralleled the observance of the commandments. Yet, unlike the *mitzvot*, or 'commandments', prayer is independent of action and can become a process of mediation. Mystical prayer, which is accompanied by meditative *kavvanot*, or 'intention', focusing on each prayer's Kabbalistic content, became a feature of various stems of Kabbalah. For the Kabbalist, prayer was understood as the ascent of human beings into the higher realm where the soul can integrate with the higher spheres. By using the traditional liturgy in symbolic fashion, prayer repeats the hidden processes of the cosmos.

HASIDISM

In the 19th century, Hasidim incorporated Kabbalistic ideas into their understanding of prayer. According to Hasidic thought, the Kabbalistic type of kavvanot brings about an emotional involvement and attachment to God. In Hasidism, prayer is seen as a mystical encounter with the divine in which the human heart is elevated towards its ultimate source. Frequently the act of prayer was seen as the most important religious activity.

MODERN JUDAISM

In modern times the emergence of various Jewish movements led to the reinterpretation of the liturgical tradition. Reform Jews modified the worship service through eliminating various prayers, and introducing the organ and communal singing as well as addresses in the vernacular. The aim of Reform Judaism was to adapt Jewish worship to contemporary needs. Within the Conservative and Reconstructionist movements, prayer books adhered more closely to the traditional *siddur*, or 'prayer book'. Yet, despite such a diversity of approaches, prayer continues to serve as a focal point of the faith.

Below In the Synagogue, c.1900, the focus of divine worship and service.

CHAPTER 3

THE SPIRITUAL PATH

The Bible serves as a guide to Jewish spirituality. Later Jewish sources – including the midrash and the Talmud – similarly provide a basis for the spiritual path. In this context, ethical values are of primary importance. Through their election, the Jewish people are to serve as God's servants, proclaiming God's truth and righteousness. Jews are called to action, to turn humanity away from wickedness and sin. In this quest, the Jewish nation is to become holy, just as God is holy. Through moral living, Jews are to reflect God's compassion, mercy and justice.

In the Jewish tradition, compassion is perceived as a cardinal virtue. Those who suffer are to be consoled. God's mission for his people is for them to act as comforters of the oppressed. This message is highlighted during the Passover *seder*, or 'religious meal'. The Jewish people are to remember that they were once enslaved; their responsibility is to free those who are in bondage. Yet such compassionate care is to be tempered by the quest for justice. By choosing such a moral life, the Jew is to complete God's work of creation.

Opposite Synagogue Service Imploring Divine Favour and Grace. *A devout Jew pictured by 19th-century Russian painter Nikolai Bogdanoff-Bjelski.*

Above Simchat Torah is the holy day on which the completion of the annual reading of the Torah is *celebrated. This particular festival procession took place at Livorno synagogue, Italy, in 1850.*

BIBLE

The Bible serves as the bedrock of the Jewish faith. In the Hebrew Scriptures, known as the Tanakh, the ancient Israelites recorded their history and religious beliefs.

For the Jewish people, the Hebrew Scriptures serve as the basis of belief and practice. Through the ages the nation has looked to the Bible for inspiration and sustenance. In times of tribulation as well as joy, Jews have turned to this sacred literature as a source of comfort and hope.

THE HEBREW SCRIPTURES

The Jewish faith is a revealed religion. Its basis is the Bible. The Hebrew name for the canon of Scripture is *Tanakh*: the Hebrew term is an abbreviation of the principal letters of the words standing for its divisions: *Torah*, or 'teaching'; *Neviim*, or 'prophets'; *Ketuvim*, or 'writings'. The Torah consists of Genesis, Exodus, Leviticus, Numbers and Deuteronomy. According to

Below Samuel, prophet and judge in the Bible, beheads Agad, king of the Amalekites. From the North French Hebrew Miscellany, compiled in 1278 at a time of upheaval for European Jews.

tradition, these five books were revealed by God to Moses on Mount Sinai. The second division of the Hebrew Bible – the Prophets – is divided into two parts. The first – Former Prophets – contains the books of Joshua, Judges, 1 and 2 Samuel and 1 and 2 Kings. The second part – Latter Prophets – is composed of the major prophets (Isaiah, Jeremiah and Ezekiel) and the minor prophets (Hosea, Joel, Amos, Obadiah, Jonah, Micah, Nahum, Habakkuk, Zephaniah, Haggai, Zechariah and Malachi). The third division consists of a variety of divinely inspired books: Psalms, Proverbs, Job, Song of Songs, Ruth, Lamentations, Ecclesiastes, Esther, Daniel, Ezra, Nehemiah and 1 and 2 Chronicles.

NON-CANONICAL LITERATURE

During the Second Temple period and afterwards, a large number of other books were written by Jews in Hebrew, Aramaic and Greek that were not included in the biblical canon. None the less, these texts did gain canonical status in the Roman Catholic and Eastern Orthodox churches. Known as the Apocrypha, they had an important impact on Christian thought. The most substantial is the Wisdom of Jesus Son of Sirah (also known as Ben Sira or Ecclesiasticus). Other works include: the Wisdom of Solomon, 1 and 2 Maccabees, Tobit and Judith. Additional literary sources of the Second Temple period are known as the Pseudepigrapha – these non-canonical books consist of such works as the Testament of the Twelve Patriarchs, 1 and 2 Enoch and Jubilees.

Above Samson, an Israelite judge and man of great strength, defeats a lion in a German illustration from 1360.

RABBINIC JUDAISM

In rabbinic literature a distinction is drawn between the revelation of the Pentateuch (Torah in the narrow sense) and the prophetic writings. This is frequently expressed by saying that the Torah was given directly by God, whereas the prophetic books were given by means of prophecy. The remaining books of the Bible were conveyed by means of the holy spirit rather than through prophecy. Nevertheless, all these writings constitute the canon of Scripture.

According to the rabbis, the expositions and elaborations of the *Torah She-Bi-Ketav*, or 'Written Law',

Below The Judgement of Solomon, greatest of the judges, by Valentin de Boulogne, 1625.

Left *The text of every Sefer Torah, kept in the synagogue, is identical because it is copied from an original by a* sofer *(scribe).*

'Torah from Sinai', is a fundamental principle of the faith: 'The Torah was revealed from heaven. This implies our belief that the whole of the Torah found in our hands this day is the Torah that was handed down by Moses, and that it is all of divine origin. By this I mean that the whole of the Torah came unto him from before God in a manner which is metaphorically called "speaking"; but the real nature of that communication is unknown to everybody except to Moses to whom it came.'

Above The Book of Exodus recounts that the Israelites built cities for Pharaoh. From a Hebrew Haggadah, 1740.

were also revealed by God to Moses on Mount Sinai. Subsequently they were passed from generation to generation, and through this process additional legislation was incorporated. This process is referred to as the *Torah She-Be-Al-Peh*, or 'Oral Torah'. Thus traditional Judaism affirms that God's revelation is twofold and binding for all time. Committed to this belief, Orthodox Jews pray in the synagogue that God will guide them to do his will as recorded in their sacred literature.

THE MEDIEVAL PERIOD

In the Middle Ages this traditional belief was affirmed. Thus the 12th-century Jewish philosopher Moses Maimonides (1135–1204) declared that the belief in *Torah MiSinai*, or

Below The coming of the prophet Elijah, from the Washington Haggadah, created in Italy by Joel ben Simeon, 1478.

THE ZOHAR

The medieval mystical work the Zohar asserts that the Torah contains mysteries beyond human comprehension. According to Simeon ben Yohai, traditionally identified as the author of the Zohar: 'Alas for the man who regards the Torah as a book of mere tales and everyday matters! If that were so, even we could compose a Torah dealing with everyday affairs, and of even greater excellence. Nay, even the princes of the world possess books of greater worth which we could use as a model for composing such Torah. The Torah, however, contains in all its words supernal truths and sublime mysteries.'

MODERN JUDAISM

Orthodox Judaism remains committed to the view that the Written as well as the Oral Torah were imparted by God to Moses on Mount Sinai. This act of revelation serves as the basis for the entire legal system as well as doctrinal beliefs about God. Yet despite such an adherence to tradition, many modern Orthodox Jews pay only lip service to such a conviction. The gap between traditional belief and contemporary views of the Torah is even greater in

the non-Orthodox branches of Judaism. Here there is a general acceptance of biblical scholarship. Such a non-fundamentalist approach rules out the traditional belief in the infallibility of Scripture and thereby provides a rationale for changing the law and reinterpreting the theology of the Hebrew Scriptures.

THE PENTATEUCH

Like Maimonides, the 13th-century philosopher Nahmanides (1194–1270) in his *Commentary to the Pentateuch* argued that Moses wrote the Five Books of Moses at God's dictation. It is likely, he observed, that Moses wrote Genesis and part of Exodus when he descended from Mount Sinai. At the end of 40 years in the wilderness he completed the rest of the Pentateuch. Nahmanides observed that this view follows the rabbinic tradition that the Torah was given scroll by scroll. For Nahmanides, Moses was like a scribe who copied an older work.

MISHNAH, MIDRASH AND TALMUD

IN THE 2ND CENTURY CE, THE MISHNAH WAS COMPILED BY YEHUDA HA-NASI AS THE FIRST COLLECTION OF RABBINIC LAW. IN LATER CENTURIES, THE PALESTINIAN AND BABYLONIAN TALMUDS WERE PRODUCED.

With the rise of rabbinic Judaism, scholars engaged in the exposition of the biblical text and the interpretation of Jewish law. In academies in Erez Israel and Babylonia, sages devoted themselves to interpreting God's will and edifying the Jewish people. Initially their teachings were passed on orally, but in time they were written down in the Mishnah, Talmud and midrashic sources.

EARLY RABBINIC JUDAISM
During the early rabbinic period – between the 1st century BCE and the 6th century CE – rabbinic scholars referred to as Tannaim (70–200 CE) and Amoraim (200–500 CE) engaged in the interpretation of the biblical

Below The Talmud is a compilation of Jewish laws. This page, from a German Talmud of the early 1300s, shows when God created his world.

text. According to tradition, both the Written and the Oral Torah were given by God to Moses on Mount Sinai. This belief implies that God is the direct source of the *mitzvot*, or 'commandments', recorded in the Five Books of Moses and is also indirectly responsible for the legal judgements of the rabbis. Such a conviction serves as the justification for the rabbinic exposition of scriptural ordinances.

Alongside this halakha, or 'exegesis of Jewish law', Jewish sages also produced interpretations of Scripture in which aggadah, or 'new meanings of the text', were expounded in midrashim, or 'rabbinic commentaries', and in the Talmud. Within aggadic sources is found a wealth of theological speculation about topics such as the nature of God, divine justice, the coming of the Messiah and the afterlife. In addition, ethical considerations were of considerable importance in the discussions of these teachers of the faith.

MISHNAH
During the age of the Tannaim, Jewish scholars produced teachings dealing with Jewish law which were codified in the Mishnah by Yehuda Ha-Nasi (135–220CE) in about 200 CE. This work is a compilation of oral traditions (Oral Law); it is divided into six orders (which are subdivided into 63 tractates). The first order, Zeraim, or 'seeds', deals largely with agricultural law, although it begins with a section about prayer. The second order, Moed, or 'season', deals with the sacred calendar. In the third order,

Above Menorah, or seven-branched candlestick, and sarcophagus at Beit She'arim, where the great Mishnah scholar Yehuda Ha-Nasi lived.

Nashim, or 'women', matrimonial law is discussed in extensive detail. The fourth order, Nezikim, or 'damages', contains both civil and criminal law and also contains a tractate of Avot, or 'moral maxims'. The fifth order, Kodashim, or 'holy things', gives a detailed account of the rules for sacrifice. Finally, the sixth order, Tohorot, or 'purity', is concerned with ritual purity.

MIDRASH
Parallel with the legal tradition, Jewish sages also expounded the narrative parts of Scripture. In the Tannaitic period such midrashim dealt with the Five Books of Moses. Some of these traditions allegedly derive from the School of Akiva; others are attributed to the School of Ishmael. These midrashic sources are: the *Mekilta* on the book of Exodus; the *Sifra* on Leviticus; and the *Sifrei* on Numbers and Deuteronomy. Other midrashic sources deal with material from the Amoraic period.

Like the tannaitic midrashim, some are in the form of running commentaries known as exegetical midrashim. Others are collections of sermons arranged according to the

Above Studying the Scriptures with rabbinic commentary is an integral part of Jewish life. Photo taken in the Great Synagogue in Moscow, 1987.

sabbaths or festivals for which they were written. These are known as homiletical midrashim. The largest collection of midrashim is *Midrash Rabbah*, consisting of works that were separate commentaries on the Torah plus the Five Scrolls (the Song of Songs, Ruth, Lamentations, Ecclesiastes, Esther). Homiletical midrashim are exemplified by *Pesikta de-Rav Kahana*, *Pesikta Rabbati* and *Midrash Tanhuma* (known also as *Yelammedenu*).

TALMUD

In the centuries following the composition of the Mishnah and the early midrashim, Jewish sages in Palestine and Babylonia continued to expand Jewish law. By the 4th century CE scholars in Erez Israel had collected together the teachings of generations of sages in the academies of Tiberius, Caesarea and Sepphoris. The extended discussions of the Mishnah became the Palestinian Talmud. The text of this multi-volume work covers four sections of the Mishnah (seeds, set feasts, women and damages), but here and there various tractates are missing. No doubt the discussions in these academies included matters on these missing tractates, but it is

not known how far the recording, editing and transmission of these sections had progressed before they were lost.

The views of these sages had an important influence on scholars in Babylonia, though their work never attained the same prominence as that of the Babylonian Talmud. In Babylonia, sages completed the redaction of the Babylonian Talmud by the 6th century CE – an editorial task begun by Ashi in the 5th century CE. This massive work is largely a summary of the discussions that took place in the Babylonian academies. Although the Babylonian Talmud deals with slightly fewer

Mishnaic tractates, it is nearly four times larger than the Palestinian Talmud and came to be regarded as more authoritative.

The texts of these Talmuds consists largely of summaries of rabbinic discussion: a phrase of Mishnah is interpreted, discrepancies are resolved and redundancies are explained. In this compilation, conflicting opinions of the earlier sages are contrasted, unusual words are explained and anonymous opinions are identified. Frequently, individual teachers cite specific cases to support their views, and hypothetical eventualities are examined to reach a solution on the discussion. Debates between outstanding scholars in one generation are often cited, as are differences of opinion between members of an academy or a teacher and his students. The range of talmudic explorations is much broader than that of the Mishnah, and includes a wide range of teachings about such subjects as theology, philosophy and ethics.

Below A painting of a Jewish Wedding by Italian Pietro Longhi (1701/2–85). A section of the Mishnah concerns women, marriage, divorce and vows.

ETHICS

ETHICAL CONCERNS ARE OF PARAMOUNT IMPORTANCE IN THE JEWISH TRADITION. ALONGSIDE THE ETHICAL TEACHING IN SCRIPTURE, A WIDE RANGE OF MITZVOT DEAL WITH THE MORAL LIFE.

In the Jewish faith, ethical values are of primary importance. For Jews, moral action is fundamental – since it is through the rule of the moral law that God's kingdom on earth can be realized. This is the goal of the history of the world in which God's chosen people have a central role. It is their destiny to be a light to the nations.

THE MORAL LIFE

Through the centuries Judaism did not separate religion from life. Rather, the Jewish people were called to action. It was their duty to turn men and women away from violence, wickedness and falsehood. In this quest it was not the hope of bliss in a future life that was the

Right When God destroyed humanity with a flood because of its great wickedness, Noah's family were saved in an ark, shown here under a rainbow, in a mosaic from Kykko, Cyprus.

primary goal – rather, the aim was to establish a kingdom of justice and peace on earth. Ethical action is thus at the heart of the tradition. Each Jew was to be like the creator, mirroring the divine qualities revealed to Moses: 'The Lord, the Lord, a God merciful and gracious, slow to anger, and abounding in steadfast love and faithfulness, keeping steadfast love for thousands, forgiving iniquity and transgression and sin' (Exodus 34:6–7).

THE TORAH

In the Hebrew Scriptures, deeds and events involving ethical issues are found in abundance: the punishment of Cain for murdering his brother; the violence of the generation that brought about the flood; the early prohibition against murder; the hospitality of Abraham and his plea for the peoples of Sodom; the praise of Abraham for his ethical character; the condemnation of Joseph's brothers; Joseph's restraint in Egypt in the house of Potiphar; Moses' plea for the exploited.

Yet it is in the legal codes of the Torah that we encounter moral guidelines formulated in specific laws. The Ten Commandments in particular illustrate the centrality of Jewish ethics. The first commandments are theological in nature, but the last six deal with relationships between human beings. These *mitzvot*, or 'commandments', provide a means of expressing love of others. The Decalogue thus makes it clear that moral standards are fundamental to the Jewish faith.

Left Moses receives the Ten Commandments, a central part of Jewish ethics. From a 1305 Bible Historiale, *the predominant medieval translation of the Bible into French.*

THE PROPHETS

Ethical principles are at the core of prophetic teaching. The books of the prophets are rooted in the Torah of Moses. The prophets saw themselves as messengers of the divine word – their task was to denounce the nation for its transgressions and call it to repentance. In all this they pointed to concrete ethical action as the only means of sustaining their covenantal relationship with God. In their view, God demands righteousness and justice above all else.

Emphasis on the moral life was reflected in the prophetic condemnation of cultic practices that were devoid of ethical concern. These passages illustrate that ritual laws are of instrumental value – morality is intrinsic and absolute. The primacy of ethics was also reflected in the prophetic warning that righteous action is the determining factor in the destiny of the Jewish nation. Moral transgressions referred to in such contexts concern exploitation,

Below Jewish women in New York package excess donated produce from the Greenmarket. This was for delivery to programmes serving the hungry for the Rosh Hashanah holiday, 2010.

oppression and the perversion of justice. These transgressions have the potential to bring about the destruction of the nation.

PROVERBS

The Book of Proverbs reinforces the teaching of the Torah and the prophets. Here wisdom is conceived as a capacity to act morally. It is a skill that can be learned. Throughout the book of Proverbs dispositional traits are catalogued: positive moral types include the righteous person, the wise individual and the upright; negative ones include the evil person, the fool, the mocker and the simpleton. Thus, here as in the rest of Scripture, the moral life is seen as the basis of the faith. Theology is defined in relation to action – it is through the moral life that humanity encounters the divine.

RABBINIC LITERATURE

Rabbinic sages continued this emphasis on the moral life. Convinced that they were the authentic expositors of the Bible, the rabbis amplified scriptural law. In their expansion of the mitzvot, rabbinic exegetes differentiated between the laws governing human relationships to God and those that concern relationships to others. By choosing the moral life, the Jew is able to complete God's work of creation. To accomplish this task the sages formulated an elaborate system of traditions that

Above An old man blessing a child. Such ritual is a feature of Jewish ethical teaching on the relationship between children and adults.

were written down in the Mishnah, subsequently expanded in the Talmud and eventually codified in the Code of Jewish law. According to rabbinic Judaism, this expansion of biblical law is part of God's revelation. Both the Written and Oral Torah are binding on Jews for all time. Such a conviction implies that the entire corpus of moral law is an expression of the divine will and must be obeyed.

THE CODE OF JEWISH LAW

For Jews the moral law is absolute and binding. In all cases it was made precise and specific – it is God's word made concrete in the life of the nation. The commandment to love one's neighbour embraces all humanity. In the code of Jewish law the virtues of justice, honesty and humane concern are regarded as central to community life. Hatred, vengeance, deceit, cruelty and anger are condemned. The Jew is to exercise loving kindness to all: to clothe the naked, feed the hungry, care for the sick and comfort the mourner. By fulfilling these ethical demands, the Jewish nation can help bring about God's kingdom on earth in which exploitation, oppression and injustice are eliminated.

SIN AND REPENTANCE

IN THE JEWISH TRADITION, REPENTANCE IS REGARDED AS A VIRTUE. SINNERS ARE TO RECOGNIZE THEIR WICKEDNESS, REPENT OF THEIR ACTIONS, AND RESOLVE TO CHANGE THEIR EVIL WAYS.

According to the Jewish tradition, sin is understood in terms of the rejection of God's will. Human beings are thought of as being pulled in two directions: the *yetzer ha-tov*, or 'good inclination', draws individuals towards the good, whereas the *yetzer ha-ra*, or 'evil inclination', binds them in sin. Sin occurs when the evil inclination is overpowering in this struggle.

THE LEGAL SYSTEM

According to Jewish law, there are two types of sin: sins of commission and sins of omission. The former are more serious, but in some cases a positive commandment pushes aside

Below The serpent tempts Adam and Eve leading to their expulsion from the Garden of Eden. French manuscript of Ovid's Metamorphoses, *1494.*

a negative one if this is the only way that it can be carried out. Sins involving the transgression of negative precepts are of two types: offences against God and offences against one's neighbour. Yom Kippur, the Day of Atonement brings about forgiveness for those sins committed against God. But for offences against other human beings, the wrong done to the victim must be put right.

THE EVIL INCLINATION

The yetzer ha-ra is often identified with sexual lust, but the term also applies to physical appetites in general and aggressive desires. It is perceived as the force in human beings that drives them to gratify their instincts. Although it is referred to as 'evil' because it can lead to wrong-doing, it is essential to life. As the midrash remarks: 'Were it not for the yetzer

Above The shofar is blown at the end of Yom Kippur, to remind Jews of their sins during the previous year. From a 1400s German manuscript.

ha-ra, no man would build a house or marry or have children or engage in commerce.' This is the reason why Scripture states: 'And God saw everything that he had made and behold, it was very good' (Genesis 1:31). In a similar vein, there is a legend that the Men of the Great Synagogue wished to kill the yetzer ha-ra. But the yetzer ha-ra warned them that if they were successful, then the world would be destroyed.

REPENTANCE

Given the ever-present danger of sin, how are human beings to repent of their sinfulness? This is the constant theme of prophetic literature, and it continued into the rabbinic period. According to the 12th-century Jewish philosopher Moses Maimonides (1135–1204), if a person wittingly or unwittingly transgresses any commandment, he is required to repent and turn away from his wickedness and confess his sins to God. How should one confess one's sins? Maimonides wrote: 'He says, "O God! I have sinned, I have committed iniquity. I have transgressed before you by doing such and such. Behold now I am sorry for what I have done and am ashamed and

I shall never do it again." ' True repentance takes place if the sinner has the opportunity of committing once again the sinful act, but he refrains from doing so. The sinner must strive to relinquish his sin, remove it from his thoughts and resolve never to repeat it.

LITERARY WORKS

In addition to the numerous references to repentance in rabbinic sources, there exist medieval works devoted to this theme. One of the most important, *Shaare Teshuvah* (Gates of Repentance) by Jonah ben Abraham Gerondi (1200–64), lists 20 essential features of sincere repentance: remorse; relinquishing the sin; pain for the sin; affliction of the body in fasting and weeping; fear of the consequences of the sin and of repeating it; shame for the sin; submission to God in humility and contrition; gentleness in future conduct; breaking the physical lusts by asceticism; the use by the sinner of that organ with which he sinned to do good; constant self-scrutiny; reflection by the sinner on the pun-

Right The Kapparot ceremony, in which a chicken is slaughtered and given to the poor, is performed before Yom Kippur, the annual Day of Atonement for sin.

ishment he deserves; the treatment of minor sins as major; confession; prayer; putting right the sin; almsgiving; the sinner should be conscious of his sin to refrain from repeating the sinful act when the opportunity presents itself; leading others away from sin.

PHYSICAL MORTIFICATION

For the rabbis, repentance is effected by such sincere resolve. There is no need for physical mortification in order to win pardon. The need for such mortification came into Jewish thought in the Middle Ages. The self-tortures required for true repentance are detailed in the ethical work *Rokeah* by Eleazer of Worms (1160–1238). No doubt Christian monasticism of the period influenced such practices. It is recorded that sages used to roll naked in the snow in the depths of winter, smear their bodies with honey and allow

themselves to be stung by bees and fast for days on end. However, such extreme practices were only carried out by a relatively few pietists, and in later centuries mortification of the flesh was condemned by the teachers of the Hasidic movement.

Below Penitence in a German synagogue, 1723. Flagellation was a practice influenced by Christian monks.

THE HUMAN STRUGGLE

According to rabbinic Judaism, human beings are engaged in a constant struggle against the evil that exists within themselves. The means whereby they can overcome this destructive force is provided by the Torah and its precepts. In the Talmud we read that when a person submits to the discipline provided by the Torah and studies it, then he will become free of morbid guilt. His life is then unclouded by the fear that the evil within will drag him down and bring his ruin. God has wounded human beings by creating the evil inclination – but the Torah serves as a plaster on the wound.

COMPASSION

JUST AS GOD IS COMPASSIONATE, JEWS ARE TO TREAT OTHERS WITH
COMPASSION. ALONGSIDE BENEVOLENCE AND MODESTY, IT IS REGARDED
AS AN IDENTIFYING CHARACTERISTIC OF THE JEWISH NATION.

Within the Jewish faith, compassion is regarded a central virtue. Empathy for the suffering of others and the desire to remove their pain are extolled as moral imperatives.

THE TRADITION OF COMPASSION

In Hebrew the word for compassion is *rahmanut*; this has the same root as the word *rehem*, or 'womb'. It denotes the tenderness and pity a mother should have for her child. According to the rabbis, compassion is one of the three distinguishing marks of Jews (the others being benevolence and modesty). This does not imply that non-Jews are less compassionate; rather compassion is understood as part of human nature. When compassion is ascribed to

Below Giving charity at the entrance to the grave of the Moroccan rabbi and Kabbalist Baba Saki in Netivot, Israel.

Right Compassion for the displaced. Fleeing anti-Semitism in the USSR in 1979, a Soviet Jewish child refugee and her mother arrive at Vienna.

Jews, this simply means that the Jewish people should be true to this basic element of human nature.

The Torah trains Jewry in the ways of compassion; the rabbis maintain that the ancestors of a person lacking in compassion did not stand at the foot of Mount Sinai. Just as God is described in the Bible as compassionate, so too should Jews strive to resemble the creator and be God-like in their sympathy for others.

THE CONCEPT

Rahmanut, or compassion, is understood as the tear which is shed for the sick and the poor; the hand that is outstretched in friendship; concern for the handicapped; commiseration with failure; and prayer for human-

ity overwhelmed with suffering. Even though rahmanut should result in action, it is in itself desirable. When a person is described as kind and sympathetic, this is compassion. Its opposite is indifference.

DIVINE COMPASSION

A common phrase used in the Talmud for 'God states' is 'The Compassionate says'. The second benediction of the Amidah prayer declares God's compassion for his creatures: 'Thou sustainest the living with loving kindness, revivest the dead with great compassion. Thou supportest the falling, healest the sick, loosest the bound, and keepest thy faith to them that sleep in the dust.'

One of God's names in the Jewish liturgy is *Av ha-Rahamin*, or 'Father of compassion'. The Grace after Meals speaks of God as feeding the world with goodness, with grace, with loving kindness, and with compassion. The end of the Amidah prayer refers twice to God's compassion.

UNIVERSAL RESPONSIBILITY

In Judaism, compassion is regarded as a virtue for all peoples. The prophets criticized non-Israelites for their lack of compassion to one another. Thus Jeremiah described people of the north country who 'lay hold on bow and spear, they are cruel and have no compassion' (Jeremiah 6:23). Amos pronounced God's verdict of doom on those nations who committed atrocities against one another, among them

Edom, who 'pursued his brother with the sword, and cast off all pity' (Amos 1:11).

COMPASSION FOR ANIMALS

According to the Jewish tradition, compassion must be extended to all of God's creatures. The principle of compassion toward animals is expressed by the Hebrew concept *tza'ar baalei hayyim*, or 'causing pain to living creatures'.

In the rabbinic tradition, this notion is developed in detail. Hence, according to the dietary laws, the purpose of *shehitah*, or 'ritual slaughter', is to adopt as painless a form of killing as possible. It is the principle of tza'ar baalei hayyim which underlies biblical prohibitions to avoid: muzzling the ox while ploughing (Deuteronomy 25:4), yoking an ox with an ass (22:10), taking the young before sending away the mother bird (22:76-7), and killing an animal and its young on the same day (Leviticus 22:28).

THOSE IN NEED OF COMPASSION

Judaism teaches that those whom fate has treated harshly should become objects of compassion. This applies particularly to the stranger, the widow and the orphan. According to rabbinic Judaism, it is wrong to suggest to those who mourn or suffer in other ways that this is the result of sin.

Although it is important to be self-critical, the temptation to be hard on others should be resisted. It is important in showing compassion that others should not be put to shame. Steps should always be taken not to cause distress. The Talmud, for example, asserts that in the presence

Right A 15th-century miniature showing sheitah*, the ritual slaughter of animals, which is carried out as painlessly as possible. According to Jewish law, animals are to be treated humanely.*

of a family of a criminal who has been hanged for murder, one should refrain from referring to anything that is hanging from the ceiling. Even when it is necessary to rebuke someone for his or her action, this should be done with tact.

THE LIMIT OF COMPASSION

Despite the importance of compassion, Judaism rules that there are limits. If a judge comes to the conclusion that a person is in the right and another in the wrong, it would be a perversion of justice if in feeling compassion for the guilty, there should be a miscarriage of justice. Thus the Talmud rules there must be no compassion in a law suit. The law must be decided objectively. What the judge must never do is to bend the law through a miscalculation based on sympathy for the accused.

Compassion is also misapplied when it is expressed to individuals who are deliberately cruel. There is a rabbinic dictum which states that whoever has compassion on the cruel will in the end be cruel to the compassionate.

BENEVOLENCE

LIKE THE ATTITUDE OF COMPASSION, THE PRACTICE OF BENEVOLENCE
IS OF KEY IMPORTANCE IN THE JEWISH FAITH. COMPASSION SHOULD
LEAD TO BENEVOLENCE – THE JEWISH IDEAL IS TO PRACTISE BOTH.

*Above A man begs for alms in Israel.
Giving to the needy is a means of
exercising benevolence.*

There are two related concepts of benevolence in Judaism. The first is *gemilut hasadim*, or 'bestowing loving kindness', and *tzedakah*, 'charity'. In the Bible, *tzedakah* means righteousness, and is synonymous with *mishpat*, or 'justice'. Yet, by rabbinic times, the word had assumed the meaning of charity. The Talmud states that there are three main differences between gemilut hasadim and tzedakah. Tzedakah is for the benefit of the poor, whereas gemilut hasadim is for everyone. It is not possible to contribute charity to the rich, but gemilut hasadim can be extended to all including the rich. Further, tzedakah refers to a contribution of money. The poor need financial assistance, but gemilut hasadim implies the giving of oneself. Finally, tzedakah is given to the

living. One cannot give charity to the dead. But gemilut hasadim can be extended to those who have died by burying them and attending their funerals.

RABBINIC SOURCES

There are numerous examples of gemilut hasadim in rabbinic literature. Prominent among acts of benevolence is visiting the sick. An entire section of the Shulkhan Arukh, or 'Code of Jewish Law', is devoted to the rules for visiting the sick. The rabbis declared that the Shekhinah, or 'divine presence', is with the sick because God shares in that person's suffering. Comforting mourners is another example of gemilut hasadim. In talmudic times it was a custom to take gifts of food to those who had suffered loss. To attend a funeral is an act of benevolence. Other examples include lending money to help a person with a financial difficulty, speaking words

of encouragement, greeting others warmly, helping the aged, and providing hospitality.

RELIEF FOR THE POOR

In giving charity, there should always be an element of benevolence. The poor should be spoken of kindly, and whatever is given should come from the heart without being patronizing. In ancient times there was a complex system of tzedakah: charity overseers made separate collections. One was for a weekly distribution; the other was for those who were passing through a town. Jewish communities provided a number of societies, each with its own charitable

*Below Comforting mourners at a
funeral is an example of gemilut
hasadim. Italian painting, 1750.*

According to the medieval philosopher Moses Maimonides, there are eight degrees of charity:

1 A man gives, but is glum when he gives. This is the lowest degree of all.

2 A man gives with a cheerful countenance, but gives less than he should.

3 A man gives, but only when asked by the poor.

4 A man gives without having to be asked, but gives directly to the poor who know therefore to whom they are indebted, and he, too, knows whom he has benefited.

5 A man places his donation in a certain place and then turns his back so that he does not know which of the poor he has benefited, but the poor man knows to whom he is indebted.

DEGREES OF CHARITY

6 A man throws his money into the house of a poor man. The poor man does not know to whom he is indebted but the donor knows whom he has benefited.

7 A man contributes anonymously to the charity fund, which is then distributed to the poor. Here the poor man does not know to whom he is indebted, neither does the donor know whom he has benefited.

8 Highest of all is when a man gives money to prevent another person from becoming poor, as by providing him with a job or by lending him money to tide him over during a difficult period. There is no charity greater than this because it prevents poverty in the first instance.

Above Charitable giving is a sign of benevolence. Donation box in Elijah's Cave synagogue, Haifa, Israel.

purposes. The education of poor children and other religious needs of the poor were also provided.

WHO ARE 'THE POOR'?

In determining who qualifies as a poor person, the Jewish tradition specifies that someone who has 200 zuz (an ancient silver coin) in ready cash or 50 zuz invested in business can no longer be considered poor and entitled to public assistance. A person who has a smaller amount does

qualify since he meets the terms of the law. The official rabbinic view concerning the amount to be given is that a person should give a tenth of his income. However, the rabbis discourage giving more than a fifth of their income in case they might become poor themselves. Regarding the question who should come first in terms of preference, the rabbis state that when it is a question of food, a man should come before a woman because he has a family to

support. If it is a question of clothing, a woman should take precedence because she suffers greater deprivation if she does not have proper clothes to wear. A person should help his poor relatives before he helps others; similarly, the poor of one's own town should be helped first.

Below Benevolence includes being with the sick. An Orthodox woman with a baby at the neonatal ICU in Shaarei Tzedek hospital, Jerusalem, Israel.

Below Russian Jewish refugees in the Poor Jews Temporary Shelter, Leman Street, east London, 1891.

JUSTICE

THE CONCEPT OF JUSTICE IS FUNDAMENTAL TO THE JEWISH TRADITION.
WITHIN RABBINIC SOURCES, JUSTICE IS UNDERSTOOD IN TERMS OF LAW.
THE PRACTICE OF GIVING A JUST RULING IS OF CENTRAL IMPORTANCE.

In legal cases, justice comes into operation when two parties are in conflict. For example, two individuals (A and B) might claim ownership of land: one (A) inherited the property from his father, while the other (B) claims he bought it from A and produces evidence to support this assertion. (A), however, denies ever having sold the land and rejects the evidence. In many instances, the available evidence does not provide a basis for reaching a just solution. Yet even here there is a possibility of solving the problem. Jewish law gives the benefit of the doubt to the person who is in possession of the disputed property. The general rule in such a dispute is that, in the absence of factual evidence, the court would not be justified in removing the property from where it is for this would be deciding, without sufficient cause, in favour of one of the parties. Where evidence is insufficient, the court has no right to decide in favour of either party. The only fair procedure is to leave the property where it is until further evidence is available.

CRIME AND PUNISHMENT

In cases of crime, justice involves weighing the claims of society against the criminal. In a just society, the right of the criminal to prey on others should be rejected in favour of the right of society to protect itself. However, justice is involved when society has to determine how far to punish the offender. As far as the punishment affords such protection, it is just. But if it exceeds the degree of protection required, it is unjust to the criminal.

COURTS

Proper courts are necessary for the administration of justice. According to rabbinic sages, this is one of the demands of the Torah made even to non-Jews – it is one of the seven commandments of the sons of Noah to have a legal system. The Hebrew term for a court is *bet din*, or 'house of justice'. For civil cases, a bet din is composed of three Jewish scholars.

Above The bet din *shown here is the court of justice of the Sephardic Orthodox community in Israel.*

Here the decision of the majority is followed. Judges must be unbiased, and no one should serve as a judge if one of the parties is a friend or enemy. The laws regarding judges is contained in Deuteronomy 16:18–19: 'Judges and officers shalt thou make thee in all thy gates, which the Lord thy God giveth thee, tribe by tribe; and they shall judge the people with righteous judgement. Thou shalt not wrest judgement; thou shalt not show partiality; neither shalt thou take a bribe, for a bribe doth blind the eyes of the wise, and pervert the words of the righteous.' Scripture rules that judges must never take bribes, but the rabbis extend this ruling to include any form of gift even from the party he thinks is in the right.

Below The Bible records that after God had judged the world and sent the Great Flood, Noah emerged from the Ark. 13th-century mosaic, St Mark's, Venice.

COMPROMISE

According to rabbinic Judaism, if both parties to a dispute are willing to compromise, this is a form of justice. It is especially desirable in a complicated case, where it is unlikely right is solely on one side, for the parties to compromise with one another. In marital disputes, both parties may be right in some respects and wrong in others. In such cases, the path of compromise is often the best solution.

Above Arbitration at a bet din *(Jewish court that deals with religious questions) in a Czech Jewish community, 1925.*

Witnesses in a law suit must be respectable individuals who can be relied on to tell the truth. Anyone who has a bad reputation in money matters is disqualified. No relative is permitted to serve as a witness.

THE VIRTUE OF JUSTICE

In the Mishnah, the first chapter of the Ethics of the Fathers concludes with a statement from Simeon ben Gamaliel: 'On three things the world rests: on justice, truth and peace.' Here the words of the prophet Zechariah are quoted: 'These are the things that ye shall do: Speak ye every man the truth with his neighbour; execute the judgment of truth and in your gates' (Zechariah 8:16). Commentators on this passage remark that where there is truth, there is justice; and where there is justice, there is peace. A peace based on injustice is no peace and will not endure.

JUSTICE IN PRACTICE

It is not only in courts that justice should be found – Judaism demands that Jews must be just in their dealings with one another. The relationship between employer and employee must

Right A horrifying vision of Hell by Renaissance painter Hieronymus Bosch. Belief in punishment in the Hereafter is a feature of rabbinic theology.

be based on fairness. Shopkeepers should charge fair prices and not take advantage of customers – they should have just weights and measures. A principle of everyday justice is the demand that no one should take advantage of another's helplessness. The Bible declares: 'Thou shalt not curse the deaf, nor put a stumbling block before the blind, but thou shalt fear thy God: I am the Lord' (Leviticus

Above The tombs of Zechariah and Jehoshaphat in the Kidron Valley, Israel. The prophet Zechariah stressed the importance of justice.

19:14). This principle is extended in rabbinic sources to cover every instance of causing harm to another by allowing someone to err through weakness. Thus, the rabbis forbid giving advice one knows to be bad.

HOLINESS

WITHIN THE JEWISH FAITH, THE TERM HOLINESS REFERS TO WHAT IS ELEVATED ABOVE THE MATERIAL PLANE. THE CONCEPT RELATES TO A WIDE RANGE OF TOPICS INCLUDING GOD HIMSELF.

According to the Bible, holiness is a characteristic of God. He is apart from the universe and beyond its limitations. In the Book of Isaiah, the Serafim declare: 'Holy, holy, holy is the Lord of Hosts: the whole earth is full of his glory' (Isaiah 6:3). Here Scripture asserts that God is apart from the world he created, yet there are intimations of his holiness everywhere. Anything that is dedicated to God is called holy, such as the Temple or the synagogue. The implication is that to be near God it is necessary to be holy – such an idea is expressed in Leviticus 19:12: 'Speak unto all the congregation of the children of Israel, and say to them: Ye shall be holy; for I the Lord your God am holy.'

Below A 19th-century drawing of the Western Wall in Jerusalem by Alexandre Bida. Popularly known as the Wailing Wall, Jews regard it as a central holy site of pilgrimage.

THE JEWISH PEOPLE

According to the Jewish tradition, Jewish communities are referred to as holy: a community is called *kehillah kedoshah*, implying that where Jews are gathered together for sacred purposes, holiness is present. Holiness is not reserved for select individuals, but for persons living normal lives. Jews become holy through their involvement with spiritual affairs: this involves the willingness to give up worldly things as well as a separation from physical pleasures.

SELF-CONTROL

While it is true that Judaism does not encourage asceticism, self-denial is regarded as a virtue. Thus the rabbis stated: 'Sanctify yourself by denying yourself even something of that which is otherwise permitted.' This dictum implies that self-control must be exhibited even when doing what the Torah permits. Whatever the Torah forbids is

Above Seraphim with wings (Isaiah 6) decorated with an all-seeing eye motif, from a 1537 Romanian fresco.

forbidden; but this does not mean that one should indulge oneself. Each person must exercise restraint. It is ultimately left to each individual to determine how much self-control should be exercised so that worldly pleasure does not become a barrier to spiritual growth.

THE QUEST FOR HOLINESS

For ordinary people, Judaism prescribes various aids to holiness. Prominent among these are the 'holy days', which include the Sabbath and festivals when secular concerns are set aside and there is time for spiritual refreshment. Yom Kippur (the Day of Atonement) in particular is referred to as Yom ha-Kodesh (the Holy Day); this is a time when the needs of normal physical life are transcended and Jews are called to be near to God. Classical Jewish sources are called 'holy' – by studying these it is possible for the individual to achieve a degree of spirituality. Further, there are various symbols of the Jewish religion including *tefillin*, or 'phylacteries', the *Sefer Torah*, or 'Torah scroll', and the

Right Among the Hasidim, the Rebbe is revered as a holy leader. The Tish (Yiddish: 'table') is a meal taken by the Rebbe with his followers. Seen here in the Betz Yeshiva in Mea Shearim, Jerusalem, 2005.

mezuzah, or 'rolled parchments with scriptural references', which are connected with holiness. Conversely, there is the need to avoid the opposite of what is holy.

SELF-DENIAL

According to the Talmud, there are two views of self-denial. One is that those who deny themselves are sinners, presumably because they reject legitimate gifts of food and drink which God has given to them. The second is that on the contrary those who pursue self-denial are holy. A number of thinkers hold that it all depends on one's motives. If a person is sincere in the quest for God and appreciates how necessary it is to forego many of life's pleasures to attain a spiritual state, then he is holy.

Below Blowing the shofar to signal the end of the Yom Kippur fast, London, 1929. The High Holy Days begin with Rosh Hashanah and end with Yom Kippur.

But if his reasons are a hatred of life or a wish to demonstrate religious superiority, he is a sinner.

PRAISE OF HOLINESS

Rabbinic sources extol the state of holiness. Hence, the rabbis ruled that before carrying out a *mitzvah*, or 'commandment', it is essential to recite the benediction: 'Blessed art thou, O Lord our God, King of the universe, who has sanctified us with his commandments.' Through observing God's laws we become holy. In rabbinic

sources the usual name for God is *Ha-Kadosh Barukh Hu*, or 'The Holy One, blessed be he'. There are degrees of holiness and one should make an attempt to ascend to a higher level. The Zohar states nothing is more holy than the Torah, and both students of the Torah and those who help them to study are to be called holy.

THE GIFT OF HOLINESS
According to the tradition, the attainment of holiness is not possible through one's own efforts. Rather, it is a gift from God. According to the Talmud, a person who makes a little effort to be holy is given much holiness from on high. In this quest, there are stages of development. As the 2nd-century CE teacher Phinehas ben Yair explained: 'The knowledge of the Torah leads to watchfulness, watchfulness to zeal, zeal to cleanliness, cleanliness to abstinence, abstinence to purity, purity to saintliness, saintliness to humility, humility to the fear of sin, and the fear of sin to holiness. Holiness leads to the holy spirit and the holy spirit leads to the resurrection of the dead.'

CHAPTER 4

MESSIAH AND THE HEREAFTER

For thousands of years the Jewish people have longed for messianic deliverance; sustained by this belief the community has endured persecution and suffering, confident that they will ultimately be rescued from earthly travail. In the Hebrew Bible, God declared to Abraham, Isaac and Jacob that their descendants will inherit a land of their own. In biblical times, such deliverance was understood as pertaining to human history. Yet, with the emergence of rabbinic Judaism, the concept of the Messiah was transformed. In rabbinic sources, sages maintained that prior to the coming of the Messiah, the world would be subject to a series of tribulations defined as the 'birth pangs of the Messiah'. The Messiah would then usher in a period of deliverance, and all Jewish exiles would be returned to Zion. This messianic age would usher in the concept of perfect peace in the end of days. At the end of this messianic period, all human beings would undergo judgement and either be rewarded with heavenly bliss or punished everlastingly.

Opposite The Resurrection of the Dead, *an important expectation of the messianic tradition. From the* Très belles heures of Notre Dame, *1410, commissioned by the Duc de Berry.*

Above *Section of* The Last Judgment *showing the deceased in Paradise. A painting c. 1465 by Giovanni di Paolo, one of the most important painters of the Sienese School.*

BIBLICAL MESSIAH

IN SCRIPTURE THE MESSIAH IS CONCEIVED OF AS THE REDEEMER OF
ISRAEL. AS GOD'S ANOINTED, HE WILL USHER IN A PERIOD OF PEACE
IN WHICH ALL PROPHECIES WILL BE FULFILLED.

Biblical history foretells of a future redemption, which will be brought about through an appointed agent of the Lord. According to the early prophets, such a kingly figure will be a descendant of David. Eventually there arose the view that the house of David would rule over Israel as well as neighbouring peoples. Later prophets predicted the destruction of the nation because of its iniquity, yet they were convinced that God would eventually deliver the Israelites and usher in a new redemption of the nation.

THE CONCEPT OF THE MESSIAH

The term 'Messiah' is an adaptation of the Hebrew *Ha-Mashiah*, or 'the anointed'. In time it came to refer to the redeemer at the End of Days.

Below Ethiopian icon from the 18th–19th century, showing the Messiah celebrating Passover with his disciples.

Although there are no explicit references to such a figure in the Torah, the notion of the redemption of the Jewish nation is alluded to in the promises made to the patriarchs. Such references form the background to the development of the doctrine of deliverance.

It was in the Book of Samuel that the notion of redemption through a divinely appointed agent was explicitly expressed; here Scripture asserts that the Lord had chosen David and his descendants to rule over Israel to the end of time.

This early biblical doctrine assumed that David's position would endure throughout his lifetime and would be inherited by a series of successors who would carry out God's providential plan. With the fall of the Davidic empire after the death of King Solomon in the 10th century BCE, there arose the view that the house of David would eventually rule over the two divided

Above The Prophet Amos, who foretold the coming of the Day of the Lord, by Juan de Borgoña, 1535.

kingdoms as well as neighbouring peoples. Yet despite such a hopeful vision of Israel's future, the pre-exilic prophets were convinced that the nation would be punished for its iniquity. Warning the people of this impending disaster, the Northern 8th-century BCE prophet Amos spoke of the Day of the Lord when God would unleash his fury against those who had rebelled against him. None the less, the prophets predicted that those who had been led away into captivity would eventually return to their own land.

Below Prophet Jonah rests under a gourd vine in Nineveh; a 4th-century CE mosaic pavement from the basilica in Aquileia, northern Italy.

Above The Earthly Paradise, 1607, Jan Brueghel the Elder. *According to tradition, the Messiah will bring about God's kingdom on earth.*

REDEMPTION AND REBIRTH

In the Southern Kingdom the 8th-century BCE prophet Isaiah predicted that the inhabitants of Judah would be destroyed because of their iniquity. None the less, he predicted the eventual triumph of God's kingdom on earth. In his view, only a faithful remnant will remain, from which a redeemer will issue forth to bring about a new epoch in the nation's history. A contemporary of Isaiah, the prophet Micah, also predicted that the nation would not be cut off. God, he stated, had a purpose for them in the future. Confident of the restoration of the people, he looked forward to an age of fulfilment and prosperity. Like Isaiah, he predicted a time of messianic redemption. All nations will go to the mountain of the Lord and dwell together in peace. In those days swords will be turned into ploughshares and each man will sit under his vine and fig tree.

POST-EXILIC PROPHECY

Dwelling in Babylon in the 6th-century BCE, the prophet Ezekiel castigated Israel for their iniquity – because they had turned away from

God further punishment would be inflicted on them. Yet, despite the departure of God's glory from the Temple, the prophet reassured the nation that it will not be abandoned. In his view, God takes no delight in the death of sinners; what he requires instead is a contrite heart. Using the image of a shepherd and his flock, Ezekiel reassuringly declared that God will gather his people from exile and return them to the Promised Land. In a vision of dry bones, Ezekiel predicts that, although the nation had been devastated, it will be renewed in a future

deliverance: a future king will rule over his people and under his dominion Jerusalem will be restored. In a similar vein Second Isaiah offers words of consolation to those who had experienced the destruction of Judah. In place of oracles of denunciation, the prophet offered the promise of hope and restoration.

The Bible thus presents a picture of destruction that is followed by redemption. According to the prophets, the Lord will have compassion upon his chosen people and return them to their former glory. Reassured by these words of comfort, the ancient Israelites were secure in the knowledge that they had not been forsaken. The Messiah will usher in an era of peace and tranquillity. God will be reunited with his people and Zion will undergo future glory. These words of comfort provided the framework for the evolution of the concept of messianic deliverance, which was expanded by Jewish writers during the Second Temple period.

Below The prophet Samuel anoints David. *From a wall painting in the Dura-Europos synagogue, Syria, c. 2nd century CE.*

POST-BIBLICAL MESSIAH

DRAWING ON BIBLICAL THEMES, POST-BIBLICAL JEWISH LITERATURE
DEVELOPED THE CONCEPT OF THE MESSIAH. IN THESE WRITINGS THE
STAGES OF MESSIANIC DELIVERANCE ARE DESCRIBED IN DETAIL.

In post-biblical Jewish literature, which is known as the Apocrypha and Pseudepigrapha, the concept of a future redemption was not forgotten, and there are frequent references to the ingathering of the exiles. Although the messianic predictions in these writings vary considerably, they bear witness to the deep longing for divine deliverance and redemption.

MESSIANIC ANTICIPATION
Throughout the book of Ben Sira composed in the 2nd century BCE, the love of Israel is manifest. In this work the author outlines the various stages of messianic anticipation – the destruction of Israel's enemies, the sanctification of God's name by elevating the Jewish nation, the performance of miracles, the ingathering of the exiles, the glorification of Jerusalem and the Temple, reward for the righteous and punishment for the wicked, and the fulfilment of prophetic expectations. Although Ben Sira does not specify that redemption will come through Davidic rule or an individual Messiah, the author does specify that the house of David will be preserved.

RETURN OF THE EXILES
In the Apocryphal Baruch, which was also written in the 2nd century BCE, there is a reference to the idea that God will bring about the return of the exiles to the land of their fathers once they have turned from their evil ways. Later in the book the author describes Jerusalem,

Above Head of the Messiah, *1648, by Rembrandt, who lived in the Jodenbreestraat in Amsterdam, in what was then becoming the Jewish quarter.*

which is to be renewed. The book continues with a description of the return of the exiles: 'Arise, O Jerusalem, and stand upon the height; And look about thee toward the east; And behold thy children gathered from the going down of the sun unto the rising thereof.' Alluding to Second Isaiah's vision of the ingathering of the exiles, the author depicts the re-establishment of Zion in glowing terms.

THE MESSIANIC AGE
Composed after the destruction of the Temple, the author of the Apocryphal Baruch presented a variety of reflections about the messianic age beginning with the Day of Judgement. During this period the Day of the Lord was identified with the 'birth pangs of the Messiah' – this did not refer to any suffering of the Messiah himself, but to the tribulations of the messianic age. In his view the Holy Lord will come from his dwelling, appear from the highest

---

THE WORLD TO COME

Unlike other post-biblical work, the Wisdom of Solomon is preoccupied with the world to come, eternal life, and divine retribution. In chapter 3 the author describes the reward for the righteous: 'But the souls of the righteous are in the hand of God; and no torment shall touch them. In the eyes of fools they seemed to die; and their departure was accounted to be their hurt; and their going from us to be their ruin: but they are in peace.' Turning to the destruction of the wicked, he described the future Day of the Lord: 'He shall sharpen stern wrath for a sword: and the world shall go forth with him to fight against his insensate foes; shafts of lightning shall fly with true aim; and from the clouds, as from a drawn bow, shall they leap to the mark.'

Left The Last Judgement *by Hieronymus Bosch, 1500.*

their spirits will grow strong when they see the Messiah, and heaven and earth will be transformed. The elect will then dwell in a new and blessed earth upon which sinners and evildoers will not set foot. The Messiah will be a staff to the righteous and holy and a light to the gentiles. All who dwell on earth will worship and bless him and praise the God of Spirits.

REDEMPTION

Another work of this period, *The Testaments of the Twelve Patriarchs*, consists of stories about the tribal patriarchs. In the Testament of Judah, there are vivid descriptions of messianic redemption. The star of peace

will arise and walk in meekness among men. The heavens will be opened and pour out their blessings. The spirit of truth will come upon the children of Judah. A shoot will come forth from the stock of Judah and the rod of righteousness will be in his hand to judge and save all those who call upon him. All the tribes will become one people and have one language. Those who died in grief will arise and awake to everlasting life.

Below German engraving of the Tribes of Israel around the Ark of the Covenant, c. 1630. Tradition says the Messiah will transport the scattered people of Israel back to Zion.

Above Satan Arousing the Rebel Angels, 1808. An illustration by English visionary William Blake for John Milton's poem Paradise Lost.

of heavens and tread on Mount Sinai. Not only will the wicked be chastised, so too will Satan and the angels who have corrupted the earth be brought to judgement. At the end of days the righteous will be delivered, beget a thousand children, and complete all their days in peace. The whole earth will be filled with righteousness and the fields prosper. The Lord will open the storehouses of heavenly blessing, which he will pour out upon the faithful.

THE MESSIAH

The Ethiopic Book of Enoch, another apocryphal work, continues with a description of the Messiah himself. According to the author, the Messiah existed before the creation of the world, and his dwelling place is under the wings of the God of Spirits where the elect shall pass before him. On that day the Elect One will sit on the throne of glory and choose the occupations of men and their dwelling places;

RABBINIC MESSIAH

DURING THE RABBINIC PERIOD, JEWISH SAGES DEVELOPED THE CONCEPT OF THE MESSIAH: MESSIANIC REDEMPTION WOULD BE DIVIDED INTO A SERIES OF STAGES LEADING TO THE WORLD TO COME.

Once the Temple had been destroyed and the Jewish people driven out of their homeland, the nation was bereft. In their despair the rabbis longed for a kingly figure who would deliver them from exile and rebuild their holy city. Drawing on messianic ideas that are found in Scripture, the Apocrypha and Pseudepigrapha, they foresaw the coming of a future deliverance when all peoples would be converted to the worship of the one true God.

THE COMING OF THE MESSIAH

In rabbinic sources, sages elaborated the themes found in Scripture as well as in Jewish literature of the Second Temple period. In midrashic collections and the Talmud they formulated a complex eschatological scheme divided into a series of stages. In their view, this chain of

Right This 1400s Russian icon shows the Messiah's entry into Jerusalem.

events will begin with devastation. As in the Pseudepigrapha, such sufferings are referred to as the 'birth pangs of the Messiah'. As the Talmud states: 'With the footprints of the Messiah, insolence will increase and death reach its height; the vine will yield its fruit but the wine will be costly. There will be none to offer reproof, and the whole empire will be converted to heresy.'

Not only will natural disasters come upon the land, the word of the Lord will also be forgotten during the time of messianic travail. As the Talmud states: 'When our teachers entered the vineyard (school) at Yabneh, they said: "The Torah is destined to be forgotten in Israel, as it is written (Amos 8:11): 'Behold the days come, saith the Lord God, that

I will send a famine in the land, not a famine of bread, nor a thirst for water, but of hearing the words of the Lord.'"'

THE PROPHET ELIJAH

Despite these dire predictions, the rabbis maintained that the prophet Elijah will return prior to the coming of the Messiah to solve all earthly problems. In addition, his role in the messianic era will be to certify the ritual uncleanliness of families that suffered from mixed marriages or forbidden unions, and also to grant permission to hitherto excluded peoples from marrying Jews. Moreover, Elijah's task will be to bring back to the Jewish people those who had been wrongfully excluded from the community. All this is to be done in anticipation of the coming of the Messiah. As a forerunner of messianic redemption, Elijah will announce from the top of Mount Carmel that the Messiah is coming who will initiate the end of history and the advent of God's kingdom on earth.

Left Gog and Magog. A woodcut for the Martin Luther Bible of 1534, from the workshop of Lucas Cranach the Elder. According to tradition, the Messiah will engage in battle with Gog and Magog.

MESSIAH BEN JOSEPH

Drawing on earlier conceptions, the rabbis formulated the doctrine of a second Messiah – the son of Joseph – who will precede the King-Messiah, the Messiah ben David. According to legend, this Messiah will engage in battle with God and Magog, the traditional enemies of Israel, and be slain. Only after his defeat will the Messiah ben David arrive in glory. As a hero, the Messiah ben Joseph will be mourned by the Jewish people. As the Talmud states, quoting Scripture: 'And the land shall mourn, every family apart; the family of the house of David apart, and their wives apart' (Zechariah 12:12).

In this final struggle against the nation's enemies, God will act on behalf of Israel. Thus in the midrash, the rabbis maintain that: 'There are four shinings forth: the first was in Egypt, as it is written (Psalm 80:1), "Give ear, O Shepherd of Israel, thou that leadest Joseph like a flock, thou that art enthroned upon the cherubim shine forth"; the second was at the time of the giving of the Law, as it is written (Deuteronomy 33:2), "He shone forth from Mount Paran"; the third will take place in the days of Gog and Magog, as it is

Below The Return to Jerusalem, after Raphael. Tradition is that the Messiah will bring about the return of all Jews to the Holy Land.

Above The beloved city. View of Jerusalem, *Russian painting, 1821, by Maxim N. Vorobyev.*

written (Psalm 94:1), "Thou God to whom vengeance belongeth shine forth"; the fourth will be in the days of the Messiah (ben David) as it is written (Psalm 50:2), "Out of Zion, the perfection of beauty, shall God shine forth."'

Regarding this struggle, the rabbis speculated that God had already revealed the defeat of Gog and Magog to Moses. Hence Rabbi Nehemiah stated that in Numbers 11:26 Eldad and Medad prophesied concerning this battle: 'As it is written (Ezekiel 38:17), "Thus saith the Lord God: Art thou he of whom I spoke in old time by my servants the prophets of Israel, that prophesied in those days [from many] years that I would bring thee against them?"' and so on. According to Simeon ben Yohai (2nd century CE), the war with Gog and Magog was one of the most terrible evils to befall humanity. Yet after Israel is delivered from this struggle, the King-Messiah will come to bring about the messianic age.

MESSIAH BEN DAVID

During the early rabbinic period, numerous legends emerged about the names and personality of this glorious figure. His moral character and spiritual integrity were frequently exalted and with his coming the dispersion would cease. Thus Simeon ben Yohai proclaimed: 'Come and see how beloved is Israel before the Holy One, blessed is he; for wherever they went into exile the Shekinah [God's presence] was with them, as it is written (I Samuel 2:27), "Did I indeed reveal myself unto the house of thy father when they were in Egypt." They went into exile in Babylonia, and the Shekinah was with them, as it is written (Isaiah 43:14), "For your sake I was sent to Babylonia." Likewise, when they shall be redeemed in the future, the Shekinah will be with them, as it is written (Deuteronomy 30:3), "Then the Lord thy God will return with thy captivity." It does not say "will bring back thy captivity" but "will return with thy captivity" – teaching that the Holy one, blessed is he, returns with them from the places of exile.'

Here God is described as accompanying his chosen people in exile, sharing their sufferings. Yet with messianic redemption, the exiles will return to Zion in triumph with God at their head. Clouds of glory shall be spread over them, and they will come singing with joy on their lips.

THE MESSIANIC AGE AND HEAVEN

AT THE CULMINATION OF THE MESSIANIC AGE, ALL WILL BE JUDGED. THE RIGHTEOUS WILL ENTER HEAVEN. THIS IS DIVIDED INTO A SERIES OF CHAMBERS FOR VARIOUS CLASSES OF INDIVIDUALS.

Rabbinic literature contains frequent speculation about the Days of the Messiah (also referred to as 'The World to Come'). At the end of this messianic period, all human beings will undergo judgement and either be rewarded with heavenly bliss or punished everlastingly. This vision of a future hope was animated by the Jewish conviction that God will not abandon his people.

THE MESSIANIC AGE
In their depictions of the messianic age, Jewish sages stressed that the Days of the Messiah will be totally different from the present world. Concerning the fruitfulness of the harvest, for example, they stressed his

Below Adam and Eve driven from the Garden of Eden by James Tissot. In the tradition, Heaven is referred to as Gan Eden *(Garden of Eden).*

Right Detail of a Turkish Jewish rug showing Adam and Eve, late 19th century. The Garden of Eden symbolizes heavenly bliss.

era 'is not of this world. In this world, there is the trouble of harvesting and treading [grapes]; but in the world to come a man will bring one grape on a wagon or in a ship, put it in the corner of his house, and use its contents as if it had been a large wine cask...There will be no grape that will not contain 30 kegs of wine.'

Speculating on the length of this period, the early rabbinic sages differed as to its duration. Eliezer, for instance, stated: 'The Days of the Messiah will be 40 years; for it is written in one place (Deuteronomy 8:3), "And he afflicted thee, and suffered thee to hunger and fed thee with manna", and in another place it is written (Psalm 90:15), "Make us

HEAVEN
The principal qualification for divine reward is obedience to God's law; those who are judged righteous will enter into Heaven (Gan Eden). One of the earliest descriptions is in a compilation called Midrash Konen:

There are five chambers for various classes of the righteous. The first is built of cedar with a ceiling of transparent crystal. This is the habitation of non-Jews who become true and devoted converts to Judaism. The second is built of cedar, with a ceiling of fine silver. This is the habitation of the penitents, headed by Manasseh, king of Israel, who teaches them the Law. The third chamber is built of silver and gold, ornamented with pearls ... [here] rest Abraham, Isaac, and Jacob, the tribes, those of the Egyptian exodus, and those who died in the wilderness, headed by Moses and Aaron ...The fourth chamber is made of olive-wood and is inhabited by those who have suffered for the sake of their religion... The fifth chamber is built of precious stones, gold and silver, surrounded by myrrh and aloes. ... This chamber is inhabited by the Messiah ben David, Elijah and the Messiah ben Joseph.

Above Vine of the Promised Land. 12th-century Romanesque enamel from the Rhenish School.

glad according to the days wherein thou hast afflicted us according to the years wherein we have seen evil."' Dosa said: 'Four hundred years; for it is written in one place (Genesis 15:13), "And they shall serve them, and they shall afflict them 400 years"; and in another place it is written (Psalm 90:15), "Make us glad according to the days wherein thou has afflicted us."' Jose the Galilean said: 'Three hundred and sixty-five years, according to the number of days in the solar year, as it is written (Isaiah 63:4), "For the day of vengeance was in my heart, and my year of redemption has come."'

According to another Baraitha: 'It was taught in the school of Elijah: The world will endure 6,000 years;

Right The Valley and Lower Pool of Gihon, Jerusalem, c.1870, by W. Dickens. According to tradition, the exiles will return to Jerusalem at the time of Messianic redemption.

2,000 in chaos, 2,000 under the Law and 2,000 during the messianic age; but because of our many iniquities time has been lost from the last period (that is, 4,000 years have already passed, yet the Messiah has not yet arrived).' Other traditions, however, stress that such reckoning is fruitless. Hence the Talmud records: 'Seven things are hidden

from men. These are the day of death, the day of consolation, the depth of judgement, no man knows what is in the minds of his friend; no man knows which of his business ventures will be profitable, or when the kingdom of the house of David will be restored or when the sinful kingdom will fall.'

WORLD TRANSFORMATION

Despite such disagreement about the length of this period, there was a general acceptance among the sages that at the end of the Days of the Messiah all will be changed. At the close of this era, a final judgement will come upon all humankind. Yet for such judging to take place, all those who have died will need to be resurrected. Given that there is no explicit belief in eternal salvation in the Bible, the rabbis of the post-biblical period were faced with the difficulty of proving that the doctrine of resurrection of the dead is contained in Scripture that they regarded as authoritative. To do this, they employed a number of principles of exegesis based on the assumption that each word of the Torah was transmitted by God to Moses.

HELL

ACCORDING TO JEWISH SAGES, THOSE WHO SIN WILL BE CONDEMNED TO ETERNAL TORMENT. RABBINIC LITERATURE DEPICTS THEIR SUFFERING IN GRAPHIC DETAIL.

As with heaven, we find extensive and detailed descriptions of hell in Jewish literature. In the Babylonian Talmud, Joshua ben Levi deduces the division of hell from biblical quotations. This talmudic concept of the sevenfold structure of hell was greatly elaborated in rabbinic sources.

DIVISIONS OF HELL
According to one midrashic source, it requires 300 years to traverse the height or width or the depth of each division, and it would take 6,300 years to go over a tract of land equal in extent to the seven divisions. Each of these seven divisions of hell is in turn divided into seven subdivisions, and in each compartment there are seven rivers of fire, and seven of hail. The width of each is 100 ells (measurement equivalent to about 114cm/45in), its depth 1,000, and its length 300. They flow from each other and are supervised by the Angels of Destruction. Besides, in each com-

partment there are 700 caves, and in each cave there are 7,000 crevices. In each crevice there are 7,000 scorpions. Every scorpion has 300 rings, and in every ring 7,000 pouches of venom from which flow seven rivers of deadly poison. If a man handles it, he immediately bursts, every limb is torn from his body, his bowels are cleft, and he falls upon his face.

PUNISHMENT
Confinement to hell is the result of disobeying God's Torah as is illustrated by a midrash concerning the evening visit of the soul to hell before it is implanted in an individual. There it sees the Angels of Destruction smiting with fiery scourges; the sinners all the while crying out, but no mercy is shown to them. The angel guides the soul and then asks: 'Do you know who these are?' Unable to respond the soul listens as the angel continues: 'Those who are consumed with fire

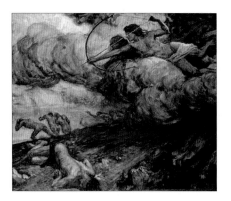

Above The Ungodly Shall Not Stand *by the 19th-century French artist James Tissot.*

were created like you. When they were put into the world, they did not observe God's Torah and his commandments. Therefore they have come to this disgrace, which you see them suffer. Know, your destiny is also to depart from the world. Be just, therefore, and not wicked, that you may gain the future world.'

VISIT TO HELL
According to this midrash, the soul was not alone in being able to see hell; a number of biblical personages entered into its midst. Moses, for example, was guided through hell by an angel, and his journey there gives us the most complete picture of its torments: 'When Moses and the Angel of Hell entered hell together, they saw men being tortured by the Angels of Destruction. Some sinners were suspended by their eyelids, some by their ears, some by their hands, and some by their tongues. In addition, women were suspended by their hair and their breasts by chains of fire. Such punishments were inflicted on the basis of sins that were committed: those who

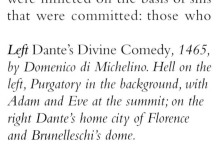

Left Dante's Divine Comedy, *1465, by Domenico di Michelino. Hell on the left, Purgatory in the background, with Adam and Eve at the summit; on the right Dante's home city of Florence and Brunelleschi's dome.*

Right Fire, the devil and separation in
a 19th-century Japanese painting of Hell.

Right Fire, the devil and separation in
a 19th-century Japanese painting of Hell.

hung by their eyes had looked lust-fully upon their neighbours' wives and possessions; those who hung by their ears had listened to empty and vain speech and did not listen to the Torah; those who hung by their tongues had spoken slanderously; those who hung by their hands had robbed and murdered their neigh-bours. The women who hung by their hair and breasts had uncovered them in the presence of young men in order to seduce them.

In another place, called Alukah, Moses saw sinners suspended by their feet with their heads down-wards and their bodies covered with long black worms. These sinners were punished in this way because they swore falsely, profaned the Sabbath and the Holy Days, despised the sages, called their neighbours by unseemly nicknames, wronged the orphan and the widow, and bore false witness. In another section, Moses saw sinners prone on their

Below The Angel of Death and
Destruction visits Rome during a plague.
Painting by Jules-Elie Delaunay, 1869.

faces with 2,000 scorpions lashing, stinging and tormenting them. Each of these scorpions had 70,000 heads, each had 70,000 mouths, each mouth 70,000 stings, and each sting 70,000 pouches of poison and venom. So great was the pain they inflicted that the eyes of the sinners melted in their sockets. These sin-ners were punished in this way because they had robbed other Jews, were arrogant in the community, put their neighbours to shame in pub-lic, delivered their fellow Jews into the hands of the gentiles, denied the Torah, and maintained that God is not the creator of the world.

THE NATURE OF HELL

This eschatological scheme, which was formulated over the centuries by innumerable Jewish scholars, should not be seen as a flight of fancy. It was a serious attempt to explain God's ways. Israel was God's chosen peo-ple and had received his promise of reward for keeping his law. Since this did not happen on earth in this life, the rabbis believed it must occur in the World to Come. Never did the rab-bis relinquish the belief that God would justify Israel by destroying the power of the oppressing nations. This would come about in the messianic age. The individual who had died without seeing the justification of God would be resurrected to see the ultimate victory of the Jewish peo-ple. And just as the nations would be judged in the period of messianic redemption, so would each individ-ual. Those deemed wicked would be punished everlastingly. In this way, the vindication of the righteous was assured in the hereafter.

JEWISH MESSIAHS

OVER THE YEARS VARIOUS PSEUDO-MESSIAHS APPEARED, EACH CLAIMING
THEY HAD COME TO USHER IN THE MESSIANIC AGE. THEY ALL FAILED
TO FULFIL THE EXPECTATIONS OF DELIVERANCE AND REDEMPTION.

JESUS THE MESSIAH
From the Gospels it appears that a
Jewish sect of Christians emerged in
the 1st century BCE. In consonance
with messianic expectations of this
period, these believers expected their
Messiah to bring about the fulfilment of human history. According
to the New Testament, Jesus of
Nazareth spent most of his life in
Galilee where he preached the coming of the Kingdom of God. After a
brief association with John the
Baptist, he attracted disciples from
among the most marginalized sec-
tors of society to whom he
proclaimed his message.

Despite his popularity among the
masses, he soon aroused suspicion
and hostility from both Jewish and
Roman officials and was put to
death during the reign of Pontius
Pilate in about 30CE. Afterwards his

followers believed he had risen from
the dead, appeared to them and
promised to return to usher in the
period of messianic rule. The Jewish
community, however, rejected these
claims; in their view, Jesus did not
fulfil the messianic role as outlined
in Scripture and portrayed in rabbinic sources. Despite the growth of
the Christian community in the
years after Jesus' death, Jews continued to wait for the advent of a
Messiah-King who would return the
exiles to Zion, resurrect the dead
and usher in a period of messianic
redemption.

EARLY MESSIAHS
The destruction of Jerusalem and
the Temple in 70CE profoundly
affected Jewish life and led to intensified longing for messianic
deliverance. With the loss of both the

*Above Jesus talking to Moses and
Elijah with his disciples Peter, John
and James below, c. 1278, by Duccio
di Buoninsegna.*

Northern and Southern Kingdoms,
Jews looked to the advent of the
messianic age when the nation
would be restored to its ancient
homeland. Although mainstream
Jewry rejected Jesus as the long-
awaited Messiah, the Jewish
community continued to long for
divine deliverance.

In 132CE a messianic revolt
against Rome was led by the war-
rior Simeon bar Kochba. This
rebellion was inspired by the conviction that God sought to
overthrow Roman oppression.
When this uprising was crushed,
Jews put forward the year of messianic deliverance until the 5th
century CE. In fulfilment of this pre-
diction, a figure named Moses
appeared in Crete, declaring that he
would be able to lead Jews across the
seas to Judaea. However, after this
plan failed, Jews continued to engage
in messianic speculation, believing
that they could determine the date
of their deliverance on the basis of
scriptural texts.

*Left Herodium, the ancient palace-
fortress built by Herod the Great on a
Judean hilltop, who lived at the time of
Jesus, the Christian Messiah.*

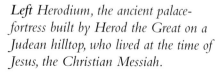

MEDIEVAL MESSIAHS

During the early medieval period a series of messianic pretenders appeared such as Abu Isa al-Isphani, Serene and Yugdhan, and the traveller Eldad Ha-Dani brought reports of the ten lost tribes, an event which stimulated the Jewish desire to return to Zion. At the end of the 11th and throughout the 12th century a number of pseudo-Messiahs appeared in the Jewish world. In 1096 the arrival of the Crusaders gave rise to widespread excitement among Jews living in the Byzantine empire. As a consequence, the French Jewish community sent a representative to Constantinople to obtain information about the advent of the Messiah. In Khazaria 17 communities marched to the desert to meet the ten lost tribes. In Salonika the arrival of the prophet Elijah was announced. During this period a proselyte, Obadiah, journeyed to northern Palestine, where he

Below Shabbetai Tzvi, a Jewish rabbi and Kabbalist who claimed to be the long-awaited Jewish Messiah, 1670s.

encountered the Karaite Solomon ha-Kohen who declared he was the Messiah and would soon redeem the Jewish nation. In Mesopotamia another messianic figure, ben Chadd, appeared but was subsequently arrested by the caliph of Baghdad.

In the next century a messianic forerunner in Yemen was described by the 12th-century Jewish philosopher Moses Maimonides. But the most important pseudo-Messiah of this period was David Alroy who appeared in 1147 at the time of the Second Crusade. Born in Amadiya, his real name was Menahem ben Solomon, but he called himself David owing to his claim to be king of the Jews. The movement to recognize his messiahship probably began among mountain Jews of the north-east Caucasus before 1121 and gathered momentum in the ferment accompanying the struggles between Christianity and Islam following the First Crusade and during the wars preceding the Second Crusade.

EARLY MODERN MESSIAHS

In the following centuries other messianic pretenders appeared, including Solomon Molko, a 16th-century Kabbalist and mystic. When Rome was sacked in 1527 he believed he saw the signs of impending redemption. In 1529 he preached about the coming of the Messiah. To fulfil the talmudic legend about the suffering

Above Bishop John of Speyer (r. 1090–1104) protecting Jews from Crusaders, from A Popular History of Germany, *1878. Messianic expectations increased during the Crusades.*

of the Messiah, he dressed as a beggar and sat for 30 days, fasting among the sick on a bridge over the Tiber. Eventually he was burned at the stake for refusing to embrace Christianity. After his death, many of his disciples refused to accept that he had died and remained loyal to the belief that he was the long-awaited Messiah.

THE MYSTICAL MESSIAH

At the beginning of the 17th century, Lurianic mysticism had made a major impact on Sephardi Jewry, and messianic expectations had become a central feature of Jewish life. In this milieu, the arrival of Shabbetai Tzvi brought about a transformation of Jewish life and thought. In 1665 his messiahship was proclaimed by Nathan of Gaza. Eventually Shabbetai was brought to court and given the choice between conversion and death. In the face of this alternative, he converted to Islam. Despite this act of apostasy, a number of his followers remained loyal, justifying his action on the basis of Kabbalistic ideas. In subsequent years such belief was continued by various branches of the Shabbatean movement.

ANTI-MESSIANISM

DESPITE THE CENTRALITY OF BELIEF IN THE MESSIAH IN THE JEWISH TRADITION, IN RECENT TIMES THE WORLD HAS WITNESSED THE EROSION OF SUCH CONVICTION.

With the conversion of Shabbetai Tzvi in the 17th century, the Jewish preoccupation with messianic calculation diminished. As time passed, many Jews found it increasingly difficult to believe in a miraculous divine intervention that will change the course of human history.

DISILLUSIONMENT

Not surprisingly the failure of the Messiah to appear through thousands of years of history coupled with the repeated appearance of false messiahs throughout the centuries led to widespread disillusionment with the Jewish eschatological hope. As a consequence,

Below A Rabbinical Disputation *by Jacob Toorenvliet (1640–1719). As messianic expectations faded, Jews debated whether a Jewish homeland should be established in Palestine.*

the longing for the Messiah who will bring about the end of history appeared to many Jews as a misguided aspiration. Instead, 18th- and early 19th-century Jewry hailed the breaking down of the ghetto walls and the elimination of social barriers between Jews and Christians. In this milieu the belief in the Kingdom of God inaugurated by the Messiah-King receded in importance; in its place the clarion call for liberty, equality and fraternity signified the dawning of a golden age for the Jewish people.

REFORM JUDAISM

Within Reform Judaism in particular, the doctrine of messianic redemption was radically modified in the light of these developments. In the 19th century, Reform Jews interpreted the new liberation in the Western world as the first step

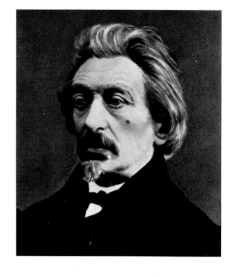

Above Moses Hess (1812–75), German socialist who argued for the creation of a Jewish homeland.

towards the realization of the messianic dream. For these reformers messianic redemption was understood in this-worldly terms. No longer, according to this view, is it necessary for Jews to pray for a restoration in Erez Israel. Rather, Jews should view their own countries as Zion, and their political leaders as bringing about the messianic age.

Such a conviction was enshrined in the Pittsburgh Platform of the Reform movement, which was formulated in 1885. As a central principle of the Platform, the belief in a personal Messiah was replaced by the concept of a messianic age, which will come about through social causes: 'We recognize in the modern era of universal culture of heart and intellect the approach of the realization of Israel's great messianic hope for the establishment of the kingdom of truth, justice and peace among all men. We consider ourselves no longer a nation but a religious community, and therefore expect neither a return to Palestine, nor a sacrificial worship under the administration of the sons of Aaron, nor a restoration of any of the laws concerning the Jewish state.'

Right *Jewish ghetto in Rovigo, Italy, 1867, by Giovanni Biasin. At the end of the 19th century, Zionists pressed for the creation of a Jewish state to solve the problem of discrimination against Jews in Europe and elsewhere.*

ZIONISM

These sentiments were shared by secular Zionists who similarly rejected the traditional belief in the coming of the Messiah and the in-gathering of the exiles. The early Zionists were determined to create a Jewish homeland, even though the Messiah had not yet arrived.

Rejecting the religious categories of the Jewish past, such figures as Moses Hess (1812–75), Leo Pinsker (1821–91) and Theodor Herzl (1860–1904) pressed for a political solution to the problem of anti-Semitism. In their view there is no point in waiting for a supernatural intervention to remedy Jewish existence.

As Pinsker explained: 'Nowadays, when in a small part of the earth our brethren have caught their breath and can feel more deeply for the sufferings of their brothers; nowadays, when a number of other dependent and oppressed nationalities have been allowed to regain their independence, we, too, must not sit even one moment longer with folded hands; we must not admit that we are doomed to play on in the future the hopeless role of the "wandering Jew" ... it is our bounded duty to devote all our remaining moral force to re-establish ourselves as a living nation, so that we may finally assume a more fitting and dignified role.'

BEYOND MESSIANISM

Such attitudes are representative of a major transformation in Jewish thought. In the past, Jews longed for the advent of a personal Messiah who would bring about the messianic age, deliver the Jewish people to their homeland, and inaugurate the fulfilment of human history.

Although this doctrine continues to be upheld by a large number of devout Orthodox Jews, it has been largely eclipsed by a more secular outlook. Most contemporary Jews prefer to interpret the messianic hope in naturalistic terms, abandoning the belief in the coming of the Messiah, the restoration of the sacrificial system, and the idea of direct divine intervention. On this view, it is argued that Jews should free themselves from the absolutes of the past. Jewish views about the Messiah should be seen as growing out of the life of the people. In the modern world, these ancient doctrines can be superseded by a new vision of Jewish life, which

Right *This Israeli poster of Theodor Herzl celebrates the 50th anniversary of the meeting of the first Zionist Congress in Basle, Switzerland, in 1897, which later became the World Zionist Organization.*

is human-centred in orientation. Rather than await the coming of a divinely appointed deliverer who will bring about peace and harmony on earth, Jews should themselves strive to create a better world for all peoples.

DEATH OF THE AFTERLIFE

IN THE PAST JEWS BELIEVED EARTHLY LIFE WAS NOT THE END. AFTER DEATH THE RIGHTEOUS WOULD BE REWARDED AND THE WICKED PUNISHED. SUCH A CONVICTION HAS LOST ITS HOLD ON MODERN JEWISH CONSCIOUSNESS.

On the basis of the scheme of salvation and damnation – which is at the heart of rabbinic theology throughout the centuries – it might be expected that modern Jewish theologians of all shades of religious observance and opinion would attempt to explain contemporary Jewish history in the context of traditional eschatology. This, however, has not happened: instead many Jewish thinkers have set aside doc-

Below A 19th-century photograph of the city of Lydda, where the Council of Lydda ruled c. 135 CE that in certain circumstances the laws of the Torah could be transgressed in order to save life.

trines concerning messianic redemption, resurrection, final judgement and reward for the righteous and punishment for the wicked.

JEWISH THEOLOGY

This shift in emphasis is in part due to the fact that the views expressed in the narrative sections of the midrashim and Talmud are not binding. All Jews are obliged to accept the divine origin of the law, but this is not so with regard to theological concepts and theories expounded by the rabbis. Thus it is possible for a Jew to be religiously pious without accepting all the central beliefs of mainstream Judaism. Indeed,

Above Joseph Hertz (1872–1946) was born in Hungary, became chief rabbi of Great Britain, and wrote on the theme of resurrection.

throughout Jewish history there has been widespread confusion as to what these beliefs are. In the 1st century BCE, for example, the sage Hillel stated that the quintessence of Judaism could be formulated in a single principle: 'That which is hateful to you, do not do to your neighbour. This is the whole of the Law; all the rest is commentary.' Similarly, in the 2nd century CE, the Council of Lydda ruled that under certain circumstances the laws of the Torah may be transgressed in order to save one's life, with the exception of idolatry, murder and unchastity.

PRINCIPLES OF JEWISH FAITH

In both the above cases, the centre of gravity was in the ethical rather than the religious sphere. However, in the medieval period Moses Maimonides (1135–1204) formulated what he considered to be the 13 principles of the Jewish faith. Other thinkers, though, challenged this formulation. Hasdai Crescas (1340–1410), Simon ben Zemah

Above Sigmund Freud (1865–1939), Austrian Jewish psychologist, was critical of traditional Jewish theology.

Duran (1361–1444), Joseph Albo (c.1380–c.1444) and Isaac Arami elaborated different creeds, and some thinkers argued that it is impossible to isolate from the whole Torah essential principles of the Jewish faith. As David ben Solomon Ibn Abi Zimra (c.1479–1573) stated: 'I do not agree that it is right to make any of the perfect Torah into a "principle" since the whole Torah is a "principle" from the mouth of the Almighty.' Thus when formulations of the central theological tenets of Judaism were propounded, they were not universally accepted since they were simply the opinions of individual teachers. Without a central authority whose opinion in theological matters was binding on all Jews, it has been impossible to determine the correct theological beliefs in Judaism.

REINTERPRETING MESSIANIC REDEMPTION

Given that there is no authoritative bedrock of Jewish theology, many modern Jewish thinkers have felt fully justified in abandoning the various elements of traditional rabbinic eschatology, which they regard as untenable. The doctrine of messianic redemption, for example, has been radically modified. In the 20th century, Reform Jews interpreted the new liberation in the Western world as the first step towards the realization of the messianic dream. But messianic redemption was understood in this-worldly terms. No longer, according to this view, was it necessary for Jews to pray for a restoration in Erez Israel; rather they should view their own countries as Zion and their political leaders as bringing about the messianic age. Secular Zionists, on the other hand, saw the return to Israel as the legitimate conclusion to be drawn from the realities of Jewish life in Western countries, thereby viewing the State of Israel as a substitute for the Messiah himself.

THE JEWISH HOPE

Traditional rabbinic eschatology has thus lost its force for a large number of Jews in the modern world, and in consequence there has been a gradual this-worldly emphasis in Jewish thought. Significantly this has been accompanied by a powerful

RESURRECTION

The earlier doctrine of the resurrection of the dead has in more recent times been largely replaced by the belief in the immortality of the soul.

The original belief in resurrection was an eschatological hope bound up with the rebirth of the nation in the Days of the Messiah, but as this messianic concept faded into the background, so did this doctrine. For most Jews, physical resurrection is simply inconceivable in the light of a scientific understanding of the world. As the former Chief Rabbi of Great Britain, Joseph Herman Hertz (1872–1946) wrote: 'Many and various are the folk beliefs and poetical fancies in the rabbinical writings concerning Heaven, Gan Eden, and Hell, Gehinnom. Our most authoritative religious guides, however, proclaim that no eye hath seen, nor can mortal fathom, what awaiteth us in the Hereafter; but that even the tarnished soul will not forever be denied spiritual bliss.'

attachment to the Jewish state. For many Jews, the founding of Israel is the central focus of their religious and cultural identity. Jews throughout the world have deep admiration for the astonishing achievements of Israelis in reclaiming the desert and building a viable society. As a result, it is not uncommon for Jews to equate Jewishness with Zionism, and to see Judaism as fundamentally nationalistic in character – this is a far cry from the rabbinic view of history that placed the doctrine of the hereafter at the centre of Jewish life and thought.

Left Partying in a Tel Aviv nightclub. For many young Jews, enjoying this life is more important than the afterlife.

PART II

JEWISH PRACTICE

According to the Jewish heritage, God revealed the Five Books of Moses to Moses on Mount Sinai. Traditional Judaism maintains that in addition Moses received the Oral Tradition. This was passed down from generation to generation and was the subject of rabbinic debate. This first authoritative compilation of the Oral Law was the Mishnah, composed by Yehuda Ha-Nasi in the 2nd century CE. In subsequent centuries sages continued to discuss the content of Jewish law; their deliberations are recorded in the Palestinian and Babylonian Talmuds.

In time, Jewish scholars felt the need to produce codes of Jewish law so that all members of the community would have access to the legal tradition. The most important code, the *Shulkhan Arukh*, was composed in the 16th century by Joseph Caro, together with glosses by Moses Isserles. This has served as the standard Code of Jewish Law for Orthodox Jewry until the present day. Alongside the Orthodox community, the various non-Orthodox branches of Judaism draw on this sacred tradition in their reinterpretation of Jewish observance for the modern world.

Opposite Members of a Hasidic community dancing on Simchat Torah as the scrolls of the Torah are carried round a synagogue at Bnei Brak, Israel.

Above A 17th-century illustration from the Barcelona Haggadah of the Passover Seder meal, celebrated in Jewish homes each year.

CHAPTER 5

WORSHIP

Throughout the history of the nation, Jews have turned to God for comfort and support. In ancient times the Tabernacle and the Temple served as the focus of religious life; subsequently the synagogue became the place for public worship.

The Jewish year consists of 12 months based on the lunar cycle, and is 354 days long. Throughout the year, believers gathered together to recite the traditional liturgy. According to Scripture, God rested on the Sabbath day; as a consequence, the Jewish people are to rest from all forms of labour on *Shabbat*, or 'the Sabbath'. During the rabbinic era, Jewish sages formulated 39 categories of work that were later interpreted by scholars as forbidding a wide range of activities. For Orthodox Jews these regulations are authoritative and binding. Alongside the Sabbath, the pilgrim festivals (Passover, Sukkot and Shavuot) occupy a central place in the Jewish calendar. In ancient times pilgrims went to offer sacrifices in the Temple in Jerusalem. Later special prayers were recited in the synagogue, and each festival has its own special liturgical characteristics, ceremonies and customs.

***Opposite** Morning service in a synagogue in Teaneck, New Jersey, USA.
Young boys gather round the Scrolls of the Law.*

***Above** Jews praying in the Portuguese Sephardic Synagogue in Amsterdam, the
Netherlands, built in 1671 by Jews who escaped from the Inquisition in Iberia.*

JEWISH CALENDAR

RUNNING FROM NISAN TO ADAR, A VARIETY OF FESTIVALS ARE CELEBRATED THROUGHOUT THE JEWISH YEAR, MANY OF WHICH COMMEMORATE HISTORICAL EVENTS IN THE LIFE OF THE NATION.

According to tradition, the first work of chronology is the *Seder Olam* attributed to Yose ben Halafta (2nd century CE). In this work, calculation is based on biblical genealogical tables, the length of lives recorded in the Hebrew Bible, and the creation of the world in six days. On this basis the year of creation was 3761BCE. The Jewish calendar is lunar, not solar, consisting of a lunar year of 12 months of 29 or 30 days. The year is thus 354 days. The shortage of 11 days between lunar and solar years is made up by adding a 13th month (Adar 2) in certain years. In 356CE the sage Hillel II introduced a permanent calendar based on mathematical and astrological calculations.

CALENDAR REFORM

In modern times there have been several attempts at calendar reform so as to arrange a calendar with the same number of days in each month.

This would result in a uniform pattern so that the same date would fall on the same day of the week each year. The year would be divisible into two equal halves and four quarters. The main objection to such an alteration is that it would disturb the regularity of a fixed Sabbath after every six working days. If the reform were carried out, it would fall on a different day each year.

THE MONTHS

There are 12 months in the Jewish calendar. New Year (Rosh Hashanah) takes place in the seventh month in autumn and begins the spiritual year.

1 NISAN

Shabbat ha-Gadol This Sabbath takes place before Passover.
14 The Fast of the First-Born A fast is observed by every male first-born in gratitude for God's deliverance during the Exodus.
15–22 Passover Passover lasts for eight days and commemorates God's deliverance of the Israelites from Egypt. It is also referred to as the festival of unleavened bread. This term refers to the unleavened bread which the Israelites baked when they fled from the Egyptians.
16 The Counting of the Omer The Israelites were commanded to count 49 days from the second day of Passover when the omer was brought to the Temple. The 50th day was celebrated as a wheat harvest.
17–20 Hol Hamoed Intermediate days of Passover and Sukkot which are observed as semi-holy days.

Left Rabbis drinking with pilgrims at Lag B'Omer at the El Ghriba synagogue, Djerba, Tunisia.

Above Passover lamb being taken into a synagogue. Copper plate from the Verdun Altar, Klosterneuburg, of 1181 made by Nicholas of Verdun.

23 Isru Hag Day after the festival of Passover.
28 Yom Yerushalaim Jerusalem Reunification Day.

2 IYYAR

5 Yom ha-Atsmaut Celebration of the day of the State of Israel's independence.
Second, fifth and seventh days of the week During the month of Iyyar and Marheshvan these days are kept as fast days to atone for any sins committed during the preceding Passover or Sukkot.
14 Second Passover The Paschal lamb was to be sacrificed only on 14 Nisan. Those who were unable to make this sacrifice because they were in a state of ritual impurity or a long way from home could make this offering on 14 Iyyar.
18 Lag B'Omer The period between Passover and Shavuot was a time of tragedy. During the days of Akiva a plague occurred among his disciples and only stopped on 18 Iyyar. This day became known as the Scholars' Feast. The day itself is a time of joy when pilgrims go to Meron where Simeon ben Yohai (2nd century CE) is buried.

3 SIVAN

3–5 Three Days of Bordering This day commemorates the time when the Israelites prepared themselves for the revelation on Mount Sinai.

6–7 Shavuot This festival is celebrated seven weeks after the bringing of the omer on the second day of Passover. It commemorates the giving of the law on Mount Sinai.

8 Isru Hag Day after Shavuot.

4 TAMMUZ

17 The Fast of the 17 of Tammuz This fast commemorates the day when the walls of Jerusalem were breached by the Romans as well as other disasters.

5 AV

Sabbath of the 'Vision' The Sabbath before Tishah B'Av.

9 Tishah B'Av This fast commemorates the day when the Temple was destroyed by Nebuchadnezzar (604–561BCE), and the Second Temple by Titus (ruled 79–81CE).

Sabbath of 'Comfort Ye' The Sabbath after Tishah B'Av.

15 The 15 of Av A joyous day in ancient times when the people participated in a wood offering.

6 ELLUL

7 TISHRI

1–10 Ten Days of Penitence The period begins with Rosh Hashanah and concludes with Yom Kippur. It is a time for spiritual cleansing.

1–2 Rosh Hashanah The New Year festival.

3 Fast of Gedaliah This fast commemorates the assassination of Gedaliah, the Governor of the Jews appointed by Nebuchadnezzar.

10 Yom Kippur Day of Atonement.

15–21 Sukkot This festival commemorates God's protection of the Israelites in the wilderness. Sukkot, or 'booths', are built during this festival to symbolize the temporary shelter used by the Israelites.

17–21 Hoi Hamoed Atzeret Intermediate days of the festival, observed as semi-holy days.

21 Hoshanah Rabbah Name given to the seventh day of Sukkot since seven circuits are made around the Torah while Hoshanah prayers are recited.

22–3 Shemini Atzeret This two-day festival is observed at the end of Sukkot. A special prayer for rain is recited during the Musaf or additional service.

23 Simchat Torah On this festival the annual cycle of Torah readings is completed and begun again.

24 Isru Hag The day after the Sukkot festival.

8 MARHESHVAN

Second, fifth and seventh During Iyyar and Marheshvan these days are kept by some as fast days to atone for sins committed during Sukkot.

9 KISLEV

25–2/3 of Tevet Hanukkah This festival is celebrated for eight days. It commemorates the re-dedication of the Temple by the Maccabees after the Seleucids were defeated in 165BCE.

10 TEVET

10 The Fast of 10 Tevet This day commemorates the siege of Jerusalem by Nebuchadnezzar.

11 SHEVAT

15 New Year for Trees Joyous festival celebrated in Israel by the planting of trees.

Sabbath relating to the shekels Sabbath that takes place before or on 1 Adar.

12 ADAR

Sabbath of 'Remember' Sabbath before Purim.

13 Fast of Esther This fast commemorates Queen Esther's fast before she asked Ahasuerus (486–465BCE) to revoke his decree against the Jews.

14 Purim This festival commemorates the defeat of Haman's plot against the Jews.

15 Shushan Purim This festival commemorates the victory of the Jews of Shushan.

Sabbath of the Red Heifer Sabbath that occurs on the first or second Sabbath after Purim.

Sabbath of the Month Sabbath that occurs before or on 1 Nisan.

NAMES OF THE MONTHS

The names of the months in the Jewish year are of Babylonian origin. In the pre-exilic books they are identified by their numerical order. Concerning the days themselves, they begin at sunset and end at nightfall on the next day. As a result, the Sabbath begins at sunset on Friday and ends the next night when three stars appear. This same pattern apples to all holy days. The Hebrew date is normally given by indicating the name of the month first; this is followed by the date and then the year. When the year is written in Hebrew, it is usual to omit the thousands.

Above Calendar page from a Spanish Bible manuscript of 1301.

PLACES OF WORSHIP

AT FIRST, JEWISH WORSHIP TOOK PLACE IN THE SANCTUARY. LATER THE TEMPLE BECAME THE CENTRAL PLACE OF PRAYER. AFTER ITS DESTRUCTION IN 70CE, IT WAS REPLACED BY THE SYNAGOGUE.

Throughout their history Jews have gathered together for worship. In the desert the ancient Israelites transported a portable shrine; this was subsequently superseded by the Temple built in Jerusalem by King Solomon (10th century BCE). In later centuries the synagogue served as a meeting place for prayer and study.

SANCTUARY

Scripture relates that Moses made a portable shrine (sanctuary) following God's instructions in the Book of Exodus. This structure travelled with the Israelites in the desert and was placed in the centre of the camp in an open courtyard. The fence surrounding it consisted of wooden pillars from which a cloth curtain was suspended. Located in the eastern half of the courtyard, the Sanctuary measured 50 cubits by 10

Below A modern synagogue in Teaneck, New Jersey, USA, with a beautiful stained-glass window.

cubits (about 75 x 15 ft/23 x 4.5m; at its end stood the Holy of Holies, which was separated by a veil hanging on five wooden pillars on which were woven images of the cherubim. Inside the Holy of Holies was the Ark of the Covenant, the table on which the shewbread was placed, the incense altar, and the *menorah*, or 'candelabrum'. In the courtyard there was also an outer altar on which sacrifices were offered, as well as a brass laver for priests.

TEMPLE

In time this structure was superseded by the Temple, which was built by King Solomon in Jerusalem in the 10th century BCE. From the time of Solomon's reign, the Temple served as the site for prayer and the offering or sacrifices to God. In addition to the communal sacrifices made daily, there were additional communal sacrifices offered on the Sabbath, festivals, and the New Moon. The Temple was also the site to which the *omer*, or the first barley measure harvested on the second day of Passover, and the first fruits were brought on Shavuot. On Passover all families were required to come to Jerusalem to offer the paschal sacrifice.

ORIGINS OF THE SYNAGOGUE

In the 6th century BCE the Temple was destroyed by the Assyrians when they invaded the country. After the exile during the same century, Jews in Babylonia established a new institution for public worship: the synagogue (meaning 'assembly' in Greek). There they came together to study and pray. On their return to Jerusalem in the latter part of the 6th century BCE, the Jewish populace

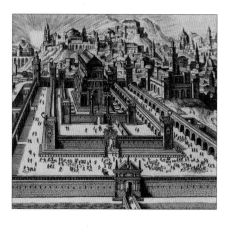

Above Am imaginary view of the Temple of Solomon. Copper engraving by Pierre Mariette, 1670.

continued to gather in synagogues as well as offer sacrifice in the Temple. Thus the synagogue developed alongside the Second Temple.

THE SYNAGOGUE

In the synagogue itself, there are a number of elements, which parallel the Sanctuary and the Temple. Firstly, there is the Holy Ark – this is symbolic of the Holy of Holies, the most important part of the Sanctuary and the Temple. The Ark itself is located on the eastern wall so that Jews are able to pray in the direction of the Temple in Jerusalem. Secondly, the eternal light hangs before the Ark. This represents the lamp that burned continually in the Sanctuary.

The third major element in the synagogue is the Torah scroll, which is placed in the Ark. The Torah is written in Hebrew by a scribe who uses a special ink on parchment. A breastplate covers the Torah, and over it hangs a pointer, which is used for the chanting or recitation of the Torah. There are two rollers on which the Torah scroll is wrapped; in addition, various ornaments, usually in silver, adorn the Scroll. These are symbolic of the ornaments of the High Priest in Temple times.

A fourth feature of the synagogue is the *bimah*, or 'platform', which was in previous times used only for the

Above Siege of Jerusalem by Assyrians *under Nebuchadnezzar, 587*BCE. *From* Merian's Illustrated Bible, *c.1627.*

reading of the Law and the Prophets, as well as for rabbinical sermons. Finally, men and women sit separately; the women are usually seated in a balcony during the service.

SYNAGOGUE HISTORY

According to tradition, there were about 400 synagogues in Jerusalem when the Second Temple fell. Although this figure may be exaggerated, there is considerable evidence of synagogue building in the Jewish world during the Second Temple period. By the 5th century BCE it was widely attested that wherever Jews lived they built structures which became the focus of Jewish life and thought. Unlike the Temple, where ritual was carried out exclusively by priests, the only requirement for synagogue worship was the presence of a *minyan*, or 'quorum of ten men'. Any service could be led by a lay person. This shift away from Temple hierarchy marked a fundamental democratization of Jewish life.

THE MIDDLE AGES

The medieval synagogue dominated Jewish life; in most communities it

Right Moses receives the Tablets of the Law, builds the Ark of the Covenant and makes offerings. From the medieval Bible by Guiars de Moulins.

was at the heart of the Jewish quarter. Men attended services three times a day, and the local rabbinic court frequently convened there. Classes took place in the sanctuary or in an annexe, and oaths as well as banns of excommunication were pronounced in its environs. In addition, communal offices, the ritual bath, a library, a hospice for travellers and a social hall were located in synagogue rooms or adjacent buildings.

THE MODERN PERIOD

In the early modern period, synagogues were constructed in Western European ghettos; Poland's wooden synagogues influenced synagogue architecture all over Eastern Europe. From the 19th century, reformers influenced major innovations. Reform synagogues (temples) were large, imposing buildings with organs. The section for women was abolished, and decorum during the service was

Above Eternal light *or* Ner Tamid *burns before the Ark in a synagogue in Westchester County, New York.*

emphasized. Head coverings for men were abandoned, and the reader's platform was shifted from the centre to the area in front of the Ark.

Yet, despite such changes, Reform temples, together with Orthodox synagogues have reassumed a major role in Jewish life.

WORSHIP

ACTS OF WORSHIP MAY BE PERFORMED INDIVIDUALLY OR IN A GROUP
WITH OR WITHOUT A LEADER. THROUGH IT JEWS EXPRESS THEIR JOYS,
SORROWS AND HOPES, ESPECIALLY IN TIMES OF CRISIS AND CALAMITY.

Above An engraving by Bernard Picart showing the Simchat Torah ceremony at an Amsterdam synagogue, Holland.

In the Hebrew Bible, the patriarchs often addressed God through personal prayer. Abraham, for example, begged God to spare Sodom since by destroying the whole population the righteous as well as the wicked would be destroyed. At Beth-El Jacob vowed: 'If God will be with me, and will keep me in this way that I go,

and will give me bread to eat, and raiment to put on ... then shall the Lord be my God (Genesis 28:20–1). After Israel made a golden calf to worship, Moses begged God to forgive them for this sin (Exodus 32:31–2).

THE TEMPLE
In ancient times the Temple in Jerusalem served as the central focus for worship. Twice daily – in the morning and afternoon – the priests offered sacrifices while the Levites

chanted psalms. Additional services were added on Sabbaths and festivals. As time passed it became customary to include other prayers with the recitation of the Ten Commandments and the Shema (Deuteronomy 6:4–9, 11, 13–21; Numbers 15:37–41). When the Temple was destroyed in 70CE, sacrificial offers were replaced by the prayer service in the synagogue. To enhance uniformity, the sages introduced fixed periods for daily prayer, which corresponded with the times sacrifices had been offered in the Temple. By the completion of the Talmud in the 6th century CE, the major elements of the synagogue service were established. In the 8th century CE the first prayer book was composed by Rav Amram, Gaon of Sura.

THE ORDER OF SERVICE
Jews are commanded to recite the Shema during the morning and evening services in accordance with the commandment, 'You shall take of them when you lie down and when you rise' (Deuteronomy 6:7), The first section (6:4–9) opens with 'Shema Yisrael' ('Hear, O Israel: the Lord our God is one Lord'). This teaches the unity of God, and emphasizes the duty to love God, meditate on his commandments and impress them on one's children. In addition, it contains laws about the tefillin and the mezuzah.

Below A watercolour by Richard Moser of the elaborately decorated interior of a synagogue in Vienna, 1920.

Above Amsterdam Jews at Yom Kippur, 1723, in the Second Synagogue built when the Great Synagogue proved too small.

Tefillin consists of two black leather boxes containing scriptural verses, which are bound by black leather straps on the arm and forehead in accordance with the commandment 'you shall bind them as a sign upon your hand, and they shall be frontlets between your eyes' (Deuteronomy 6:8). They are worn by men during morning prayer except on the Sabbath and festivals. The mezuzah consists of a piece of parchment containing two paragraphs of the Shema, which is placed into a case and fixed to the right-hand side of an entrance. Male Jews wear an undergarment with

Below Stained-glass window featuring the menorah at the Great Synagogue in Jerusalem, Israel.

fringes (the smaller tallit) and a larger tallit, or 'prayer shawl', for morning services. The silk or wool shawl has black or blue stripes with tzizit, or 'fringes', at each of the four corners.

A central feature of the synagogue service is the *Shemoneh Esreh*, or '18 Benedictions' or the Amidah. Composed over a long period of time, the prayers received their full form in the 2nd century CE. They consist of 18 separate prayers plus an additional benediction dealing with heretics. The first and last three benedictions are recited at every service; the 13 other prayers are recited only on weekdays. On Sabbaths and festivals they are replaced by one prayer dealing with the Holy Day. Other prayers are added on special occasions.

THE SYNAGOGUE SERVICE

From earliest times, the Torah was read in public gatherings; later regular readings of the Torah on Sabbaths and festivals were instituted. The entire Torah is divided into 54 sections, each of which is known as a *sidrah*. Each of these sections is subdivided into parashot, or 'portions'. Before the reading of the Torah in the synagogue, the Ark is opened and the Torah Scroll is removed.

The number of men called up to the reading on the Sabbath is seven; on other occasions the number varies. In former times those who were called up to the Torah read a section of the weekly sidrah; later an expert in Torah reading was appointed to recite the entire sidrah, and those called up recited blessings instead. After the reading of the Torah, a section from the *Haftarah*, or 'prophetic books', is recited. Once the Torah scroll is replaced in the Ark, a sermon is usually delivered based on the sidrah of the week. Another central feature of the synagogue service is the kaddish prayer. Written in Aramaic, it takes several forms in the prayer book and expresses the hope for universal

peace under the kingdom of God – this prayer is recited by mourners at the end of the service.

THE MODERN PERIOD

The traditional liturgy was essentially the same until the Enlightenment. Reformers in Central Europe then altered the worship service and introduced new prayers into the liturgy. They decreed that the service should be shortened and conducted in the vernacular as well as in Hebrew. In addition, they introduced melodies accompanied by a choir and organ and replaced the chanting of the Torah with the recitation of the sidrah. Prayers viewed as anachronistic were abandoned, and prayers of a particularistic character were amended so they became more universalistic in scope.

In recent years, all groups across the Jewish spectrum have produced new liturgies. Moreover, a wide range of occasional liturgies exist for camps, youth groups and *havurot*, or 'informal prayer groups'. Among non-Orthodox denominations there is a growing emphasis on more egalitarian liturgies with gender-free language and an increasing democratic sense of responsibility.

Below Rabbi carries the Torah scrolls during a Yom Kippur service in the Great Synagogue, Budapest, Hungary.

SABBATH

WITHIN THE JEWISH FAITH, SABBATH DAY OBSERVANCE IS OF PARAMOUNT IMPORTANCE. JEWS GATHERED TOGETHER TO COMMEMORATE THE CREATION OF THE UNIVERSE AND GOD'S SPECIAL DAY OF REST.

According to Genesis, God finished the work he had made on the seventh day. He blessed the seventh day and hallowed it and ceased his labour. Genesis 2:1–3 is the basis of the decree no work is to be done on the Sabbath.

During their time in the wilderness, the Israelites were commanded to observe the Sabbath. They were told to work on five days and collect a single portion of manna. On the sixth day they were told to collect a double portion for the following day, was to be 'a day of solemn rest, a holy sabbath of the Lord' (Exodus 16:23). On the seventh day when several people looked for manna, the Lord said: 'How long do you refuse to keep my commandments and my laws? See! The Lord has given you the sabbath, therefore on the sixth day He gives you bread for two days; ... let no man go out of his place on the seventh day' (Exodus 16:23–9).

Below Table set for the Sabbath meal with candles, wine and a challah loaf.

Several weeks later God revealed the Ten Commandments, including regulations concerning the Sabbath day: 'Remember the sabbath day, to keep it holy. Six days you shall labour, and do all your work, but the seventh day is a sabbath to the Lord your God; in it you shall not do any work, you, or your son, or your daughter, your manservant, or your maidservant, or your cattle, or the sojourner who is within your gates; for in six days the Lord made heaven and earth, the sea, and all that is in them, and rested the seventh day; therefore the Lord blessed the sabbath day and hallowed it' (Exodus 20.8–11).

RABBINIC JUDAISM

By the time of the Sanhedrin, Sabbath observance was regulated by Jewish law. Following Exodus 20:10, the primary aim was to refrain from work. In the Torah only a few provisions are delineated. Such regulations were expanded by the rabbis who listed 39 categories of work.

According to the Mishnah, the 39 categories of work are: sowing; ploughing; reaping; binding sheaves; threshing; winnowing; sorting; grinding; sifting; kneading; baking; shearing sheep; washing wool; beating wool; dyeing wool; spinning; sieving; making two loops; weaving two threads; separating two threads; tying; loosening; sewing two stitches; tearing in order to sew two stitches; hunting a deer; slaughtering; flaying; salting; curing a skin; scraping the hide; cutting; writing two letters; erasing in order to write two letters; building; pulling down a structure; extinguishing a fire; lighting a fire; striking with a hammer; and, finally, moving something.

Above A Jewish woman lighting Sabbath candles. A 17th-century Dutch woodcut.

In the Talmud these 39 categories were discussed and expanded to include within each category a range of activities. In order to ensure that individuals did not transgress these prescriptions, the rabbis enacted further legislation, which serves as a fence around the law.

SABBATH OBSERVANCE

The Sabbath begins on Friday at sunset. Candles are lit by the woman of the house about 20 minutes before sunset, as she recites the blessing: 'Blessed are you, O Lord our God, King of the universe, who has hallowed us by your commandments and commanded us to kindle the Sabbath light.' In the synagogue service preceding Friday *maariv*, or 'who brings on twilight', takes place at twilight. Known as Kabbalat Shabbat, it is a late addition dating to the 16th century when Kabbalists in Safed went to the fields on Friday afternoon to greet the Sabbath queen.

Traditionally, when the father returns home from the synagogue he blesses his children. With both hands placed on the head of a boy, he says: 'May God make you like Ephraim and Manasseh'; for a girl: 'May God make you like Sarah, Rebekah, Rachel and Leah.' In addition, he recites the priestly blessing.

Those assembled then sing Shalom Aleikhem, which welcomes the Sabbath angels. At the Sabbath table the father recites the Kiddush prayer over a cup of wine. This is followed by the washing of the hands and the blessing of the bread. The meal ends with the singing of *zemirot*, or 'table hymns', and concludes with the *Birkhat ha-Mazon*, or 'grace after meals'.

SYNAGOGUE SERVICE

On Sabbath morning the liturgy consists of a morning service, a reading of the Torah and the *Haftarah*, or 'selective readings from the prophets', and the additional service. In the service itself, introductory prayers prior to the Shema differ from those of weekdays, and the Amidah is also different. Seven individuals are called to the reading of the law, and an eighth for the reading from the prophets. In the Reform movement the worship is abridged and has no additional service. On returning home, the morning Kiddush and the blessing over bread are recited, followed by the Sabbath meal and then the grace after meals. In the afternoon service, the Torah is read prior

Below A woman praying before the Shabbat candles.

Above Abraham sees Sodom in Flames by James Tissot, shows the importance of keeping God's law.

to the Amidah; three persons are called to the Torah, and the first portion of the reading of the law for the following week is recited. Customarily three meals are to be eaten on the Sabbath day; the third meal is known as the Seudah Shelishit. It should take place just in time for the evening service. At the end of the Sabbath, the evening service takes place and is followed by the Havdalah service.

HAVDALAH

The Havdalah ceremony marks the conclusion of the Sabbath period; it is divided and consists of four blessings. Three are recited over wine, spices and lights, and the service concludes with the Havdalah blessing. The final blessing opens with the phrase, 'Blessed are you, O Lord our God, King of the universe, who distinguishes'; it is followed by a series of comparisons: between the holy and the profane, light and darkness, Israel and the nations, between the seventh day and the six days of the week. The hymn Ha-Mavdil follows the Havdalah ceremony and asks for forgiveness of sins and for the granting of a large number of children. A number of customs, including filling

a cup and extinguishing the Havdalah candle in wine poured from it, are associated with the Havdalah ceremony. Within Reform Judaism an alternative Havdalah service incorporates additional readings with traditional blessings.

Below An Orthodox Jew at daily prayer at the Western Wall in Jerusalem.

SPECIAL SABBATHS

IN THE JEWISH CALENDAR, A NUMBER OF SABBATHS ARE OF SPECIAL IMPORTANCE AND CELEBRATED IN TRADITIONAL SYNAGOGUES. ON THESE OCCASIONS, THE WORSHIP SERVICE ALTERS IN VARIOUS WAYS.

Throughout the Jewish year, special sabbaths are held to mark the coming or ending of a festival.

THE SABBATH OF BLESSING
On this Sabbath before a New Moon, worshippers using the Ashkenazi liturgy recite a formula based on sage Rav's prayer that 'it will be God's will to renew the coming month for good service' and with four expressions of hope it will be God's intention to re-establish the Temple, rescue his people from all afflictions, maintain Israel's sages and grant a month of good tidings. The service continues with the prayer 'He who performs miracles', an announcement of the date of the New Moon, and a benediction.

SHABBAT MAHAR HODESH
This Sabbath, which falls on the eve of the New Moon, has a biblical origin (1 Samuel 20:18). The Torah reading

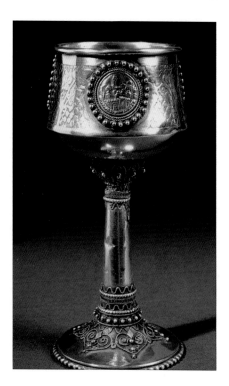

Left Silver goblet used for Kiddush, a prayer recited before the meal on the eve of Shabbat and Jewish holidays.

is that for the week. The Haftarah (1 Samuel 20:18-42) depicts the covenant between Jonathan and David on the eve of the New Moon.

SABBATH OF THE NEW MOON
In the Sabbath service which falls on the New Moon the Hallel is recited after the morning service. The Torah reading is that for the week and the additional reading is Numbers 28:9–15. The Haftarah is Isaiah 66:1–24.

SABBATH OF RETURN
The origin of the name of this Sabbath is derived from the opening words of the Haftarah: 'Return [*shuvah*], O Israel, to the Lord your God.' Since this Sabbath occurs during the Days of Penitence, it is also known as the Sabbath of Repentance.

SABBATH DURING SUKKOT
In the service for this Sabbath, which occurs during the intermediate days of Sukkot, the Hallel and the Book of Ecclesiastes are read after morning service. In some traditional congregations, religious poems are recited.

SABBATH OF GENESIS
The origin of the name of this Sabbath is derived from the opening words of the Book of Genesis which are included in the reading of the law for this Sabbath (which follows the Simchat Torah festival): 'In the beginning God created ...' On this Sabbath the annual reading cycle of the Torah commences with Genesis 1:1–6,8, and the Haftarah is that for the week. Included among

Above David's Farewell from Jonathan by Rembrandt, commemorated on Shabbat Mahar Hodesh.

those who are called to the Torah is the person chosen as 'bridegroom of Genesis' on Simchat Torah. He normally provides a festival meal to which all are invited after the Sabbath morning service.

SABBATH OF HANUKKAH
This Sabbath takes place during the Hanukkah festival. After the morning service, the Hallel is recited. The Torah reading is that for the week. The additional reading is Numbers 7:1–7. If the Sabbath also falls on the eighth day of Hanukkah the weekly portion is Genesis 41:1–44.17 and the additional reading is Numbers 7:54–8.4. If this Sabbath coincides with the New Moon, Numbers 28:9–15 is recited from a second scroll before the additional reading.

SABBATH OF THE SONG
The origin of the name of this Sabbath is the song Moses and the Israelites sang at the Red Sea (Exodus 15:1–18), which is included in the Torah reading. In some congregations special religious poems are also recited. The Torah reading is the weekly portion (Exodus 13:17–17:16).

Above The Parting of the Red Sea, *an 18th-century lithograph by Becquet for a French catechism, forms a part of the Exodus story. The Hallel and Song of Songs are recited on the Sabbath during Passover.*

SABBATH OF THE SHEKEL TAX

The origin of the name of this Sabbath, which precedes or coincides with the New Moon, Rosh Hodesh Adar, is derived from the Mishnah that states that 'on the first day of Adar they gave warning of the shekel dues.' The additional reading concerns the half-shekel levy, which was used to support the Sanctuary. In some congregations the rabbi urges that contributions be made to religious institutions in Israel.

SABBATH OF REMEMBRANCE

On the Sabbath before Purim, the additional reading emphasizes the obligation to 'remember what Amalek did to you' (since traditionally Haman was regarded as a descendant of Amalek).

SABBATH OF THE RED HEIFER

This Sabbath precedes the Sabbath of the New Moon. The additional reading deals with the red heifer whose ashes were used for ritual purification by the ancient Israelites.

SABBATH OF THE MONTH

The origin of the name for this Sabbath is derived from the opening words of the additional reading: 'This month [*ha-Hodesh*] shall mark for you the beginning of the months.'

THE GREAT SABBATH

The origin of the name of this Sabbath is uncertain but it may derive from the last verse of the Haftarah: 'Lo, I will send the prophet Elijah to you before the coming of the awesome [*gadol*], fearful day of the Lord '(Malachi 4:5).

SABBATH DURING PASSOVER

This Sabbath takes place during the intermediate days of Passover. In the service the Hallel and Song of Songs are recited after the morning service.

SABBATH OF PROPHECY

The Sabbath precedes the ninth day of Av. Its name is derived from the Haftarah, which refers to Isaiah's vision [*hazon*] about the punishments that will be inflicted on Israel.

SABBATH OF COMFORT

The origin of this name is derived from the opening words of the Haftarah: 'Comfort [*nahamu*], O comfort my people.' The Torah reading is Deuteronomy 3:23–7:11 which includes the Ten Commandments and the first paragraph of the Shema.

Below Jewish high priests, a 14th-century fresco from Ohrid, Macedonia. The high priesthood ended with the fall of the Temple, and synagogue services took the place of Temple worship.

PASSOVER

THE FESTIVAL OF PASSOVER COMMEMORATES THE EXODUS FROM EGYPT. THE SEDER MEAL TAKES PLACE ON THE FIRST NIGHT. DURING THE PASSOVER CELEBRATIONS, JEWS ARE COMMANDED TO EAT MATZAH.

Through the centuries the Jewish people celebrated the festival of Passover, which commemorates the exodus from Egypt. The term 'passover' is derived from the account of the tenth plague in Egypt when first-born Egyptians were killed, whereas God passed over the houses of the Israelites (whose doorposts and lintels were sprinkled with the blood of the paschal lamb).

THE FESTIVAL OF UNLEAVENED BREAD

Passover is also known as the festival of unleavened bread. Once the Egyptian Pharaoh gave permission for the Israelites to go, they were in such a hurry to leave that they did not wait for their bread to rise. Subsequently God commanded that no leaven was to be eaten at future Passover celebrations, nor should any leaven be found in the house. As a consequence, it became the custom just before the festival to conduct a

thorough spring-clean. All leavened foods were removed, and special Passover cutlery and crockery were brought out. This was accompanied by a final ritual search for leaven.

FESTIVAL CELEBRATIONS

Passover is also described as the festival of spring – this refers back to its traditional agricultural connections. Primarily the festival is perceived as a celebration of liberation. Traditionally it is kept for eight days and its main focus is the Passover Seder (meal), which takes place on the first night. Even the most secular Jews often attend a Passover Seder: it is an opportunity for the extended family to meet one another in an atmosphere of fellowship and joy.

PREPARATION

In preparation for Passover, Jewish law stipulates that all leaven must be removed from the house. On the

Above Three matzahs. The unleavened breads play an important part in the Seder meal.

14th of Nisan a formal search is made for any remains of leaven. This is then put aside and burned on the following morning. The first night of Passover is celebrated in the home; the ceremony is referred to as the Seder. This is done to fulfil the biblical commandment to relate the story of the Exodus to one's son: 'And you shall tell thy son on the day, saying: "It is because of what the

Below Passover Seder, from a 15th-century missal; manuscript attributed to the school of Van Eyck.

Below Father distributing loaves of unleavened bread and haroset, from the Spanish Golden Haggadah, c.1320.

ORDER OF THE SEDER

At the Seder, the Haggadah, or 'Passover prayer book', details the order of service. It is as follows:

The Kiddush is recited.
The celebrant washes his hands.
Parsley is dipped in salt water.
Celebrant divides the middle matzah and sets the afikoman aside.
Celebrant recites the Haggadah narration.
Participants wash their hands.
Blessing over bread is recited.
Blessing over matzah is recited.
Bitter herbs are eaten.
The matzah and *maror*, or 'bitter herbs', are combined.
The meal is eaten.
The afikoman is eaten
Grace after meals is recited.
The Hallel is recited.
The service is concluded.
Hymns and songs are sung.

Right *Passover in the London Hasidic Jewish community. Hasidim dip their cutlery and crockery in a ritual bath of fresh rainwater to purify them.*

Lord did for me when I came out of Egypt'" (Exodus 13:8). The order of the service dates back to Temple times. During the ceremony celebrants traditionally lean on their left sides – this was the custom of freemen in ancient times.

MATZAH

Three *matzot*, or 'unleavened bread', are placed on top of one another, usually in a special cover. The upper and lower matzot symbolize the double portion of manna that provided for the Israelites in the wilderness. The middle matzah (which is broken in two at the beginning of the Seder) represents the 'bread of affliction'.

The smaller part of the matzah is eaten to comply with the ancient commandment to eat matzah. The larger part is set aside for the *afikoman*, which recalls Temple times when the meal was completed with the eating of the paschal lamb. These

Below *Clockwise from top: Plague of the first born, the Israelites leave Egypt, the passage of the Red Sea and the pursuit by the Egyptians. From the Golden Haggadah, c.1320.*

three matzot also symbolize the three divisions of the Jewish people: Cohen, Levi and Yisrael.

FOUR CUPS OF WINE

According to tradition, each Jew must drink four cups of wine at the Seder. The first is linked to the recital of Kiddush; the second with the account of the Exodus and the Blessing for Redemption; the third with the grace after meals; and the fourth with the *Hallel*, or 'psalms', and prayers for thanksgiving. These cups also symbolize four expressions of redemption in Exodus 6:6–7. Today the cups are usually small.

CUP OF ELIJAH

This cup symbolizes the hospitality awaiting the passer-by and wayfarer. According to tradition, the Messiah will reveal himself at the Passover, and Malachi declared that he will be preceded by Elijah. The cup of Elijah was also introduced because of the doubt as to whether five cups of wine should be drunk rather than four.

THE SEDER PLATE

The Seder plate displays a number of other symbols for Passover in addition to the matzah. Bitter herbs symbolize the bitterness of Egyptian slavery. Parsley is dipped in salt water and eaten after the Kiddush, or 'prayer over wine'. It is associated with spring. Haroset is a mixture of apples, nuts, cinnamon and wine. It is a reminder of the bricks and mortars that Jews were forced to use in Egypt. A roasted shankbone symbolizes the paschal offering. A roasted egg commemorates the festival sacrifice in the Temple. Salt water recalls the salt that was offered

Above *Table set for Seder meal with foods associated with Passover.*

with all sacrifices. It also symbolizes the salt water of the tears of all ancient Israelites.

SHAVUOT

THE FESTIVAL OF SHAVUOT COMMEMORATES THE GIVING OF THE LAW ON MOUNT SINAI. IT CULMINATES THE PROCESS OF LIBERATION OF THE JEWISH NATION WHICH BEGAN WITH THE EXODUS AT PASSOVER.

The festival of Shavuot, or 'Festival of Weeks', is based on Leviticus 23:15: 'and from the day you bring the *omer*, or 'sheaf offering', of 'wave offering', you shall count off seven weeks [Shavuot].' Through the centuries, this festival has been observed as a celebration of the giving of the law.

ORIGINS

On the second day of Passover a meal offering was brought to the Temple, consisting of a sheaf of barley that was waved by the priest. This accounts for the fact that it is referred to as a 'wave offering'. Strictly speaking, the word *omer* is the name of a 'measure'. A sheaf that had this measure was brought as an offering in thanks for the barley harvest. Seven weeks were counted from the second day of Passover. At the end of seven weeks (on the 50th day), Shavuot was celebrated.

Below A mid-19th-century image of a festival procession at a synagogue at Livorno, Italy.

Initially, Shavuot was a harvest festival. However, the revelation on Mount Sinai took place during the month of Sivan according to Exodus 19: the date of Shavuot (on the sixth of Sivan) and Sinaitic revelation thus occurs at the same time. For this reason Shavuot came to be seen as a celebration of revelation, rather than a harvest festival. During the prayers for the day, Shavuot is referred to as 'the season of the giving of the Torah'.

SHAVUOT RITUALS

There are no special rituals for Shavuot as there are for Passover and Sukkot. Originally, Shavuot appears to have been an adjunct of Passover. But an adjunct festival does not require its own rituals. Further, even when Shavuot became the festival celebrating the giving of the law, new rituals expressing this theme were not created. Yet, during the Middle Ages, Shavuot customs began to develop. It is the practice, for example, to decorate the synagogue

Above Children celebrate Shavuot in a kindergarten in Jerusalem.

with flowers and plants. This symbolizes what occurred on Mount Sinai when the Torah was given. When God gave the law, it was covered with luxuriant plants and fragrant flowers.

Another custom is to eat dairy dishes. One of the reasons given is that the Torah is like milk, which soon turns sour if it is left in vessels of gold or silver. Students of the Torah who have golden opinions of themselves and lack humility are not true representations of Jewish scholarship. They turn sour the nourishing milk of the Torah.

Below Ruth harvesting, from the 1520s Latin Bible of St Amand Abbey, France. The Book of Ruth is read on Shavuot.

Above A boy learning how to fire an arrow from a bow. Archery plays a part in the celebration of Lag B'Omer.

CELEBRATION

Shavuot is celebrated for two days on the 6th and 7th of Sivan. Seven weeks are counted from the bringing of the omer on the second day of Passover. The festival is also referred to as Pentecost, a Greek word meaning 50, since it was celebrated on the 50th day. Symbolically, the day commemorates the culmination of the process of emancipation, which began with the Exodus at Passover. It is concluded with the proclamation of the Law on Mount Sinai.

During the Temple period, farmers set out for Jerusalem to offer a selection of the first ripe fruits as a thanks-offering. In post-Temple times, the festival focuses on the giving of the law on Mount Sinai. In some communities it is a practice to remain awake during Shavuot night. In the 16th century, Solomon Alkabets and other Kabbalists began the custom of *tikkun*, in which an anthology of biblical and rabbinic material was recited. Today in the communities where this custom is observed, this lectionary has been replaced by a passage of the Talmud or other rabbinic literature.

Right Poem for the first day of Shavuot from Laudian Mahzor, a German book of Jewish liturgy for festivals, c.1275.

Some congregations in the Diaspora read a book of psalms on the second night. Synagogues are decorated with flowers or plants. Jews should count the days until the Law was given on Sinai. This is like a slave counting the days to his freedom, or lovers counting the days until reunion. In the Middle Ages, the omer period was one of mourning. One reason given for this is that the disciples of Akiva died during this period. It is the custom not to have a haircut during this time, except on certain days. In addition, weddings are not to be celebrated except at specific times.

LAG B'OMER

The word 'lag' has the numerical equivalent of 33. This day, which is the 33rd day of the omer, is a minor festival because Simeon ben Yohai, traditionally viewed as the author of the Zohar, died on this day. The ascent of his soul to Heaven is described as his wedding, the reunion of the soul with God. Weddings are permitted on this day, even though it takes place during the omer. Lag B'Omer became a scholars' festival, celebrated as a day of joy. In some communities, teachers and students go out into the woods to shoot bows and arrows.

SUKKOT

THE FESTIVAL OF SUKKOT COMMEMORATES THE WANDERING OF THE ISRAELITES IN THE DESERT. DURING THIS FESTIVAL JEWS ARE COMMANDED TO CONSTRUCT SUKKOT (BOOTHS) AND DWELL IN THEM.

Sukkot is a pilgrim festival prescribed in the Bible: 'On the 15th of the month and for seven days is the feast of tabernacles to the Lord' (Leviticus 23:34). Beginning on the 15th of Tishri, it commemorates God's protection of the Israelites during their sojourn in the desert. Leviticus demands that Jews are to construct booths during this period as a reminder that the people of Israel dwelt in booths when they fled from Egypt (Leviticus 23:42–3).

BIBLICAL LAW

The Book of Leviticus goes on to explain how the festival of Sukkot is to be celebrated: 'You shall take on the first day the fruit of goodly trees, branches of palm trees and boughs of leafy trees and willows of the brook; and you shall rejoice before

Below An Orthodox Jew and a secular youth blessing the four species during the Feast of Tabernacles in Jerusalem.

the Lord your God for seven days ... You shall dwell in booths for seven days ... that your generation may know that I made the people of Israel dwell in booths when I brought them up out of the land of Egypt' (Leviticus 23:40, 42–3).

THE SUKKAH

The feast of tabernacles was thus ordained to remind Jews of their wandering in the wilderness before they reached the Promised Land. This was a time when they were particularly close to God. Today Jews are expected to build their own *sukkah*, or 'tabernacle', and the sages of the Talmud explained how this is to be done. The sukkah has to be at least four square cubits in size (a cubit is about 45cm/18in). It must have at least three walls and it should have a covering of things that were once growing. However, this does not imply that it should have a complete roof. When pious Jews stand in

Above Serving food at a Sukkot celebration in the Grand Choral Synagogue, St Petersburg, Russia.

the sukkah, they should be able to see the stars through the branches of the covering. Meals should be eaten in the sukkah for the duration of the festival, although in cold climates there is no obligation to sleep in it or even to remain in it if it rains.

LULAV

In addition to constructing a sukkah, Jews are to perform a ceremony involving the fruit and the branches. This is done by holding an *etrog*, a citron, which is a large citrus fruit, in one hand and branches of palm, willow and myrtle (which are collectively known as the *lulav*) in the other. During the synagogue service, the lulav is waved in six directions: north, south, east, west, up and down. In all likelihood this symbolizes God's control of all the points of the compass and space.

Various explanations have been given regarding the composition of the lulav: possibly the most attractive is that it symbolizes the different types of Jews that make up the community, that all are necessary and should work in harmony while keeping their individuality. In any case, the lulav is waved while the Hallel (Psalms 113–118) is recited, and it is taken in a circuit around the synagogue while a prayer is recited for a good harvest.

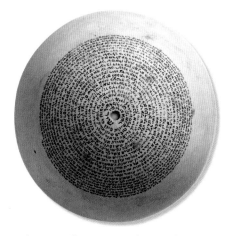

Above Hollow eggs with sacred texts were used to decorate European sukkahs for the holiday of Sukkot. This 19th-century Polish egg is decorated with text from the Song of Solomon.

THE GREAT HOSHANAH

On the seventh day of the festival known as the Great Hoshanah (God saves), seven circuits are made in the synagogue. This is often viewed as the culmination of the whole season of repentance (the New Year, the Ten Days of Penitence and the Day of Atonement). Since Sukkot is celebrated during the course of the Tabernacles

Below Jews eating in a public sukkah during Sukkot. Some congregations build community sukkahs.

festival, it is a mixture of joy and solemnity. The next day, the day of the holy convocation, is Shemini Atzerert (the eighth day of the solemn assembly) and Simchat Torah (the rejoicing of the law). Shemini Atzeret and Simchat Torah are traditionally commemorated on the same day, but it has become customary for Shemini Atzeret to be observed on the eighth day and Simchat Torah on the ninth.

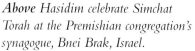

Above Hasidim celebrate Simchat Torah at the Premishian congregation's synagogue, Bnei Brak, Israel.

SIMCHAT TORAH

Simchat Torah is a time of joy. It is a holy day on which the annual reading of the Torah is finished and the whole cycle begins again with the first portion from the Book of Genesis. It is considered to be an honour to be called up to read the last section of the Book of Deuteronomy, and the person chosen is called 'Bridegroom of the Torah'. The next person who is called up to read the first section of the Book of Genesis is known as the 'Bridegroom of Genesis'.

During the service, the Torah scrolls are taken from the Ark and carried in procession around the synagogue. In Hasidic communities, the enthusiasm is overwhelming and the procession spills out into the street amid singing and dancing. Children are called up and given sweets and fruits. In some communities it is the custom for the two 'bridegrooms' to give a party for the whole community.

CHAPTER 6

FESTIVALS

Celebrating Jewish high days and holidays is a vital part of being a Jew. Communities come together to mark not just the happiest festivals but also those that commemorate sad and serious times such as Holocaust Remembrance Day and Yom Kippur. The Jewish New Year begins in the autumn of the first day of Tishri and marks the start of the Ten Days of Penitence, which end on the Day of Atonement. In the Bible, Rosh Hashanah is referred to as falling on the first day of the seventh month (Leviticus 23:24). During the rabbinic period, it came to be regarded as a day of judgement for the entire world, on which each person's fate is inscribed in the Book of Life. Today the High Holy Days can continue to serve as the focus for reflection and introspection. Throughout the Jewish year, the community also celebrates a numbers of days of joy, including Hanukkah, Purim, Rosh Hodesh, the New Year for Trees, the Fifteenth of Av and Israel Independence Day. During these celebrations, Jews remember joyous historical events and times of tragedy in the history of their nation as well as seasons of the year when thanks are due to God for his blessings.

Opposite Blowing the shofar, a ceremonial wind instrument originally made from a ram's horn, on Rosh Hashanah to mark the beginning of the Jewish New Year.

Above A late 18th-century engraving showing Jews in a synagogue in Amsterdam, Holland, celebrating Purim. At Purim, Esther delivered the Jews from Haman's plot to destroy them.

ROSH HASHANAH

ROSH HASHANAH (NEW YEAR) MARKS THE COMMENCEMENT OF THE
SPIRITUAL YEAR. AT THIS TIME JEWS ARE COMMANDED TO REPENT OF
THEIR SINS AND RESOLVE TO IMPROVE DURING THE NEXT 12 MONTHS.

The New Year is commemorated for two days on the 1st and 2nd of Tishri. It marks the beginning of the Ten Days of Penitence, which ends on Yom Kippur, or 'the Day of Atonement'. From ancient times to now, Rosh Hashanah has been seen as the start of the spiritual year. It is a time for reflection and self-examination.

BIBLICAL JUDAISM
In ancient times, the Jewish New Year took place on one day; in subsequent centuries it became a two-day festival. The term Rosh Hashanah occurs only once in Scripture – in Ezekiel 40:1. Nevertheless, this festival had three other biblical designations: (1) Shabbaton – a day of solemn rest to be observed on the first day of the seventh month; (2) Zikhron Teruah – a memorial proclaimed with the blast of the horn (Leviticus 23:24); and (3) Yom Teruah – a day of blowing the horn (Numbers 29:1). Later it

Below Sounding the shofar on Rosh Hashanah. 1723 engraving by Bernard Picart from his series on Judaism.

was referred to by the sages as Yom ha-Din (the Day of Judgement) and Yom ha-Zikkaron (the Day of Remembrance).

DIVINE JUDGEMENT
The Mishnah declares that all human beings will appear before God on the New Year. The Talmud expands this idea by stressing the need for self-examination. In rabbinic sources each individual stands before the throne of God, and judgement on each person is entered on the New Year and sealed on the Day of Atonement.

According to the Talmud, there are three ledgers opened in heaven: one is for the completely righteous, who are immediately inscribed and sealed in the Book of Life. Another is for the thoroughly wicked, who are recorded in the Book of Death. A third is for the intermediate, ordinary type of individual, whose fate hangs in the balance and is suspended until the Day of Atonement. In this light, Rosh Hashanah and Yom Kippur are called *Yamim Noraim*, or 'Days of Awe'.

Above At Rosh Hashanah it is customary to eat apples dipped in honey for 'a good and sweet year'.

SYNAGOGUE OBSERVANCE
On New Year Day, the Ark curtain, reading desk and Torah scroll mantles are decked in white, and the rabbi, cantor and person who blows the *shofar*, or 'ram's horn', all wear a white *kittel*, or 'robe'. In the synagogue service the Amidah or the Musaf service contains three sections relating to God's sovereignty, providence and revelation: Malkhuyyot deals with God's rule; Zikhronot portrays God's remembrance of the ancestors of the Jewish people when he judges each generation; Shofarot contains verses relating to the shofar, and deals with the revelation on Mount Sinai and the messianic age. Each introductory section is followed by three verses from the Torah, three from the Writings; three from the Prophets, and a final verse from the Torah.

Below A poem for Rosh Hashanah, has a drawing of the sacrifice of Isaac by Abraham. From a 14th-century German Jewish book of prayers for festivals.

Above A Central European postcard from 1900 showing the blowing of the shofar, or horn, for Rosh Hashanah.

AVINU MALKENU

Avinu Malkenu is said from Rosh Hashanah to Yom Kippur. The phrase means 'Our father, our king'.

Avinu Malkenu, we have no king but you.

Avinu Malkenu, help us for your own sake.

Avinu Malkenu, grant us a blessed New Year.

Avinu Malkenu, annul all evil decrees against us.

Avinu Malkenu, annul the plots of our enemies.

Avinu Malkenu, frustrate the designs of our foes.

Avinu Malkenu, rid us of tyrants.

Avinu Malkenu, rid us of pestilence, sword, famine, captivity, sin and destruction.

Avinu Malkenu, forgive and pardon all our sins.

Avinu Malkenu, ignore the record of our transgressions.

Avinu Malkenu, help us return to you fully repentant.

Avinu Malkenu, send complete healing to the sick.

Avinu Malkenu, remember us with favour.

Avinu Malkenu, inscribe us in the book of happiness.

Avinu Malkenu, inscribe us in the book of deliverance.

Avinu Malkenu, inscribe us in the book of prosperity.

Avinu Malkenu, inscribe us in the book of merit.

Avinu Malkenu, inscribe us in the book of forgiveness.

The Torah readings at Rosh Hashanah concern the birth (Genesis 12:1–34) and the binding of Isaac (Genesis 22:1–24). On both days the shofar is blown at three points during the service: 30 times after the reading of the Law; 30 times during Musaf; and 10 before Alenu. In the liturgy there are three variants of the blowing of the shofar: *tekiah*, or 'a long note'; *shevarim*, or 'three tremulous notes'; and *teruah*, 'nine short notes'. According to the 12th-century Jewish philosopher Moses Maimonides, the shofar is blown to call sinners to repent.

TASHLICH

Traditionally, it was the custom to go to the seaside or the banks of a river on the afternoon of the first day. The ceremony of Tashlich symbolizes the casting of one's sins into a body of water. The prayers for Tashlich and the three verses from the Book of Micah (Micah 7:18–20) express confidence

Right A Rosh Hashanah service at the Moscow Choral Synagogue, Russia.

in divine forgiveness. In the home, a piece of bread is dipped in honey followed by a piece of apple, and a prayer is recited that the year ahead may be good and sweet.

A SOLEMN DAY

The Ten Days of Penitence begin with the New Year and last until the Day of Atonement. This is regarded as the most solemn time of the year when all are judged and their fate determined for the coming year. During the Ten Days various additions are made to the liturgy, especially in the morning service. Selihot Penitential prayers are recited during the morning service, and various additions are made to the Amidah and the reader's repetition of the Amidah. The reader's repetition is followed by the Avinu Malkenu prayer.

YOM KIPPUR

YOM KIPPUR CONCLUDES THE TEN DAYS OF PENITENCE, WHICH BEGINS WITH ROSH HASHANAH. DURING YOM KIPPUR, JEWS ARE COMMANDED TO REPENT OF THEIR SINS AND SEEK FORGIVENESS.

Yom Kippur is the holiest day of the Jewish year. Observed on the 10th of Tishri, it is prescribed in Scripture: 'On the tenth day of the seventh month is the Day of Atonement; and you shall afflict yourselves. It shall be to you a sabbath of solemn rest, and you shall afflict yourselves; on the ninth day of the month, beginning at evening, from evening to evening' (Leviticus 23: 27, 32).

The rabbis stress that the Day of Atonement enables human beings to atone for sins committed against God. However, regarding transgressions committed against others, pardon cannot be obtained unless forgiveness has been sought from the persons injured. As a result, it is customary for Jews to seek reconciliation with anyone they might have offended during the year.

Below The Day of Atonement as observed by Ashkenazi Jews in the 18th century, by Bernard Picart.

KAPPAROT

The kapparot ritual takes place before Yom Kippur among Sephardi and Eastern communities as well as among some Ashkenazim. During this ceremony a fowl is slaughtered and either eaten before the fast or sold for money, which is given to charity. Its death symbolizes the transfer of guilt from the person to the bird that has been killed. In some congregations, Jews substitute coins for the fowl, and charity boxes are available at the morning and afternoon services before Yom Kippur.

Previously *malkot*, or 'lashes', were administered in the synagogue to impart a feeling of repentance, but this custom has largely disappeared.

YOM KIPPUR RITUAL

Customarily, Jews were able to absolve vows on the eve of Yom Kippur. In addition, afternoon prayers are recited earlier than normal, and the Amidah is extended by two formulae

Above Emperor Hadrian expelled the Jews from Jerusalem. His persecution is referred to in the Yom Kippur liturgy.

A DAY OF FASTING

According to the sages, afflicting one's soul involves abstaining from food and drink. Thus every male over the age of 13 and every female over 12 is obliged to fast from sunset until nightfall the next day. Sick people may take medicine, and small amounts of food and drink. Those with chronic illnesses like insulin-dependent diabetes may be forbidden to fast. During the day normal Sabbath prohibitions apply, but worshippers are to abstain from food and drink, marital relations, wearing leather shoes, using cosmetics and lotions and washing the body, except for fingers and eyes.

Below Leather shoes are not worn on the day of Yom Kippur.

Right *The Kol Nidre, the first of the Yom Kippur services, in the Great Synagogue, Budapest, Hungary.*

of confession. Some pious Jews immerse themselves in a *mikveh*, or 'ritual bath', in order to undergo purification before the fast. In the home, a final meal is eaten, and, before lighting the festival candles, a memorial candle is lit to burn throughout the day. Leather shoes are replaced by non-leather shoes. The *tallit*, or 'prayer shawl', is worn throughout all the services, and a white curtain adorns the Ark and Torah scrolls. The reader's desk and other furnishings are covered in white. Among Ashkenazim, rabbis, cantors and other officials also wear a white kittel (gown).

CONFESSION

On Yom Kippur five services take place. The first, Kol Nidre, takes place on Yom Kippur eve. Among the Orthodox, it was a custom to spend the night in the synagogue reciting the entire Book of Psalms as well as other readings. Among Sephardim and Reform Jews the memorial prayer is recited on Kol Nidre. In addition to selihot and other hymns, the morning service includes a Torah reading describing the Day of Atonement ritual in the Sanctuary. Before the Musaf service, a special prayer – Hineni He-Ani Mi-Maas – is recited. A number of liturgical hymns are included in the reader's repetition of the Amidah, including the 11th-century U-Netanneh Tokef passage, which states that prayer and charity avert judgement.

MARTYROLOGY

Interpolated among the selihot and confessions towards the end of Musaf is the Elleh Ezkerah martyrology. Based on a medieval midrash, this describes the plight of the Ten Martyrs persecuted for defying Hadrian's ban on studying of the Torah. In some rites this part of the service is expanded to include Holocaust readings. In the afternoon service, Leviticus 18 is read, dealing with prohibited marriages and sexual offences. The second reading is the Book of Jonah.

CONCLUDING SERVICE

Before the neilah, or 'concluding service', the hymn El Nora Alilah is chanted among the Sephardim. This part of the liturgy is recited as twilight approaches. In some congregations, the Ark remains open and worshippers stand throughout the service. They ask God to inscribe each person for a good life and to seal them for a favourable fate. At the end of the service, the shofar is blown, and the congregations recite *La-Shanah ha-Baah Bi-Yerushalayim*, or 'next year in Jerusalem'. After the service concludes, it is customary to begin the construction of the sukkah, or 'booth'.

Below *Jews in preparation for Yom Kipper perform the kapparot ritual, in which a chicken is sacrificed.*

FASTS

THROUGHOUT THE JEWISH YEAR, THE COMMUNITY COMMEMORATES A VARIETY OF EVENTS WITH FASTING. ALONGSIDE YOM KIPPUR, THERE IS A RANGE OF FAST DAYS WHICH HIGHLIGHT TRAGIC PAST EVENTS.

Fasting or abstinence from food plays its part in Jewish religion. Individuals may fast as a sign of repentance or mourning, or to make atonement.

THE FIRST TEMPLE

In the ritual of the First Temple, fasting was a permanent feature: the death of a national leader such as King Saul could initiate a day-long fast or even a weekly fast. The purpose of such fasting was manifold: its most important function was to avert or terminate calamities. In addition, fasting served as a means of obtaining divine forgiveness.

THE BIBLE

In Scripture, there is no record of specific fast days in the annual calendar except for the Day of Atonement. Fixed fast days were first mentioned in the post-exilic period by the prophet

Below On the 9th of Av, Jews wearing jute bags gather to pray at the Western Wall in Jerusalem, to mark the fall of the First and Second Temples.

Zechariah. According to tradition, these fasts commemorate events which resulted in the destruction of the Temple: the 10th of Tevet – the beginning of the siege of Jerusalem; the 17th of Tammuz – the breaching of the walls; the 9th of Av – the destruction of the Temple; the 3rd of Tishri – the assassination of Gedaliah, the Babylonian-appointed governor of Judah. As a result, the practice of fasting, which was initially spontaneous, later entered the calendar as a recurring event in the commemoration of historical tragedies.

OBSERVANCE

Jewish texts lay down a series of prescriptions to regularize the process of fasting. During the First Temple period, the devout offered sacrifice, confessed sins and uttered prayers. From the Second Temple period onwards, public fasts were accompanied by a reading from Scripture. On solemn fasts, four prayers were recited as well as Maariv. The Amidah of the fast day consisted of 24 benedictions (the normal 18 and six others), and the liturgy was elaborated with passages of *selihot*, or 'supplication', and prayers for mercy. During the service the shofar, or 'ram's horn', was sounded, accompanied by other horns.

In the Temple, the blowing of shofarot and trumpets was performed differently from other localities. Prayers were normally uttered in the open, and all the people tore their clothes, wore sackcloth and put ashes or earth on their heads. Holy objects were also humiliated. It was common for the altar to be covered with sackcloth and the Ark, containing the Torah scrolls, was

Above The Suicide of Saul, 1562, by Pieter Brueghel the Elder. Saul's death initiated fasting and mourning.

frequently taken into the street and covered with ashes. During the mass assembly, one of the elders rebuked the people for their failings, and the affairs of the community were scrutinized. It was normal for young children and animals to fast as well. The sages, however, exempted young children and animals, the sick, those obliged to preserve their strength and pregnant and nursing women.

ORDINARY AND IMPORTANT FAST DAYS

Ordinary fast days lasted during the daylight hours; important fasts were 24 hours in length. Fasts were held either for one day, or, on some occasions, for a series of three or seven days. In some cases they took place daily for a continued period.

In unusual cases, fasts were held on Sabbaths and festivals, but it was normally forbidden to fast on these days. So as not to mar the celebration of joyful events in Jewish history, Hananiah ben Hezekiah ben Garon (1st century CE) formulated a Scroll of Fasting which lists 35 dates on which a public fast should not be proclaimed. Eventually, however, this list was abrogated. It was customary to hold fast days on Mondays and Thursdays. After the destruction of the Second Temple, individuals took upon themselves to

5 7th of Adar is a traditional date of the death of Moses.

6 Yom Kippur Katan is a fast day which takes place on the last day of each month.

7 The Fast of the First-Born takes place on 14th Nisan to commemorate the sanctification of the first-born who were saved during the time of the last plague of Egypt.

8 Days commemorating various calamitous events in the history of the Jewish nation.

fast every Monday and Thursday. Jewish law specifies that in such cases these persons should fast during the afternoon of the preceding day. It was also possible to fast for a certain number of hours. On some occasions, the fast was only partial, with those fasting refraining only from meat and wine.

BIBLICAL FASTS

1 The Day of Atonement (Yom Kippur) is to be a fast day.

2 The Ninth of Av (Tishah B'Av) was the day when Nebuchadnezzar (fl. 7th–6th centuries BCE) destroyed the Temple in 586BCE and Titus later devastated the Second Temple in 70CE.

3 The Seventeenth of Tammuz commemorates the breaching of the walls of Jerusalem, which occurred on 9th of Tammuz in the First Temple period.

4 The Tenth of Tevet is a fast that commemorates the commencement of the siege of Jerusalem by Nebuchadnezzar.

5 The Fast of Gedaliah takes place on 3rd of Tishri to commemorate the fate of Gedaliah, the governor of Judah who was assassinated on this day.

6 The Fast of Esther takes place on the 13th of Adar, the day before Purim.

RABBINIC FASTS

1 The especially pious are encouraged to fast during the Ten Days of Penitence and for as many days as possible during the month of Elul.

2 The first Monday and Thursday and the following Monday after Passover and Sukkot are observed as fast days.

3 Shoavim Tat is observed during the Three Weeks of Mourning.

4 A fast is observed during the Three Weeks of Mourning between 17th of Tammuz and 9th of Av.

PRIVATE FASTS

1 The anniversary of the death of a parent.

2 Grooms and brides fast on the day before their wedding.

3 Fasting occurs to prevent the consequences of nightmares taking place.

4 Fasting takes place if a Torah scroll is dropped.

Below *German Jews from Nuremberg, 1734, commemorate Tishah B'Av in memory of the destruction of the Temple in Jerusalem.*

HANUKKAH

HANUKKAH IS A JOYOUS FESTIVAL COMMEMORATING THE TRIUMPH OF THE JEWS OVER THEIR ENEMIES IN ANCIENT TIMES. FOR EIGHT DAYS A HANUKKAH MENORAH IS LIT AND TRADITIONAL PRAYERS RECITED.

The festival of Hanukkah, or 'dedication', is celebrated for eight days beginning on the 25th of Kislev – it commemorates the victory of the Maccabees over the Seleucids in the 2nd century BCE. Originally a Jewish rebel army the Maccabees took control of Judea, which had been a client state of the Seleucid empire, and founded the Hasmonean dynasty, which ruled from 164BCE to 63BCE, reasserting the Jewish religion and expanding Israel's borders.

At this time the Maccabees were engaged in military conflict with the Seleucids who had desecrated the Temple. After a three-year struggle (165–163BCE), the Maccabees under Judah Maccabee (d. 160/161 BCE) conquered Jerusalem and rebuilt the altar. According to the Talmud, one day's worth of oil miraculously kept the menorah burning in the Temple for eight days.

I MACCABEES

The First Book of Maccabees 4:36–59 states that Judah Maccabee, after defeating Lysias, entered Jerusalem and purified the Temple. The altar, which had been defiled, was destroyed and a new one was constructed.

Judah then made new holy vessels including a candelabrum, an altar for incense and a table, and established the 25th of Kislev as the date for the rededication of the Temple. This day coincided with the third anniversary of the proclamation of the edicts of Antiochus Epiphanes (c.215–164BCE) in which he decreed idolatrous sacrifices should be offered in the Temple. The altar was to be consecrated with the renewal of the daily sacrificial service; this was to be accompanied by song, the playing of musical instruments, the chanting of the Hallel, and the offering of sacrifice.

Above In this scene from 1 Maccabees, Mattathias kills a Jew who comes to make a sacrifice at an altar. By Gabriel Bodenehr the Elder (1673–1765).

These festivities lasted for eight days, and Judah decreed they should be designated as a time for rejoicing.

II MACCABEES

The Second Book of Maccabees 1:8; 10:1–5 parallels 1 Maccabees. It adds that the eight-day celebration was performed on an analogy with Solomon's consecration of the Temple. The eight days were celebrated with gladness like the Feast of Tabernacles, which recalled how the ancient Israelites had been wandering like wild beasts in the mountains and caves. Thus, bearing wands wreathed with leaves, boughs and palms, they offered hymns of praise.

Hanukkah is therefore called Tabernacles or Tabernacles and Fire. Fire had descended from heaven at the dedication of the altar during the time of Moses and at the sanctification of the Temple of Solomon. At the consecration of the altar in the time of the prophet Nehemiah there was also a miracle of fire, and similarly in the days of Judah Maccabee.

Left A menorah dominates this fresco of preparations for a Jewish festival by Luigi Ademollo. In the 2nd century BCE, the Maccabees under Judah Maccabee drove out the Seleucid oppressors, rebuilt the Temple and rekindled the menorah.

Right Children playing with dreidels at Hanukkah. This traditional Jewish toy bears the initial letters of the Hebrew words 'A great miracle happened there.'

THE KINDLING OF LIGHTS

None of these early sources mention the kindling of lights on Hanukkah. This is referred to first in a *baraita*, or 'religious law outside teaching': 'The precept of light on Hanukkah requires that one light be kindled in each house; the zealous require one light for each person; the extremely zealous add a light for each person each night. According to Bet Shammai: "On the first day, eight lights should be kindled, thereafter they should be progressively reduced" while Bet Hillel held that: "On the first night one light should be kindled, thereafter they should be progressively increased."'

HANUKKAH OBSERVANCE

The main observance of this festival is the kindling of the festive lamp on each of the eight nights. This practice gave this holiday the additional

Below Hanukkah recalls when a day's oil kept the Temple menorah burning for eight days. In this 1299 Hebrew Bible from Spain, oil is poured into a menorah.

name of *Hag ha-Urim*, or 'festival of lights'. In ancient times this lamp was placed in the doorway or in the street outside; subsequently the lamp was placed inside the house. The lighting occurs after dark (except on Friday night, when it must be done before the kindling of the Sabbath lights). The procedure for lighting the Hanukkah candles is to light one candle (or an oil lamp) on the first night, and an additional candle each night until the last night when all eight candles are lit. The kindling should go from left to right. An alternative tradition prescribes that the eight candles are lit on the first night, seven on the second night and so forth. These candles are lit by an additional candle called the *shammash*, or 'serving light'. In addition to this home ceremony, candles are lit in the synagogue.

THE SYNAGOGUE LITURGY

In the synagogue this festival is commemorated by the recitation of the Al ha-Nissim prayer in the Amidah, and Grace after Meals. In the morning service the Hallel is recited, and a special reading from the law takes place on each day. In both the home and the synagogue the hymn Maoz Tsur is sung in Ashkenazi communities; the Sephardim read Psalm 30 instead. During Hanukkah it is customary to hold parties, which include games and singing. The most

well-known game involves a *dreidel*, or 'spinning top'. The dreidel is inscribed with four Hebrew letters (*nun, gimmel, he, shin*) on its side – this is an acrostic for the phrase *nes gadol hayah sham*', or 'a great miracle happened there'. During Hanukkah, *latkes*, or potato pancakes, and *sufganiyyot*, or doughnuts, are eaten. In modern Israel the festival is associated with national heroism and a torch is carried from the traditional burial site of the Maccabees at Modiin to various parts of the country.

Below Children lighting a menorah for the eight-day holiday of Hanukkah, commemorating the rededication of the Holy Temple in Jerusalem.

PURIM

THE FESTIVAL OF PURIM CELEBRATES THE DELIVERANCE OF THE JEWISH PEOPLE FROM THEIR OPPRESSORS. THE BOOK OF ESTHER IS READ DURING THE FESTIVAL.

According to Scripture, this feast was instituted by Mordecai to celebrate the deliverance of the Jews from the plot by Haman, chief minister of King Ahasuerus (486–465BCE), to kill them. The term 'purim' refers to the lots cast by Haman in order to determine the month when this massacre was to take place. Purim is celebrated on the 14th of Adar, and is a time of joy and thanksgiving.

OBSERVANCE

The central feature of this festival is the reading of the Book of Esther, from the *megillah*, or 'scroll', with special cantillation (ritual chanting or intoning). Megillot scrolls are often decorated, sometimes with scenes from the narrative. It is customary to fold the megillah over and spread it out before the reading. The

Below Mordecai and Haman. A 2nd-century fresco from Dura-Europos Synagogue, Syria.

four verses of redemption (Esther 2:5; 8:15–16 and 10:3) are read in a louder voice than other verses. It is the custom of children to make a loud noise with rattles whenever the name of Haman is read. It is the practice for the reader to recite the names of the ten sons of Haman (Esther 9:7–9) in one breath to demonstrate that they were executed simultaneously. According to one interpretation, this is done so that a person will not gloat over the downfall of one's enemies.

GIFTS

The Book of Esther (9:22) describes the practice of sending portions to friends on Purim and giving gifts to the poor. The rule is to send at least two portions of eatables, confectionery and so forth to a friend and to give a present of money to at least two poor men. A special festival meal is often consumed on Purim afternoon: among Purim foods are boiled

Above Children in Old Jerusalem dress in colourful costumes as angels, clowns and police officers for Purim.

beans and peas, which are viewed as a reminder of the cereals Daniel ate in the king's palace in order to avoid infringing dietary laws. Three-cornered pies, known as *hamantashen*, or 'Haman's hats', are also eaten. According to the Babylonian sage Rava (270–350CE), a person is obliged to drink so much wine on Purim that he becomes incapable of knowing whether he is cursing

SACRED LITERATURE

Parodies of sacred literature produced for Purim include *Massekeht Purim*, a parody of the Talmud with its theme of the obligation to drink wine and abstain from water. The institution of the Purim rabbi as a merry fool became a norm in many communities. This can be seen as an annual attempt to find psychological relief from an overwhelming burden of loyalty to the Torah. Under influence from the Italian carnival, people dressed up on Purim in fancy dress. Men were even allowed to dress as women, and vice versa.

Above Jews celebrating Purim in a synagogue in Amsterdam, Holland. A late 18th-century engraving.

Haman or blessing Mordecai. The laws concerning this festival are found in the Code of Jewish Law.

KABBALAH

In Kabbalistic and Hasidic literature much is made of Purim as a day of joy and friendship. Unlike Passover, which celebrates God's intervention in human life, God is not mentioned in the Book of Esther. The lots of Purim are compelled with the 'lots' cast on the Day of Atonement when human beings call fate and luck into being. Kabbalists esteemed Purim so highly that they reported in the name of Isaac Luria that the Day of Atonement is like Purim. Although a few Reform congregations abolished Purim, the majority continue to regard the day as one of encouragement and hope.

PURIM KATAN

Following the talmudic injunction that one must recite a special thanksgiving benediction on returning to the place where one was once miraculously saved from danger, the custom arose of celebrating the anniversary of the Jews escape from destruction by reciting special prayers with a ritual similar to that of Purim. These communal Purims are referred to as 'Purim Katan' or 'Moed Katan' or 'Purim', followed with the name of the community. In some cases special Purims were preceded by a fast comparable to the Fast of Esther.

In addition, on the Purim Katan itself the story of personal or communal salvation is recited from a scroll in the course of the synagogue service in which special prayers are recited. Sometimes the Al ha-Nissim prayer and the Hallel are inserted into the ritual. The traditional Purim observance of enjoying a festival meal and giving charity to the poor were also added to these Purims.

PURIM-SHPIL

The term *Purim-shpil*, or 'Purim play', refers to the group performances or monologues given at the traditional family meal held on the festival of Purim. There is evidence that the use of the term 'Purimshpil' was widespread among Ashkenazi communities as early as the mid-16th century. At the beginning of the 18th century, the biblical Purim-shpil reflected various trends of the contemporary European theatre in its literary style, choice of subject and design.

As time passed, the Purim-shpil became a complex drama with a large cast, comprising thousands of rhymed lines performed to musical accompaniment. The play invariably maintained a strong connection with Purim.

Below Kurdish Jews celebrating the festival of Purim wearing traditional dress and reading from a scroll of the Book of Esther.

FESTIVALS OF JOY

DURING THE YEAR JEWS CELEBRATE A NUMBER OF JOYOUS FESTIVALS. IN MODERN TIMES, ISRAEL INDEPENDENCE DAY HAS GAINED CONSIDERABLE SIGNIFICANCE IN THE JEWISH CALENDAR.

In addition to the festivals of Hanukkah and Purim, Jews celebrate several other festivals of joy. The first, Rosh Hodesh, celebrates the New Moon; the second, Tu b'Shevat, is related to tree planting; the third, 15th of Av, is a folk festival; and the fourth, Israel Independence Day, commemorates the creation of the State of Israel.

NEW MOON

Originally Rosh Hodesh, or 'new moon', was not fixed by astronomical calculations; instead it was proclaimed after witnesses had observed the reappearance of the crescent of the moon. On the 30th of every month, members of the High Court assembled in a courtyard in Jerusalem; there they waited

Above A young boy pats down the soil around a sapling he has planted for Tu b'Shevat in Herzlia, Israel.

to receive information from reliable witnesses. They then sanctioned the New Moon. If the moon's crescent was not seen on the 30th day, the New Moon was celebrated on the next day. To inform the population of the beginning of the month, beacons were lit on the Mount of Olives and from there throughout the country as well as in the Diaspora.

Later the Samaritans began to light beacons, and the High Court sent out messengers to far-removed communities. Those Jews who lived far from Jerusalem always celebrated the 30th day of the month as Rosh Hodesh. On these occasions, when they were informed of its postponement to the next day, they also observed a second day as Rosh Hodesh. By the middle of the 4th century CE, however, the sages established a permanent calendar and the public proclamation of the New Moon ceased. A relic of this original practice is retained in the synagogue custom of announcing the New Moon on the Sabbath preceding its celebration.

Although the biblical commandment of joy is not prescribed in relation to Rosh Hodesh, the rabbis

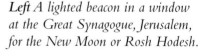

Left A lighted beacon in a window at the Great Synagogue, Jerusalem, for the New Moon or Rosh Hodesh.

ISRAEL INDEPENDENCE DAY

Israel's national day is Israel Independence Day, which commemorates the proclamation of its independence on the 5th of Iyyar 1948. The Chief Rabbinate of Israel declared it a religious holiday and established a special order of service for the evening and morning worship. This service includes the Hallel, and a reading from the Book of Isaiah. The rabbinate also suspended any fast that takes place on the day and various other restrictions. In Israel, the preceding day is set aside as a day of remembrance for soldiers who died in battle. Memorial prayers are recited, and next-of-kin visit the military cemeteries. At home, memorial candles are lit, and Psalm 9 is recited in many synagogues.

Right Celebrating Independence Day at the Western Wall, Jerusalem.

inferred its relevance from the fact that the Bible equated the New Moon with the festivals as well as from the duty to recite the following on Rosh Hodesh: 'This is the day which the Lord hath made. We will rejoice and be glad in it' (Psalm 118:24). Hence it is forbidden to fast on the New Moon, and any funeral service is abbreviated. On the New Moon it is customary to partake of a festive meal.

During the period of the First Temple, Rosh Hodesh was observed with the offering of special sacrifices, the blowing of shofars, feasting and a rest from work. By the end of the 6th century BCE, Rosh Hodesh became a semi-holiday. Eventually this status disappeared, and Rosh Hodesh became a normal working day except for various liturgical changes. In the morning service the Hallel psalms of praise are recited. The Bible reading is from Numbers

and describes the Temple service for the New Moon. An additional service is also included, corresponding to the additional sacrifice which was offered on the New Moon.

NEW YEAR FOR TREES

A further joyous festival is Tu b'Shevat (New Year for Trees), which occurs on the 15th of Shevat. Even though this festival is not referred to in the Bible, it appeared in the Second Temple period as a fixed cut-off date for determining the tithe levied on the produce of fruit trees. Once the Temple was destroyed, the laws of tithing were no longer applicable. As a consequence, this festival took on a new character. Wherever Jews resided, it reminded them of their connection with the Holy Land.

During the 15th century, a number of new ceremonies and rituals were instituted by the mystics of

Safed. Owing to the influence of Isaac Luria (1534–72), it became customary to celebrate the festival with gatherings where special fruits were eaten and hymns and readings from the Bible were included. Among the fruits eaten on Tu b'Shevat were those of the Holy Land. In modern Israel new trees are planted during this festival.

15TH OF AV

Another joyous occasion is the 15th of Av, which was a folk festival during the Second Temple period. At this time bachelors selected their wives from unmarried maidens. According to the Mishnah, on both this day and the Day of Atonement, young girls in Jerusalem dressed in white garments and danced in the vineyards where young men selected their brides. In modern times this festival is marked only by a ban on eulogies or fasting.

HOLOCAUST REMEMBRANCE DAY

THE HOLOCAUST HAS CAST A SHADOW OVER THE MODERN JEWISH COMMUNITY. HOLOCAUST MEMORIAL DAY COMMEMORATES THOSE WHO LOST THEIR LIVES AT THE HANDS OF THE NAZIS.

It is now well over half a century since the Holocaust took place. For survivors, the Holocaust is an ever-present memory, but for others it is an event of the past. To ensure that this tragedy is not forgotten, *Yom ha-Shoah*, or 'Holocaust Remembrance Day', is now commemorated throughout the Jewish world. Inaugurated in 1959, Holocaust Remembrance Day was signed into law by the Prime Minister of Israel, David Ben-Gurion (1886–1973), and the President of Israel, Yitzhak Ben-Zvi (1884–1963).

The original proposal was to hold Holocaust Remembrance Day on the anniversary of the Warsaw ghetto

Below The women's compound at Bergen-Belsen concentration camp, where Margot and Anne Frank died in March 1945. Painting by Leslie Cole.

uprising on 19 April 1943, but this was problematic since the 14th of Nisan is the day before Passover. The date was therefore moved to the 27th of Nisan, eight days before Israel Independence Day. Most Jewish communities hold a ceremony on this day but there is no institutional ritual. Generally Jews light a memorial candle and recite the Kaddish prayer for the dead.

ORTHODOX JUDAISM

After the war, the Chief Rabbinate of Israel decided that the 10th of Tevet should be a national remembrance day for victims of the Holocaust. It recommended traditional forms of remembering the dead, such as the study of the Mishnah section about ritual baths, saying psalms, lighting a yahrzeit candle and saying Kaddish. On other occasions, the Chief

Above Holocaust memorial in Miami Beach, Florida, USA, designed by Kenneth Treister.

Rabbinate recommended Tisha b'Av as the appropriate day for remembrance. In April 1951, the Knesset decreed that 27th Nisan should become Yom ha-Shoah, ignoring the Rabbinate's decision. In turn, the Chief Rabbinate decided to

COMMEMORATION

On the eve of Holocaust Remembrance Day, there is a state ceremony at Yad Vashem, the Holocaust Martyrs' and Heroes' Remembrance Authority. At 10 a.m. on Yom ha-Shoah, air-raid sirens are sounded throughout Israel for two minutes, During this time, people stop working and stand at attention. On the eve of Yom ha-Shoah and the day itself, places of public entertainment are closed by law. Documentaries about the Holocaust are screened on television and songs are played on the radio. Flags on public buildings are flown at half mast.

Above Dr Laszlo Tauber, Holocaust survivor, lights a menorah in memory of victims and survivors of the Holocaust at a service in Washington DC, 1985.

ignore the Knesset's chosen date. Although there are Orthodox Jews who commemorate the Holocaust on Yom ha-Shoah, others in the Orthodox world – especially the Hasidim – remember the victims of the Holocaust on traditional days of mourning which were in place before World War II, such as Tishah B'Av. In Israel most Orthodox Zionists stand still for two minutes during the siren. Others, especially in Haredi areas, do not pay attention to this event: most stores remain open, schools continue, and most people carry on with their activities when the siren sounds. The non-participation of the Haredim has caused friction with the rest of the Israeli population.

NORTH AMERICA

Jews in North America observe Yom ha-Shoah within the synagogue as well as in the broader American community. Commemorations range widely from synagogue services to communal vigils and educational

programmes. Some congregations find it more practical to have a commemorative ceremony on the closest Sunday to Yom ha-Shoah. It is usual to have a talk by a Holocaust survivor, recitation of songs and reading, and viewing of a film dealing with the Holocaust. Some communities stress the loss that Jews experienced during the Holocaust by reading out the names of Holocaust victims.

HOLOCAUST RITUALS

Rituals associated with Yom ha-Shoah are continually being created and vary widely. Attempts have also been made to observe this day of mourning and remembrance in the home. A common practice is to light a yahrzeit candle.

There have also been attempts to compose a Holocaust liturgy such as the 'Six Days of Destruction' produced by the Reform movement. It was intended to serve as a modern addition to the five scrolls that are read on special holidays.

It has also been suggested that a programme of observance for Yom ha-Shoah should include fasting, and a Holocaust Haggadah has been written in which the story of the Holocaust is told.

Despite the variations in practice, the overriding theme of Yom ha-Shoah or Holocaust Remembrance Day is the importance of remembering this tragedy and ensuring that it never occurs again.

Below Memorial in Berlin for the murdered Jews of Europe, designed by Peter Eisenman; comprising a field of thousands of concrete steles.

TISHAH B'AV

THE FESTIVAL OF TISHAH B'AV RECALLS THE DESTRUCTION OF THE
TEMPLE BY THE BABYLONIANS IN THE 6TH CENTURY BCE, AND LATER
THE ROMAN CONQUEST OF JERUSALEM IN THE 1ST CENTURY CE.

This day of mourning commemorates the destruction of the Temple in Jerusalem by the Babylonians and later by the Romans. In synagogues throughout the Jewish world Jews gather together to mourn this tragic event as well as other calamities in Jewish history which occurred at about the same time. Tishah B'Av serves to remind Jewry of its vulnerability throughout the ages.

HISTORICAL BACKGROUND

In 586BCE the Temple (First Temple) was destroyed by King Nebuchadnezzar of Babylonia (7th–6th century BCE) on the 10th of Av. The

Below A dramatic reconstruction of The Destruction of Jerusalem *by David Roberts (1796–1864).*

rebuilt Temple (Second Temple) was destroyed by the Romans in 70CE on the same day. In time the 9th of Av became the anniversary of both destructions. The Talmud justifies this date because a series of calamities occurred on this day throughout Jewish history in addition to the destruction on the Temples on the 10th of Av.

MOURNING RITES

It is uncertain whether the 9th of Av was observed as a day of mourning before 70CE, in memory of the destruction of the First Temple. The Talmud recounts that Eliezer ben Zadok, who lived before and after the destruction of the Second Temple, did not fast on the 9th of Av, which was deferred because of

Above Romans carrying the Menorah and Jewish holy vessels in triumph, following the destruction of the Second Temple in 70CE. From the Triumphal Arch of Titus, Rome, 81CE.

the Sabbath to the following day since it was his family's traditional holiday of wood offerings for the altar. This indicates that fasting on the 9th of Av was observed during the period of the Second Temple. In any event, fasting on the 9th of Av was observed during the mishnaic period. Some rabbis advocated

Above Rebuilding the Temple in Jerusalem, *manuscript illumination from a 13th-century Bible.*

permanent abstention from wine and meat in memory of the destruction of the Temple, but this was regarded as excessive.

The general rule in the Talmud for the mourning rites of Tishah B'Av is that a person is obliged to observe on it all mourning rites that apply in the case of the death of a next of kin. These rites have to be followed from sunset to sunset. Some mourning rites are already observed during the weeks prior to Tishah B'Av from the fast of the 17th of Tammuz. On the 1st of Av, the mourning rites are intensified. On the eve of Tishah B'Av, at the final meal before the fast, one should not partake of two cooked dishes nor eat meat nor drink wine. It is customary to eat a boiled egg at this meal, and to sprinkle ashes on it. Grace after this meal is said silently by each individual.

RULES FOR TISHAH B'AV

These rules are observed on the fast of Tishah B'Av:

1 There should be complete abstention from food and drink.
2 Bathing is forbidden. Washing of the hands and the face, however, are permissible for cleansing.
3 The use of oils for anointing or the application of perfumes is forbidden.
4 Sexual intercourse is forbidden.
5 Footwear made of leather is not to be worn.
6 One should sit on the ground or on a low stool.
7 It is customary to abstain from work.
8 The study of Torah is forbidden, except for the reading of the Book of Lamentations and its midrash, the Book of Job, the curses in the Book of Leviticus (Leviticus 26:14–42), several chapters in the Book of Jeremiah, and aggadic tales in the Talmud describing the destruction of Jerusalem.

NIGHT OF TISHAH B'AV

On the night of Tishah B'Av pious individuals used to sleep on the floor with a stone as a pillow. It was customary to fast until noon of the 10th of Av. Meat and wine should not be consumed until the afternoon of the 10th, although some of the mourning rites are lessened from Tishah B'Av afternoon onwards based on the belief that Tishah B'Av will again be a holiday since the Messiah will be born then. At the end of the 17th century, strict observance of Tishah B'Av also became a mark of adherence to traditional Judaism after Shabbetai Tzvi abolished the fast of Tishah B'Av and turned the day into a time of joyous celebration.

SYNAGOGUE OBSERVANCE

In the synagogue the following practices are observed:

1 The lights are dimmed and only a few candles lit. This is a symbol of the darkness which befell Israel.
2 The curtain of the Ark is removed in memory of the curtain in the Holy of Holies in the Temple. According to talmudic legend, it was stabbed and desecrated by Roman emperor Titus (39-81 BCE).
3 Congregants sit on low benches or on the floor.
4 The cantor recites the prayers in a monotonous and melancholy fashion.
5 Some people change their customary seats.
6 In some congregations the Torah Scroll is placed on the floor and ashes are sprinkled on it.
7 The prayer service is the regular weekday service with a number of changes.
8 In some congregations it is customary not to wear prayer shawls and *tefillin*, or 'phylacteries', during the morning service. Instead they are worn during the afternoon service.
9 It is customary to sprinkle ashes on the head as a symbol of mourning. In Jerusalem, it is customary to visit the Western Wall where the Book of Lamentations is recited.

Below Prayer with Torah scroll at the Western Wall, Jerusalem, on the 9th of Av, the anniversary of the destruction of both the First and Second Temples.

CHAPTER 7

HOME CEREMONIES

In Judaism religious observance in the home is of central importance. According to the sages, the home is a *mikdash me-at*, or 'minor sanctuary'. Like the synagogue, home continues various traditions of the ancient Temple. The Sabbath candles, for example, recall the Temple menorah and the dining table symbolizes the altar. *Kashrut* or dietary laws and the discipline of keeping a kosher kitchen, together with ritual immersion, are seen as a part of a person's freewill choices about aligning one's life with God. In this context, honouring and respecting parents is regarded as an ideal. Most significantly, in the home family life is sanctified.

This chapter also considers personal piety and duties of the heart in Jewish religious practice. A good person shows humility, compassion, mercy and justice. Alongside the home, communal life is of fundamental importance. Within the context of community and synagogue, Jews express their loyalty to the traditions of their ancestors and their dedication to God.

Opposite A father putting the Passover basket on his son's head in the ritual meal held annually to mark the Exodus from Egypt. From the Barcelona Haggadah c.1340.

Above A family in Seattle, Washington DC, USA, holding a Passover seder, to commemorate the Jews' escape from slavery in Egypt.

HOME

ACCORDING TO THE TRADITION, THE HOME IS REGARDED AS A MINOR SANCTUARY. THROUGHOUT THE YEAR VARIOUS RELIGIOUS CEREMONIES TAKE PLACE IN A FAMILY SETTING.

The Jewish home is a *mikdash me'at* or minor sanctuary. Religious observance is of fundamental importance.

THE HOME AND THE TEMPLE

Like the synagogue, the home continues various traditions of the ancient Temple. The dining table symbolizes the altar and the Sabbath candles recall the Temple menorah.

Most significantly, within the home, family life is sanctified. As head of the family, the father is to exercise authority over his wife and children. He is obligated to circumcise his son, redeem him from Temple service in a special ceremony if he is the first-born, teach him the Torah, marry him off and teach him a craft. Moreover, the father of the family is required to serve as a role model for the transmission of Jewish ideals to his offspring.

Below A Jewish woman hiding leavened bread for her husband to find, 1723. At the beginning of Passover, leavened bread must be removed from the house.

WIFE AND MOTHER

The prevailing sentiment is that the wife's role is to bear children and exercise responsibility for family life.

According to Jewish law, womanhood is a separate status with its own sets of rules. In terms of religious observance, women were classed as slaves and children, disqualified as witnesses, excluded from the study of the Torah and segregated from men. Moreover, they were viewed as ritually impure for extended periods of time. In general, they were exempted from time-bound commandments. As a consequence, they were not obliged to fulfil those commandments that must be observed at a particular time. The purpose of these restrictions was to ensure that their attention and energy be directed towards completing their domestic duties.

In the modern world, however, a growing number of women have agitated for equal treatment and the role of women has undergone a major transformation.

Above An Orthodox Jewish father from Tiberias, Israel, holding his son. Family life is central to Judaism.

CHILDREN

Young people are to carry out the commandment to honour and respect their parents. For the rabbis, the concept means providing parents with food, drink, clothing and transportation. Respect requires children do not sit in a parent's seat, interrupt them, or express an opinion in a dispute involving a parent. The Talmud extols this: 'There are three partners in man, the Holy One, blessed be He, the father and the mother. When a man honours his [parents], the Holy One, blessed be He, says, "I will ascribe [merit] to them as though I had dwelt among them and they had honoured me."'

DOMESTIC HARMONY

The ideal of home life is domestic harmony. The Talmud specifies the guidelines for attaining this goal: 'A man should spend less than his means on food, up to his means on clothes, and more than his means in honouring wife and children because they are dependent on him.' Such harmony is attained through give and take, as well as the observance of Jewish ritual. When the family follows God's commandments, the home is permeated with sanctity.

*Left Hebrew postcard from the 1920s
showing a Hungarian Jewish family
gathered around the dinner table.*

SYMBOLS AND OBSERVANCE

Mezuzahs on each doorpost characterize the Jewish home. In Scripture it is written that 'these words' shall be written on the mezuzot, or 'doorposts', of the house (Deuteronomy 6:4–9; 11:13–21). This is understood literally; these two passages are copied by hand on to parchment, put into a case and fixed to the doorpost of every room in the house.

Sabbath candles are important home ritual objects. At least two candles should be used in honour of the dual commandment to remember and observe the Sabbath day. This ceremony is performed before sunset on Sabbath eve as well as at festivals symbolizing light and joy. Lighting the candles is normally the wife's task.

The cycle of the year provides various opportunities for home observances. On Passover normal dishes are replaced. Traditional law excludes the use of all domestic utensils, crockery and cutlery. As a result sets are kept especially for this holiday. The seder, or 'religious meal',

itself is observed on the first night of Passover. On Sukkot it is customary to dwell in a *sukkah*, or 'booth', built for the festival in a yard, garden or balcony. It is covered by foliage through which the stars can be seen at night. During Hanukkah a festival lamp is kindled at home on each day of the festival in memory of the victory of the Maccabees over the Seleucids. Life-cycle events also provide an occasion for special observances in the home.

MODERN JUDAISM

In contemporary society Orthodox Judaism continues to carry out these home activities. However, within the various branches of non-Orthodox Judaism modifications have been made to those traditions and a number of home festivities have been eliminated because they are no longer viewed as spiritually significant. None the less, there is a universal recognition among Jewry that the home is central to Jewish existence and survival.

Left Mezuzah cases. Such cases contained Bible scrolls and were fixed to doorposts to protect the household.

Below Taking part in home ceremonies. A mother and father help their daughter light the Friday night candles.

COMMUNITY LIFE

IN THE JEWISH WORLD, COMMUNAL LIFE IS OF FUNDAMENTAL SIGNIF-
ICANCE. IT IS WITHIN THE COMMUNITY THAT JEWS ARE ABLE TO CARRY
OUT THEIR RITUAL AND MORAL RESPONSIBILITIES.

Through the centuries, community life had been of central importance in the Jewish faith. Alongside the home, Jews have encouraged active participation within the community. Community centres, synagogues and other venues help unite the Jewish people into a collective whole.

THE ANCIENT WORLD

In ancient Israel, Jews constituted a Hebrew clan. Later, as they changed from a nomadic to an agricultural existence, they lived in towns. As a result, their leadership became urbanized. Leaders were responsible for administering justice and towns were organized into territorial units. During the Babylonian exile, Jewish institutions established a pattern for later communal development. As early as the 2nd century BCE, Jews in Alexandria formed their own cor-

Below Conversation in the street. Polish Jews in the ghetto at Vienna, Austro-Hungary, c.1873.

poration with a council that regulated its affairs in accordance with Jewish law. It also constructed synagogues and sent taxes which were collected for the Temple in Jerusalem. In the Roman Empire, Jews were judged by their own courts: this system established the basis for legal autonomy which became a standard for Jewish life throughout the world.

THE DIASPORA

When the Temple was destroyed in 70CE, Jewish life underwent a transformation. In Israel the patriarchate together with the Sanhedrin served as the central authority. In Babylonia, on the other hand, the exilarch was the leader of the community along with the heads of the rabbinical academies. Jews were bound together by the law, and synagogues, law courts, schools, philanthropic institutions and ritual baths constituted the framework of communal life. In North Africa and Spain, the *nagid* ('prince') was the

Above A kosher butcher weighing beef in his shop at the Orthodox Jewish community headquarters in Budapest. Kosher (Kashrut) meat is required as part of Jewish dietary law.

head of the community. Later in the medieval period in the Franco-German region, rabbinical authorities exercised communal leadership. As in Babylonia, a wide range of institutions regulated daily life, and taxes were raised to provide for the needy. In this milieu the synagogue served as the centre for Jewish worship and study.

COMMUNAL STATUTES

In order to regulate communal affairs, *takkanot ha-kahal*, or 'statutes', were established; these were amplified by special ordinances and enactments. To ensure their enforcement, a *bet din*, or 'court', was presided over by a panel of *dayyanim*, or 'judges'. These courts excommunicated offenders. The parnas, or 'community's head', was recognized by the secular or church authorities. He and the local rabbi were often designated as Master of the Jews or Bishop of the Jews. From the 14th century, Polish Jewry gained dominance in Eastern Europe and communal autonomy was often invested in the Jewish community of a central town which had responsibilities for smaller communities

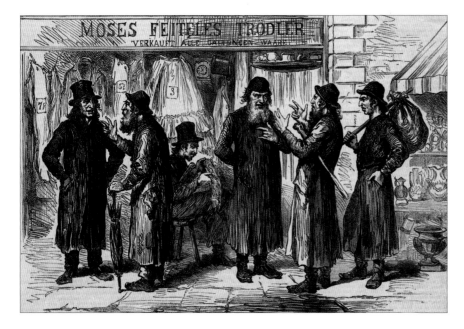

in the region. In Poland – Lithuania, the Council of the Four Lands functioned as a Jewish parliament. By contrast, in the Ottoman empire a chief rabbi was recognized as the Jewish community's representative. Each province of the empire had its own chief rabbi.

THE ENLIGHTENMENT

With the advent of the Enlightenment in the 18th century, the traditional pattern of Jewish life was fundamentally altered. Previously, Jews were unable to opt out of the community. However, with full citizenship rights, Jews assimilated into the wider community. In modern times, Jews have adjusted communal life to contemporary demands. In contrast with previous centres where Jewish life was uniform in character, the Jewish community has fragmented into a number of different religious groupings.

MODERN JUDAISM

On the far right of the Jewish spectrum, Orthodoxy has sought to preserve the beliefs and practices

Below A bet din (Jewish court dealing especially with religious questions) in London's East End, 1930s.

of the past. From the late 18th century, Orthodox Jews opposed changes to Jewish existence brought about by the Enlightenment. Moving to the centre of the religious spectrum, Conservative Judaism advocates a moderate stance in which traditional law is observed, but modified according to contemporary needs. As an offshoot of the Conservative movement, Reconstructionist Judaism rejects supernaturalism while adopting a moderately traditional approach to Jewish life. Reform Judaism has adopted a more liberal stance, intent

Above The circular city of Nahalal, Israel. An aerial view of the first moshav, a co-operative settlement consisting of small separate farms, founded in the Jezreel Valley.

on modernizing Judaism for the contemporary world. Humanistic Judaism espouses a more radical position; like Reconstructionist Judaism it rejects any form of supernaturalism and focuses on humanistic values. Alongside these movements, there are a variety of alternative approaches to Jewish existence that espouse a range of differing ideologies.

THE COMMUNAL IDEAL

Throughout Jewish history, communal life has undergone enormous change. Yet despite the variations in form, the Jewish people have been united in their determination to preserve and transmit their religious traditions. Despite their varied forms of organization, Jews remain loyal to the concept of *K'lal Yisrael*, or 'the community of Israel', and are intent on ensuring the survival of Judaism and the Jewish people. It is within the context of community that Jewry continues to gain spiritual sustenance and strength.

PRAYERS AND BLESSINGS

PRAYER IS AT THE HEART OF THE JEWISH TRADITION. THE TALMUD DESCRIBES IT AS BELONGING TO THE HIGHEST THINGS OF THE WORLD. IT LETS JEWS ESTABLISH A DIRECT CONTACT WITH THE CREATOR.

Jewish prayer is usually recited in Hebrew; this is the language of the Bible, the prophets and the sages of Israel. It is customary for prayers to be chanted, since this endows the words with a more profound meaning. The Ashkenazim and the Sephardim use different traditions of chant, and there are also different chants in the traditions of German, French, Italian, Lithuanian and Polish Jews. These forms of chanting vary depending on the context: the weekday mode of chanting differs from that of the festivals. On Rosh Hashanah and Yom Kippur the chanting is more solemn.

Below An illuminated heading from a German prayer book, c.1320, for the Day of Atonement, which is observed by praying and fasting.

Right An Ashkenazi Rabbi of Jerusalem by George S. Hunter, (1846–1919) wearing the prayer shawl.

GESTURES
Traditionally a number of movements and gestures are made during various parts of the liturgy. Bowing and prostrating the body are frequently described in the Bible. The Talmud limits bowing to four stages in the Amidah prayer, which is recited while standing. These four bows take place at the beginning and end of the first benediction and at the beginning and end of the thanksgiving benediction near the end of the Amidah. The correct procedure for bowing is to bend the head and the body from the waist while reciting *Barukh Atah*, or 'Blessed art Thou'. Then one should straighten

the head and after it the body so that head and body are upright when saying *Adonai*, or 'O Lord'.

During the biblical period it was customary for total prostration of the body to take place with the face to the ground and arms and legs outstretched. Today this only takes place during the Alenu prayer on Rosh Hashanah and Yom Kippur and while reciting the account of the Temple service on Yom Kippur. Some Jews also cover the eyes with the right hand while reciting the first verse of

SWAYING

It is customary for traditional Jews to sway while reciting prayer. In Yiddish this is known as *shocklen*. In the past some sages were opposed to swaying since they believed it lacked decorum. Other scholars permitted a gentle form of swaying of the head as an aid to concentration. Others, such as the Hasidim, however, advocated the use of violent movements and gestures. Advocates of such a practice cite Psalm 35: 10 to emphasize the necessity of swaying: 'All my bones shall say, Lord who is like unto Thee' – in their view, this verse suggests that the entire body should move in praise of God.

Above Tashlich prayer by the Yarkon River, Israel. On the first day of Rosh Hashanah, prayers are recited near water.

the Shema: 'Hear, O Israel, the Lord our God, the Lord is One.' This is done so that one is not distracted during the recitation of this prayer.

TEMPLE AND SYNAGOGUE

Since the destruction of the Temple in Jerusalem in the 1st century CE, the synagogue has become the central place of prayer. No longer are sacrifices offered as they were in ancient times, and the use of incense, which was associated with the Temple cult, has been abandoned. It is also incorrect to have a seven-branched menorah in the synagogue like the one used in the Temple. However, since the 19th century, Reform Jews have referred to their place of worship as a 'temple', but such a designation is regarded by traditional Jews as a misnomer.

COVERING THE HEAD

During the talmudic period, it was a mark of piety to cover the head. This is because heaven is described as above in both spatial and spiritual terms. For this reason it has become customary for Jewish men to cover their head; by doing so they create a barrier between themselves and the heavenly domain. Both Orthodox and non-Orthodox men cover their head during worship services, and recently this practice has been adopted by some women in non-

Above Rabbi's Blessing, *1871, by Moritz Daniel Oppenheim, one of the leading German Jewish artists.*

Orthodox synagogues. It is also common for Orthodox men (as well as some traditionalists) to wear head coverings at all times.

SYNAGOGUE DECORUM

According to tradition, the synagogue should be a place where Jews worship in a spirit of holiness. One should not eat or drink in the synagogue; conversation during prayers should be avoided unless necessary for the conduct of the service; and a synagogue should not be used as a short-cut from one place to another. Yet, despite such a spirit of decorum, traditionally the synagogue should be regarded as a familiar place where Jews gather together for religious purposes.

BLESSINGS

There are four types of blessings in Judaism. The first are blessings to be recited when enjoying God's bounty. For each type of enjoyment (such as eating bread or fruit) a specific blessing was introduced. Another group of blessings is recited before the performance of a *mitzvah* or commandment: 'Blessed art thou ... Who has sanctified us with his commandments and has commanded us to ...'. A third

type of blessing consists of those said on beholding the wonders of nature. Finally, there are blessings of general praise such as the blessing of the Kiddush on the Sabbath and festivals, or the blessings at a wedding.

PRAYERS OF THE DAY

There are three daily prayers: *shaharit* or morning prayer, *minhah* (afternoon) and *ma'ariv* (evening). Morning prayer should be recited just after sunrise; afternoon prayer can be recited from 20 minutes after midday until nightfall; evening prayer can be recited at any time during the night until dawn, but it is customary for minhah and ma'ariv to be recited one after the other. The central feature of all three prayers is the Amidah, which is arranged in three sets of blessings. First there are three in praise of God; these are followed by 11 blessings of petition; finally there are three blessings of further praise. Before the Amidah in the morning and evening service, the Shema is recited together with a number of blessings.

PARENTS AND CHILDREN

ACCORDING TO SCRIPTURE, IT IS THE DUTY OF CHILDREN TO HONOUR AND REVERE PARENTS. IN RABBINIC LITERATURE, SUCH DUTIES ARE ELABORATED IN DETAIL.

In the Jewish faith respect for parents is a cardinal virtue. Scripture uses two different expressions to describe such an attitude. In Exodus 20:12 Jews are instructed to 'honour thy father and thy mother'; Leviticus 19:3 states: 'Each one of you shall revere his mother and his father'.

RABBINIC JUDAISM
On the basis of these two passages, rabbinic sages taught that there is a double obligation to honour parents and revere them. They point out that in the verse from Exodus the father is mentioned first, whereas in the verse from Leviticus the mother is referred to first. The reason given is that children are more ready to honour their mother than their father, but are more ready to revere their father than their mother. As a result, the parent who might be neglected is mentioned first. This is as if to say, you may not need reminders to honour your father and to revere your mother. But do not forget to honour both and to revere both.

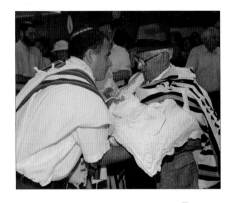

Above Father, son and great grandfather at a circumcision ceremony in Israel.

PARENTAL DUTIES
According to rabbinic Judaism, the duty to honour parents is defined as the obligation to provide them with food and drink, clothe them and escort them. The duty to revere parents is defined as the obligation not to stand or sit in their place, contradict them or take sides in a dispute involving them. The duty to honour parents is conceived as positive – to do what they require. But the duty to revere them is a negative requirement: not to do that which causes them distress.

OBLIGATIONS OF CHILDREN
These requirements require clarification. For example, to give parents food and drink and clothe them can mean either it is the responsibility of children to support their parents financially or, alternatively, it could mean simply that children should be courteous to their mother and father, serving them with their meals, and helping them on with their clothes – in such cases food and clothing would have been purchased by the parents themselves. This issue was debated by later scholars. The final ruling is that children have no obligation to support their parents financially. Yet, if their parents are too

Left The Lesson. A boy studies the Talmud in this Austrian painting of 1930 by F.X. Wolf.

Left Across the generations. Grandparents and grandchildren lighting candles for Hanukkah.

poor to provide for their own needs, then their children must support them financially. Regarding the obligation not to contradict parents or patronize them, this does not imply that children are not permitted to disagree with their mother and father. It means instead that children should not give the impression of judging their parents' opinions in a patronizing fashion. Children do not have to forfeit their own opinions; on the contrary, they have a right to their own views. The obligation not to stand or sit in a parent's place is understood both literally and figuratively. If a father has a special place at home, a child should not occupy it unless a parent has no objection. Further, the injunction means that if a parent has a special position in the community, children should not take the same role. However, it is permitted for parents to forgo their rights in these matters.

LIMITATIONS

Despite such obligations to parents, there are limits to what a mother and father can demand. The commandment to honour parents does not give parents the right to act in a dictato-

rial fashion. Children have rights, and the wishes of parents should be set aside if children are expected to commit a crime or disobey the *mitzvot*, or 'commandments'. According to a number of authorities, there is not an obligation for children to obey their parents other than in the cases specified by Jewish law. Thus, if a parent objects to the person their son or daughter chooses to marry, the parents' wishes do not have to be respected.

When parents divorce, children can be tempted to take sides, but this should be resisted. Children should avoid playing one parent against another. When there are contradictory demands to the father and mother, the children must do their best to be impartial.

HONOUR

The obligation to honour and revere parents is extended by rabbinic sages in various ways. Honour is to be paid to parents who are no longer alive. The institutions of *kaddish*, or 'reciting a prayer for the dead', and *yahrzeit*, or 'lighting a memorial candle', were introduced for this purpose. There are also other categories of individuals to whom respect is due – this is a further extension of this commandment. These include grandparents, parents-in-law, step-parents, older siblings, and teachers. Yet, duties to parents must always come first.

Below Grandfather, father, son. Three generations of Jews reading from the Torah for the son's bar mitzvah.

DIETARY LAWS

SCRIPTURE DIFFERENTIATES BETWEEN FOOD WHICH IS KOSHER AND FOOD WHICH IS FORBIDDEN. THESE REGULATIONS WERE EXPANDED IN RABBINIC SOURCES.

According to Scripture, food must be *kosher*, or 'ritually fit', if it is to be consumed. Through the centuries, Jews have observed these biblical regulations as well as rabbinic prescriptions. The laws of *kashrut* are of seminal importance in the tradition.

BIBLICAL LAW

The Bible declares that laws of kashrut were given by God to Moses on Mount Sinai. As a result, Jews are obligated to follow this legislation due to its divine origin. Nevertheless, various reasons have been adduced for such observance. Allegedly, forbidden foods are unhealthy; that is why they are forbidden. Another explanation is that those who refrain from eating particular kinds of food serve God even while eating. Thereby they are able to attain an elevated spiritual state. Some of these laws, such as refraining from eating pork,

Below A Jewish bakery in the le Marais district of Paris.

have gained such significance that Jews were prepared to sacrifice their lives rather than violate God's law.

ANIMALS, BIRDS AND FISH

The laws concerning which animals, birds and fish may be eaten are contained in Leviticus 11 and Deuteronomy 14:3–21. The Bible states that only those animals that chew the cud and have split hooves may be eaten. Such animals include cows and sheep. However, no similar formula is stated concerning which birds may be consumed; instead a list is given of forbidden birds. Although no reasons are given to explain these choices, it has been suggested that forbidden birds are in fact birds of prey. By not eating them, human beings are able to express their abhorrence of cruelty as well as the exploitation of the weak over the strong. Regarding fish, the law states that only fish that have both fins and scales are allowed. Again, no reason is given to support

Above A rabbi wearing a prayer shawl supervises production of kosher wines at a winery in Tuscany, Italy.

this explanation. Yet various explanations have been proposed, such as the argument that fish that do not have fins and scales frequently live in the depths of the sea, which was regarded as the abode of the gods of chaos.

SLAUGHTER

A further category of kashrut deals with *shehitah*, or 'the method of killing animals for food'. Even though the Torah does not specify the details of this procedure, the Talmud states this method has divine authority since it was explained by God to Moses on Mount Sinai. According to tradition, the act of slaughter must be done with a sharpened knife without a single notch, because that might tear the animal's food pipe or windpipe.

Numerous other laws govern this procedure. A person must be trained in the law if he is to act as a *shohet*, or 'slaughterer'. According to rabbinic scholars, the central idea underlying the laws of ritual slaughter is to give the animal as painless a death as is possible. Judaism does not require that the devout become vegetarians, but when animals are killed for food this must be done so as to cause the least amount of suffering possible.

Another aspect of ritual slaughter is the concern that no animal is eaten if it has a defect. In such cases it is referred to as *terefah*, or 'torn'. The prohibition against terefah is based on Exodus 22:31. This law is elaborated in the Mishnah where the sages decree that terefah refers not only to the meat of an animal torn by wild beasts but to any serious defect in an animal's or a bird's organs. On the basis of this law, the shohet is obliged to examine the lungs of an animal after it has been slaughtered to ensure that no defect is found. If any irregularity is found in an animal that has been slaughtered it should be taken to a rabbi to determine if it is kosher. In the preparation of meat, it is imperative that adequate salting takes place. This prescription is based on the biblical prohibition against consuming blood.

MILK AND MEAT

Another restriction concerning ritual food is the prohibition against eating milk and meat together. This stipulation is based on Exodus 23:19: 'Thou shalt not boil a kid in its mother's milk'. According to

Below A German Jewish slaughtering yard in the 1700s. Animals are killed according to Jewish dietary laws by cutting the animal's throat and allowing the blood to drain out.

rabbinic Judaism, this rule does not refer only to the act of boiling a kid in its mother's milk. Tradition stipulates that it is forbidden to cook meat and milk together. Later, this law was expanded to eating milk and meat products at the same time. Eventually the law was introduced that dairy dishes should not be eaten after a meal until a stipulated period of time had passed. Meat, on the other hand, may be eaten after dairy produce; none the less, it is usual to wash the mouth out beforehand. Not only should milk and meat products not be consumed at the same time, dairy food should not be cooked in meat utensils, and vice versa.

MODERN JUDAISM

Although the Bible does not attempt to explain the origin of these various dietary laws, it does associate them with holiness. The rabbis of the Talmud and midrash explored the rationale of the system of kashrut. Generally they believed that observance of such laws aids the development of self-discipline and moral conduct.

Today, kosher food is obtainable in kosher food stores and some supermarkets. Observant Jews eat in kosher restaurants, which have been inspected by supervisors.

Above Purifying dishes for Passover, an important part of the preparations, in Mea Shearim neighbourhood, Jerusalem.

Up until modern times the rules of kashrut were universally practised by Jewry. Yet, in the 19th century, the Reform movement broke with tradition. For this reason, most Reform Jews have largely ignored the prescriptions of the dietary system. Conservative Judaism, however, adheres to the laws of kashrut, although allowance is made for personal selectivity. Orthodox Judaism, on the other hand, strictly follows the tradition.

Below Seal of approval. Packaged kosher food is sealed with a label, often called a hechsher.

CONVERSION

ACCORDING TO TRADITION, A PERSON IS JEWISH IF HIS OR HER MOTHER IS JEWISH. HOWEVER, CONVERSION HAS ALWAYS BEEN A ROUTE OF ENTRY INTO THE JEWISH COMMUNITY.

Although there is no formal term for the process of conversion in the Hebrew Bible, there are several biblical terms that are suggestive of such an act. Such terms illustrate that conversion was practised during the biblical period in order to assimilate conquered peoples as well as those who came to live within the Israelite community. During the tannaitic and amoraic periods (100BCE–600CE), conversion was frequently extolled by various authorities. According to the early rabbinic sage Elazar, for example, conversion was viewed as part of God's salvationist scheme. According to Hoshiah, another early rabbinic authority, God acted righteously towards Israel when he

Above Ethiopian immigrants to Israel demonstrate against a ruling by the rabbinate that they must undergo conversion to be considered Jews, 1996.

scattered them among the nations. In another passage in the Talmud it is asserted that the proselyte is dearer to God than the Israelite since he has come of his own accord.

As a result of such openness to converts, a number of gentiles converted to Judaism during the early rabbinic period. However, the rise of Christianity led to the cessation of Jewish missionizing. None the less, during the talmudic and post-talmudic period occasional conversions did take place in accordance with rabbinic law. Eventually the regulations governing conversion were drawn together and edited by Joseph Caro (1488–1575), the compiler of the *Shulkhan Arukh*, which since its publication in 1565 has served as the authoritative Code of Jewish Law.

CANDIDATE CONVERSION

In the *Shulkhan Arukh* the requirements for conversion as laid down in the Talmud and other codes are detailed. When a man or woman appears as a candidate, the person is asked: 'What motivates you? Do you know that, in these days, Jews are subject to persecution and discrimination, that they are hounded and troubled?' If the individual replies: 'I know this and yet I regard myself as unworthy of being joined to them,' the convert is accepted immediately. The root principles of the faith, namely the unity of God and the prohibition of idol worship, are expounded to the candidate at considerable length. The proselyte is taught, too, some of the simpler and some of the more difficult commandments, and is informed of the punishment involved in violating the commandments.

Similarly, the convert is told of the rewards of observing them, particularly that by virtue of keeping the commandments he or she will merit the life of the world to come. He or she is told that no one is considered wholly righteous except those who understand and fulfil the commandments. Further, the convert is told that the world to come is intended only for the righteous. If the male convert finds these doctrines acceptable, he is circumcised immediately. After his circumcision has completely healed, he undergoes ritual immersion. Three learned Jews

Below Passover Haggadah showing Savants at the Table of Maimonides. *From left: Joseph Caro, Isaac Alfasi, Maimonides, Jacob ben Asher and Rashi. Laws regulating conversion are contained in compendiums of Jewish law compiled by such rabbinic scholars.*

Above Jews washing in a small spring mikveh *(ritual bath) outside the Tomb of the Prophet Samuel, north of Jerusalem. Traditionally, converts undergo ritual immersion in a mikveh.*

Above American entertainers Frank Sinatra and Sammy Davis Jr were members of the Rat Pack. Both championed Jewish civil rights and causes in the USA, and Davis became a Jew.

stand by while he is in the water and instruct him in some of the easy and some of the difficult commandments.

In the case of the female proselyte, Jewish women accompany her and supervise her immersion. The three learned male Jews remain outside the *mikveh*, or 'pool', and give the convert instruction while she is in the water.

THE CANDIDATE'S MOTIVES

The *Shulkhan Arukh* states: 'When the would-be proselyte presents himself, the convert should be examined lest the person be motivated to enter the congregation of Israel by hope of financial gain or social advantage or by fear. A man is examined lest his motive be to marry a Jewish woman, and a woman is questioned lest she have similar desires towards some Jewish man.' If no unacceptable motive is found, the candidate is told of the heaviness of the yoke of the Torah and how difficult it is for the average person to live up to the commandments of the Torah. This is done to give the candidate a chance to withdraw if he so desires. Once a man

Right Harvest scene from the Book of Ruth, 1320. According to Scripture, Ruth was a Moabite woman who joined the Jewish people.

is circumcised and a man or woman is ritually immersed, the convert is no longer a non-Jew. The central feature of these regulations governing the traditional conversion procedure is the emphasis on joining the Jewish community and accepting the law.

MODERN JUDAISM

Up until the present day, the procedure outlined in the *Shulkhan Arukh* has been rigorously followed. Within modern Orthodox Judaism, the emphasis is on living a Jewish way of life within the community. For this reason, converts are given extensive religious instruction. Conservative Judaism generally follows these legal requirements, but Reform Judaism has departed from the traditional practice in a variety of ways.

Emphasizing the universalistic mission of Judaism, Reform Jews very early in their history abrogated the necessity of ritual immersion for converts. On the question of circumcision, opinion was at first divided. Eventually, however, it was generally accepted that the only requirements were that the person freely seek membership, that the candidate be of good character and be sufficiently acquainted with the faith and practices of Judaism. Unlike Orthodoxy, Reform Judaism accepts conversion for the sake of marriage.

DUTIES OF THE HEART

NOT ONLY ARE JEWS OBLIGATED TO FULFIL RITUAL AND MORAL DUTIES, THEY ARE ALSO COMMANDED TO DIRECT THEIR SPIRITUAL LIFE IN ACCORDANCE WITH GOD'S WILL.

In the Middle Ages the 11th-century Jewish philosopher Bahya Ibn Pakudah wrote an important treatise *Duties of the Heart*. In this he described Jewish obligations as comprising duties which he calls practices of the limbs: these are acts a Jew is obliged to perform. In addition, he listed a second category – duties of the heart – which relate to the inner life.

SPIRITUALITY

In the past, Jewish writers promoted inwardness. What is clear is that the norm for these sages was different from the attitude of modern Jews. For example, Bahya discussed the concept of equanimity. In his view, it is essential for a person to adopt such an attitude if God is to be truly worshipped. In other words, a spiritual person must be indifferent to the praise and blame of others. Such an individual should so love God

Above Prayer at Home, c.1470. A facsimile of a Hebrew book of sacred texts painted by the Italian Renaissance master Leonardo Bellini.

that he does not care what others think. His mind and heart should be directly focused on the Divine. Yet, for most Jews today such an attitude of disinterestedness is not based on the love of God, but on a disdain of the opinions of others. Moreover, such an attitude can result in indolence. If a person does good only to satisfy others, his motivation is not adequate. On the other hand, one who aspires to do good only for the sake of heaven is leaving it up to himself to decide if and when God is satisfied. Indeed, he may in fact trying to deflect criticism by believing that his motives are for God alone. This can result in complacency and self-satisfaction.

CHARACTER

According to Judaism, one who has a good character should possess the traits of humility, compassion, love of mercy and a sense of justice. Conversely, he or she should avoid such attitudes as pride, vanity, cruelty, falsehood and bad temper. To be humble does not mean that a person should be unaware of his talents. Rather, such an individual should regard all his positive qualities as a

Left When Joseph's brothers sold him into slavery they betrayed their brotherly duty. From a painting by Raphael.

> **THE ASCETIC LIFE**
> Bahya and others' views on the ascetic life should be viewed with caution by those with no saintly pretensions. Judaism demands correct action. But there is no requirement to be a saint. Ascetics in previous centuries have denied themselves food and drink and rarely slept in a comfortable bed. At times they flogged themselves and performed other acts of self-torture. Such actions are not required; indeed, such can even lead to morbid self-hatred.

Right A cantor reads the Haggadah to illiterate members of a Spanish synagogue so that all can take part. 14th-century Sephardi manuscript.

gift from God for which he can claim no credit. In this regard, there is a religious dimension of a good character. The pursuit of truth, for example, is connected with the God of truth. Falsehood is a distortion of reality, an affront to God.

PEACE

Rabbinic sages stated that it is permitted to tell harmless lies for the sake of peace. An example of this is Joseph's statement to his brothers that their father, Jacob, had ordered him to forgive them for their wrongdoing. This was not true, but Joseph was telling a lie to preserve family peace. The rabbis also say that a lie is in order if a person is asked indelicate questions about his married life. In such a case, he has no obligation to tell the truth. Again, it is permissible to lie about how much Torah learning one has in order to avoid appearing as a braggart.

Below A woman prays at the Tomb of the Righteous Rabbi Ovadia in the Upper Galilee, Israel.

BAD TEMPER

Within the Jewish tradition, a bad temper is severely criticized. A person who breaks things in a fit of temper is compared to an idolator because the loss of self-control is due to an inadequate awareness of God's presence. Even when a parent or teacher is obliged to show disapproval, they should retain control, making only the outward signs of displeasure. As the Ethics of the Fathers states in the Mishnah: 'The man who is quick to become angry but is easily appeased, his virtue outweighs his fault. The person who rarely flies into a rage but when he does so is hard to appease – his fault outweighs his virtue. The man who is quick to be angry and hard to appease is wicked. The man who

rarely loses his temper and on the occasions when he does so is easily appeased – that person is a saint.'

THE LOVE AND FEAR OF GOD

Love and fear of God are duties of the heart that have received a range of interpretations. In the Bible, they are usually synonymous with righteous action. It is not only that justice and righteousness lead to love and fear of God, but in a sense they are the love and fear of God. In rabbinic literature the love of God generally means love of God's law; the fear of God refers to the avoidance of sin. Among medieval mystics, the love and fear of God is viewed as a yearning of the human soul for the nearness of the Creator and its dread and awe at his majesty.

RITUAL IMMERSION

A MIKVEH, OR 'COLLECTION OF WATER', REFERS TO ANY POOL OR BATH OF CLEAR WATER WHICH IS USED FOR RITUAL IMMERSION. SUCH IMMERSION RENDERS A PERSON RITUALLY CLEAN.

From ancient times to the present, the mikveh has played a central role in Jewish life. By immersing in a mikveh a person who has become ritually unclean through contact with the dead or any other defiling object, or through an unclean flux from the body, can become ritually clean. The mikveh is also used for vessels that have become unclean.

In the modern world, the chief use of the mikveh is for a woman who has just menstruated. According to Jewish law, the contracting of marital relations with a wife who is in an unclean state is a serious offence.

The mikveh is also commonly used for the immersion of proselytes, or converts to Judaism, as part of the ceremony of conversion.

In addition, immersion in the mikveh is practised by various groups as an aid to spirituality, particularly on the Sabbath and festivals, especially the Day of Atonement.

SPIRITUALITY

The purpose of immersion is not physical, but spiritual. According to the 12th-century philosopher Moses Maimonides, the laws about immersion as a means of freeing oneself from uncleanness are decrees laid down by Scripture. They are not matters that human beings can rationally comprehend. Uncleanliness thus should not be viewed as mud or filth which water can remove, but rather of a spiritual nature and depending on the intention of the heart. For this reason the sages stated: 'If a man immerses himself, but without special intention, it is as though he has not immersed himself at all.'

THE MORAL RATIONALE

There is a moral basis for immersion. Just as one who sets his heart on becoming clean becomes clean as soon as he has immersed himself (although nothing new has occurred

Above Mikveh (ritual bath) at Masada, Israel. The water in a mikveh should come from a natural spring or river.

to his body), so, too, one who sets his heart on turning away from evil becomes clean as soon as he resolves to change his ways. For this reason, Scripture states: 'And I will sprinkle clean water upon you and you shall be clean, from all your uncleanliness and from all your idols will I cleanse you' (Ezekiel 36:25).

THE WATER

All natural spring water, provided it is clean and has not been discoloured by any admixtures, is valid for a mikveh. With regard to rainwater, melted snow or ice, care must be taken to ensure the water flows freely. The water must

Left Jewish women in the mikveh or ritual bath. An engraving from 1726 by Johann Georg Puschner.

Below A non-traditional Jewish group in Pennsylvania, USA, have a mikveh (ritual bath) in a swimming pool.

the correct amount of valid water, it does not become invalid even though someone adds drawn water to it.

TYPES OF MIKVEH

When there is a plentiful supply of valid water which can replenish the mikveh, the only condition to be fulfilled is to ensure the water does not become invalidated by the construction of the mikveh, which renders it a vessel, or by going through metal pipes, which are not sunk into the ground. Since most mikvaot are constructed in urban areas where such supplies are not freely available, the technological and halakhic solution of a valid mikveh depends essentially upon constructing a mikveh with valid water and replenishing it with invalid water, taking advantage of the fact the addition of this water to an originally valid one does not invalidate it.

Below A Hungarian Orthodox Jew prays in the yard of the mikveh (ritual bath) after making his dishes kosher.

BIBLICAL LAW

According to biblical law, any collection of water, drawn or otherwise, is suitable for a mikveh as long as it contains enough for a person to immerse himself. The rabbis, however, enacted that only water which has not been drawn in a vessel or receptacle may be used. The rabbis further established that the minimum quantity for immersion is 250–1,000 litres/55–220 gallons. A mikveh containing less than this amount becomes invalid should a specified amount of drawn water be added to it. If the mikveh contains more than this amount, it can never become invalid no matter how much water is added. A mikveh may be hewn out of rock or built in or put on the ground, and any material is suitable. It must be watertight, otherwise it becomes invalid. Finally, the height must be 47in (119.3cm) to enable a person standing in it to be completely immersed even though he has to bend the knees.

not reach the mikveh through vessels made of metal or other materials. This is avoided by attaching the pipes and other accessories to the ground, which means they cease to have the status of vessels. The mikveh should be emptied from above by hand, by vacuum or by electric or automatic pumps. There is one regulation that eases the problems of constructing a valid mikveh. Once the mikveh has

CHAPTER 8

LIFE CYCLE EVENTS

The Jewish life cycle is marked by a series of religious events which celebrate various stages of development. Beginning at birth, a number of ceremonies mark the acceptance of the child into the Jewish community. For male infants, the act of circumcision symbolizes the child's identification as a Jew. The Redemption of the First-Born recalls the ancient practice of redeeming the child from Temple service. Bar and bat mitzvah constitute steps towards Jewish adulthood. Finally, the Jewish marriage service binds the bride and groom in the presence of God.

At the end of life, the utmost regard and consideration is shown to the dying. Jewish law stipulates that the body must be buried as soon as possible after death. The general pattern for funerals involves the ritual rending of garments, the funeral procession, the eulogy, either in a funeral chapel or beside the grave, and memorial prayers. Once the funeral is over, it is customary for the family to return home to begin a period of mourning.

Opposite A Jewish marriage contract from the Netherlands, 1648. The purpose of Jewish marriage is to create a Jewish home and a family and thus continue the Jewish community.

Above The Jewish Bride, 1667, by the leading artist of the Dutch Golden Age, Rembrandt van Rijn, is a portrait that explores marital tenderness.

BIRTH

IN THE BIBLE THE FIRST COMMANDMENT IS TO BE FRUITFUL AND MULTIPLY. IT IS THEREFORE AN OBLIGATION FOR JEWISH PARENTS TO HAVE CHILDREN WHO WILL CONTINUE THE TRADITION.

From ancient times there have been various ceremonies connected with childbirth.

THE BIBLE

In biblical times childbirth took place in a kneeling position or sitting on a special birthstool. Scriptural law imposes various laws on ritual purity and impurity of the mother. If she gives birth to a boy, she is considered ritually impure for seven days. For the next 33 days she is not allowed to enter the Temple precincts or handle sacred objects. For the mother of a girl, the number of days are respectively 14 and 66. According to Jewish law, if a woman in childbirth is in mortal danger, her life takes precedence over that of an unborn child. Only when

Below In this 1900 lithograph, people are giving offerings for sacrifice to the priests at the Temple in Jerusalem. First-born boys were dedicated to God.

more than half of the child's body has emerged from the womb is it considered to be fully human so that both lives are of equal worth.

THE BIRTH OF A CHILD

In ancient times the birth of a child was accompanied by numerous superstitious practices, including the use of amulets to ward off the evil eye. After the birth, family and friends gathered nightly to recite prayers to ward off evil spirits such as Lilith, the female demon who allegedly attempts to kill off all newly born children. Among German Jews it was frequently the practice for parents of a son to cut off a strip of swaddling in which the child was wrapped during his circumcision; this is known as the wimple, and it is kept until his bar mitzvah, when it is used for tying the scroll of the law. From the medieval period Ashkenazi mothers visited the synagogue after the birth

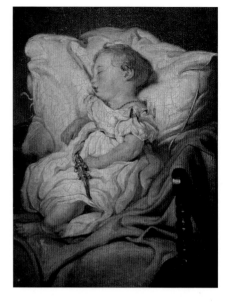

Above Painting by English Jewish painter Abraham Solomon of his brother Simeon as a baby, 1841.

of a child to recite a blessing that expresses gratitude to God as well as other prayers. It was also customary for the congregation to recite a prayer for the welfare of the mother and the child.

BABY NAMING

The naming of a child takes place either when a baby boy is named at the circumcision ceremony or when a baby girl is named in the synagogue on the first time the Torah is read after her birth. The Hebrew form of a person's name consists of the individual's name followed by *ben*, or 'son', or *bat*, or 'daughter', of the father. This form is used in all Hebrew documents as well as for the call to the reading of the Torah. In contemporary society it is still the practice to give a child a Jewish name in addition to their ordinary name. Ashkenazi Jews frequently name a child after a deceased relative; Sephardi Jews after a person who is still alive. Alternatively, a Hebrew name is selected that is related to the ordinary name either in meaning or sound, or the secular name may be transliterated in

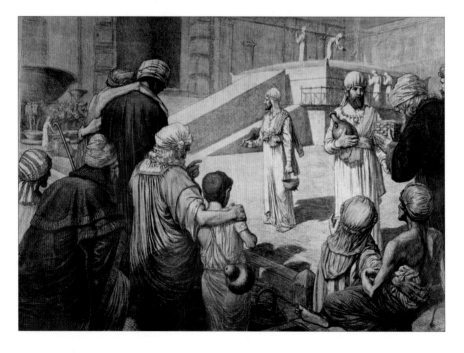

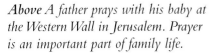

Above A father prays with his baby at the Western Wall in Jerusalem. Prayer is an important part of family life.

Hebrew characters. Traditionally it was customary to change the name of a person at the time of a serious illness. According to rabbinic Judaism, changing the name is a way of misdirecting the angel of death. On this basis, it became a custom to add a further name to the ill person's. From that point the individual was known by their original name, together with the new one.

Above The redemption of the first-born son ritual requires payment of gold to a Cohen, a member of a priestly clan that traces its paternal lineage back to Aaron, the first priest in the Jewish religion.

REDEEMING THE FIRST-BORN
The custom of redeeming first-born male children (*Pidyon ha-Ben*) is based on the scriptural prescription that first-born sons should be consecrated to the Temple. Just as first fruits and first-born animals had to be handed over to the priests, so first-born boys were dedicated to God. The obligation to

redeem first-born sons from this service is referred to in Numbers 3:44–51. Here redemption is to take place by a payment of five shekels to the priest. Detailed laws are outlined in the Mishnah tractate Bekhorot and further expanded in the talmudic commentary on this passage.

According to Jewish law, the sons of priests and Levites are exempt from redemption. Similarly, first-born sons whose mother is the daughter of either a priest or Levite are exempt. During the geonic period, a ceremony was instituted in which the father of the child declares to the priest on the 31st day after its birth that the child is the first-born son of his mother and the father, and that as a father, he is obliged to redeem him. The priest then asks the father if he prefers to give his son to the priest or redeem his son, and the father hands the priest the required amount. The father then recites a blessing concerning the fulfilment of the precept of redeeming the child, and another expressing gratitude to God. This procedure has served as the basis for the ceremony since the Middle Ages.

Left A mother reading to her young daughter in Shirat Hayam, a Gaza settlement, in 2005.

RITES OF PASSAGE

ACCORDING TO SCRIPTURE, ABRAHAM WAS COMMANDED BY GOD
TO CIRCUMCISE HIS SON ISAAC. THE PRACTICE OF CIRCUMCISION HAS
CONTINUED THROUGH THE AGES.

From ancient times, Jewish male children were circumcised; this practice was based on biblical law and was perceived as a sign of the covenant. At the age of 13, Jewish boys reach the age of adulthood, which is celebrated by a bar mitzvah ceremony. In modern times, a bat mitzvah ceremony has been introduced for Jewish girls.

CIRCUMCISION

According to Jewish law, all male children are to undergo circumcision in accordance with God's command to Abraham in the Book of Genesis. Jewish ritual involves the removal of the entire foreskin of the

Below Circumcision, from The Rothschild Miscellany, *the most lavish Hebrew manuscript of the 15th century, which details almost every custom of religious and secular Jewish life.*

penis. This act is to be performed on the eighth day after the birth of the child by a person who is qualified (*mohel*). The Jewish law specifies that this ceremony can be performed even on the Sabbath, festivals and the Day of Atonement. However, postponement is permitted if there is a danger to the child's health.

Laws concerning the ceremony are derived from both biblical and rabbinic sources. Traditionally circumcision is to take place in the presence of a *minyan*, or 'quorum of ten adult Jewish men'. On the morning of the eighth day, the child is taken from the mother by the godmother who hands him to the *sandak*, or 'godfather'. The sandak then carries the child in to the room where circumcision is to take place. He then hands him to the individual who places the child on a chair called the Chair of Elijah. Another person then takes him and passes him

Above A 17th-century circumcision set from Prague, elaborately ornamented and engraved, in gold and steel.

to the child's father who puts him on the lap of the godfather who holds the boy during the ceremony. The circumcision is performed by a mohel or specially trained person who performs circumcision. Formerly, blood was drawn orally but today an instrument is used. The infant is then handed to the person who will hold him during the ceremony of naming, and circumcision ends with a special blessing over a cup of wine, followed by the naming of the child.

BAR MITZVAH

At the age of 13, a boy attains the age of Jewish adulthood. From this point he is considered as part of a minyan. According to Jewish law, the 13th year is when a boy should observe the commandments. The essentials of the bar mitzvah ceremony involve prayer with *tefillin*, or 'phylacteries', for the first time, and reading from the Torah. It is now a universally accepted practice that the bar mitzvah boy is called to the reading at Sabbath morning services where he recites the Torah blessings, chants a maftir, or 'portion of the Law', and reads from the Prophets.

Above A bar mitzvah is held at the Western Wall in Jerusalem, a remnant of the ancient Temple.

In both Ashkenazi and Sephardi communities the bar mitzvah ceremony included a discourse by the bar mitzvah boy, which demonstrates his knowledge of rabbinic sources. In time other practices became associated with the ceremony. Some boys chanted the entire weekly reading; others were trained as prayer leaders; some conducted the Sabbath eve service on Friday night as well as the Sabbath morning. In some communities the bar mitzvah boy reads a special prayer standing before the Ark. In modern times it is usual for the rabbi to address the bar mitzvah boy after the reading of the law.

BAT MITZVAH

Unlike the bar mitzvah, there is no legal requirement for a girl to take part in a religious ceremony to mark her religious majority. None the less, a ceremonial equivalent of bar mitzvah has been designed for girls. In Orthodoxy this was an innovation in the 19th century and subsequently became widespread. In the early 20th century the Conservative scholar Mordecai Kaplan (1881–1983) pioneered the bat mitzvah

ceremony in the USA as part of the synagogue service, and since then this has become widely accepted by many American communities. In non-Orthodox congregations, a 12-year-old girl celebrates her coming of age on a Friday night or during the Sabbath morning service where she conducts the prayers, chants the Haftarah or reading from the Prophets, and in some cases also reads from the Torah and delivers an address. In Orthodox

synagogues, however, the bat mitzvah's participation in services is more limited. At a woman's minyan or quorum for prayer, she is called to the reading of the Torah and may even chant one of the portions, together with the Haftarah.

Outside the USA the bat mitzvah ceremony takes various forms. In Reform congregations the ceremony is in line with the American pattern. Orthodox girls, however, do not participate in the synagogue service. Rather, a bat mitzvah's father is called to the Torah on the appropriate Sabbath morning. His daughter then recites a prayer, and the rabbi addresses her in the synagogue or at a Kiddush reception afterwards. Alternatively, the ceremony takes place at home or in the synagogue hall on a weekday.

In Britain and South Africa the procedure is different; bat mitzvah girls must pass a special examination enabling them to participate in a collective ceremony.

Below Surrounded by friends, a Jewish girl lights candles at her bat mitzvah celebration in Manhattan, New York.

EDUCATION

IN JUDAISM EDUCATION IS OF CENTRAL IMPORTANCE. IT IS A PARENTAL DUTY TO ENSURE THEIR CHILDREN RECEIVE EDUCATION AND ARE FAMILIAR WITH THE VARIOUS ASPECTS OF THEIR RELIGIOUS HERITAGE.

Judaism stipulates that it is the responsibility of parents to educate children. The Book of Deuteronomy declares: 'And you shall teach them diligently to your children, and shall talk of them when you sit in your house, and when you walk by the way, and when you lie down and when you rise' (6:7). For this reason, Jewish education has been of paramount importance through the ages.

PARENTAL DUTY

The Hebrew Bible repeatedly refers to a father's obligation to teach his children about their religious past. The Book of Exodus states: 'You may tell in the hearing of your son and of your son's son how I have made sport of the Egyptians and what signs I have done among them' (Exodus 10:2). Exodus 13:8 says: 'And you shall tell your son on that day, "It is because of what the Lord did for me when I came out of Egypt."' The Book of Deuteronomy stipulates

Below Morning prayer in this Jewish girls' school in Jerusalem takes place in the classroom.

that 'When your son asks you in the time to come, "What is the meaning of the statutes and the ordinances which the Lord our God has commanded you?" then you shall say to your son, "We were Pharaoh's slaves in Egypt; and the Lord brought us out of Egypt with a mighty hand"' (Deuteronomy 6:20–21). In addition to such parental duties, it was the responsibility of the Levites to teach the people: 'They shall teach Jacob thy ordinances, and Israel the law' (Deuteronomy 33:10).

THE BIBLE

From the earliest times the study of the tradition was of central importance in the life of the nation. For this reason, the Hebrew Bible contains numerous references to the process of learning. The Book of Joshua, for example, states: 'This book of the law shall not depart out of your mouth, but you shall meditate on it day and night, that you may be careful to do according to all that is written in it' (Joshua 1:8). Again, the Book of Proverbs contains a number of references to the process of education:

Above Orthodox Jewish boys studying the Torah at the Yeshiva Kol Yaakov in Monsey, New York, USA.

'He who spares the rod hates his son' (Proverbs 13:24); 'Train up a child in the way he should go, and when he is old he will not depart from it' (Proverbs 22:6).

When the Israelites returned from Babylonian exile, Scripture records that Ezra gathered the people and taught them the law. When they heard his words, they vowed to observe the religious practices and festivals of their ancestors. According to the rabbis, it was Ezra who instituted the Torah reading on Monday and Thursday when people attended local markets.

Below A rabbi teaching boys Hebrew in a synagogue after school hours, 1891, from the London Illustrated News.

RABBINIC JUDAISM

According to the tradition, parents are obliged to begin a child's education as soon as possible. When the child begins to speak, he should be taught the verse: 'Moses commanded us a law, as a possession for the assembly of Jacob' (Deuteronomy 33:4). During this period the 1st century BCE sage Simeon ben Shetah (120–40BCE) established schools. However, it was his contemporary Joshua ben Gamla who is credited with the establishment of a formal system of education. He decreed that teachers had to be engaged in each locality at the community's expense and all children were to be given an education. Later the Talmud stipulated the size of classes. One teacher was permitted to handle up to 25 students. If students exceeded this number, an assistant was to be hired. More than 40 students required two teachers.

THE PALESTINIAN ACADEMY

Instruction in the law was to be carried out in the Palestinian academy. The first such institution was founded in Javneh after the destruction of the Temple in 70CE. According to tradition, Johanan ben Zakkai (fl. 1st century CE) arranged

Below A male teacher gives a lesson at a religious school for primary-level children in Jerusalem, Israel.

to have himself smuggled out of the city in a coffin. He was then brought before the Roman commander, Vespasian (9–79CE) and requested permission to found a centre of learning. This institution took over from the great Sanhedrin. Later other academies flourished under Johanan ben Zakkai's disciples.

BABYLONIAN ACADEMIES

In Babylon, schools of higher learning were also established in the 1st century CE. In the next century, under the leadership of Rav Shila and Abba bar Abba, the academy of Nehardea became the Babylonian spiritual centre, maintaining contact with the Palestinian Jewish community. When Rav returned to Babylonia from Palestine, he founded another academy at Sura in 200CE. In 259CE the Nehardea acad-

Above Boys in a classroom in Neve Michael Children's Village in Pardes Hanna, Israel, are taught by a woman.

emy was destroyed; under Judah ben Ezekiel it was transferred to Pumbedita where it remained for the next 500 years. From then it functioned in Baghdad until the 13th century.

THE POST-TALMUDIC AND MODERN PERIOD

During the period between the completion of the Talmud in the 6th century CE and the Enlightenment the majority of male Jews received some sort of education. This was generally limited to the study of sacred texts. However, in some periods secular subjects were also included. Prior to Jewish emancipation, the typical pattern of Jewish study involved a teacher with several students who studied religious texts. In the 19th century, organized *yeshivot*, or 'rabbinical seminaries', emerged in eastern Europe. In these institutions students progressed from one level to another – throughout the subject matter was Talmud and halakha, or 'Jewish law'. With the emancipation of Jewry, Jews began to study in secular schools and this has been the pattern up until the present. Jewish religion schools operating alongside secular schooling as well as Jewish day schools now serve as the primary means of Jewish education.

HIGHER EDUCATION AND COURTSHIP

AMONG THE ORTHODOX, JEWISH LEARNING CONTINUES AT A HIGH LEVEL. TRADITIONALLY, YOUNG MEN CONTINUED THEIR EDUCATION IN YESHIVOT OR ACADEMIES DEDICATED TO STUDYING SACRED TEXTS.

For the strictly Orthodox, in the modern world religious education does not end with bar or bat mitzvah. Four years of Jewish high school follow which combine secular and Jewish studies. Then young men go off to a *yeshiva* for several years.

ANCIENT ACADEMIES

A yeshiva (pl. yeshivot) is an academy dedicated to the study of the Talmud and other sacred texts. Academies of higher learning were created in Palestine and Babylonia in the 1st century CE. These institutions kept in contact with one another and attracted students from other lands. In Palestine the most famous was the academy founded by Johanan ben Zakkai (fl. 1st century CE) in Javneh after the destruction of Jerusalem in 70 CE. In Babylonia the academies of Sura and Pumbedita, founded in the 3rd century CE, exerted an enormous influence on Jewish learning.

NON-ORTHODOX YOUTH

Most young people in the Diaspora do not pursue such a rigorous course of study. They go to secular schools and attend Jewish religious schools at the weekend. In non-Orthodox congregations, boys and girls attend confirmation classes, culminating in a confirmation ceremony. Alongside such study, summer camp offers opportunities for Jewish youth to learn about the tradition. Many Jewish children go on a trip to the Holy Land, where they are given a chance to experience Jewish life in Israel.

ORTHODOX COURTSHIP

According to the tradition, marriage is a sacred institution. Jews are expected to marry. Early marriage is the norm for the strictly Orthodox. Boys and girls are taught separately,

Above An engaged couple at a meal, facsimile of Schecken Bible of 1470, painted by Leonardo Bellini of Venice.

THE YESHIVA WORLD

In the 19th century, yeshivot were organized throughout Eastern Europe, however they were destroyed in the Holocaust. After World War II, new yeshivot were set up in the United States, Israel and Europe. Today most yeshivot are organized along the traditional Lithuanian lines. Students generally study in pairs in a large hall; together they argue the meaning of ancient sources. The debate is often conducted in Yiddish as they pore over the Aramaic text. Twice a week, the head of the yeshiva will give a lecture on the portion of the Talmud that is being studied. There is also a moral tutor who gives regular talks on *musar*, or 'ethics'. Such study does not necessarily lead to a career in the practical rabbinate. The majority of graduates earn their living in secular occupations. However, almost every yeshiva has a kolel, an advanced section in which married men and their families are supported as they continue their studies.

Below Male students in a yeshiva in Efrat, an Israeli settlement established in 1983.

Above A couple under a huppah (bridal canopy), 1438, from Jacob ben Asher's Even ha'Ezer, on marriage and divorce.

and they are largely kept apart during adolescence. During a young man's final years at a yeshiva, he is expected to get married and families, friends and teachers are co-opted to find a suitable bride. In the past, in Eastern Europe villages, an official matchmaker organized the brokering between families. Today, this process is more informal. Marriages are not exactly arranged, but parents keep a close eye on the proceedings.

THE NON-ORTHODOX

Most Jewish children go to secular, co-educational schools. They then attend secular universities, often far from home. As a result, parents are able to exert far less control. According to Jewish law, certain marriages have no validity – in particular those that are incestuous, those that are adulterous, and those between a Jew and a gentile. In contemporary society intermarriage poses a major threat to Jewish life. In the past, when Jews were isolated in their own communities or when there was rampant anti-Semitism, the danger of intermarriage was small. Today in the State of Israel, Jews are likely to marry Jews. But in the Diaspora, the rate of intermarriage is very high.

INTERMARRIAGE

The religious establishment is anxious to combat this trend. Part of the drive behind the creation of non-Orthodox Jewish day schools is to help children grow up in a more Jewish milieu. Children are sent to Jewish summer camps where they meet other Jews. There are university Jewish societies, and Jewish single events take place in major cities around the globe.

Parents also exert considerable pressure. In the past, if a child married a gentile, then he or she was cut off from the Jewish community. Today this state of affairs is usually inconceivable, and most families are touched by intermarriage.

SINGLE JEWS

Despite the importance of marriage in the Jewish tradition, a significant number of Jewish men and women remain unmarried. In some cases this is because they are homosexual. Others are happier to live by themselves. Some have had a bad early experience, or simply leave it too long. Non-marriage combined with intermarriage poses a danger to the survival of the Jewish way of life. It has been calculated that if present trends continue, the Jewish community will significantly diminish in size.

Below A group of young Jews in the 1980s at a Jewish summer camp in Saratoga, California.

OUTWARD SIGNS

IN LIVING A JEWISH LIFE, JEWISH ADULTS ARE OBLIGED TO FOLLOW
A RANGE OF LAWS RELATING TO OUTWARD SIGNS. SOME OF THESE
REGULATIONS MUST BE OBSERVED BY MEN, OTHERS BY WOMEN.

All outward signs express determination to fulfil God's will as revealed to Moses on Mount Sinai and interpreted by rabbinic sages.

PHYLACTERIES

Once a Jewish boy has reached the age of maturity, he is required to wear *tefillin*, or 'phylacteries', for prayer. These consist of special boxes containing biblical verses written by hand on parchment. The verses are: (1) Exodus 13:1–10, concerning the laws relating to the dedication of the first born to God's service; (2) Exodus 13:11–16, repeating the laws of the first-born and the commandment to teach children about the miraculous deliverance from slavery in Egypt; (3) Deuteronomy 6:4–9, the first paragraph of the Shema prayer stressing the oneness of God; and (4) Deuteronomy 11:13–21, containing the second paragraph of the Shema prayer on reward and punishment. These boxes are attached to straps. One is placed over the head so that the box sits squarely upon the forehead and between the eyes. The other is wound round the left arm so that the box faces the heart. The strap is placed in a special

Above A prayer book and tefillin, worn to fulfil the law to bind the commandments on hands and before the eyes.

way so that it forms the Hebrew letter *shin*, the first letter of God's name Shaddai – God Almighty.

LAYING TEFILLIN

The action of putting on the boxes is known as laying tefillin. It is an ancient practice and should be observed by all male Jews of bar mitzvah age and above. It is performed every weekday at home or in the synagogue. Phylacteries are not worn on the Sabbath or festivals. The tradition among Ashkenazim is to wind the straps round the arm anti-clockwise whereas the Sephardim wind them clockwise. The Talmud emphasizes the importance of fulfilling this commandment, and it states that even God lays tefillin. Among the Hasidim it is said that if only every male Jew were to perform this duty then the Messiah would come.

THE BEARD

According to Leviticus, it is forbidden to cut the corners of the beard. In the medieval period, it was customary for Jewish men to have beards, and the Talmud describes the beard as the 'ornament of the face'. Later, this biblical verse was interpreted to mean Jews should not shave, but it was permissible to clip facial hair. Today many

Left Jew in Black and White, 1923, by Marc Chagall, showing the characteristic prayer shawl and tefillin.

HEAD COVERING

The skull-cap (*yarmulke* in Yiddish; *kippah* in Hebrew) is one of the most recognizable signs of male Orthodox dress. The practice goes back to the 12th century and may have been introduced to distinguish Jewish from Christian prayer. Today Orthodox men keep their heads covered at all times. Conservative and Reform Jews generally wear a head-covering in the synagogue, but go bare-headed elsewhere.

Jewish men are clean-shaven – they use an electric razor or a chemical depilatory. Among the Hasidim and the strictly Orthodox, the passage from Leviticus is also understood to mean that men should let their *peot*, or side-locks grow.

FRINGES

An element of Orthodox appearance is *tziztzit*, or 'fringes'. According to the Book of Numbers, God told the Israelites to make tassels on the corners of their garments. Orthodox men wear an undergarment with

Below The Rabbi, *1892, by Jan Styka. The leather box and straps are the tefillin and contains four Torah texts.*

fringes on the four corners; these are tied in a particular way to symbolize the numerical value of the name of God. Known as a *tallit katan*, it is largely hidden, though the fringes are brought out above the trouser waistband and are discreetly tucked into a pocket. Similar fringes are put on the four corners of the *tallit gadol*, or 'prayer shawl', which is worn in the synagogue during the morning service. A special blessing is said when both the prayer shawl and the undergarment are put on each day.

MODESTY

Women's dress is characterized by modesty. Traditionally, married women cover their heads, and the Orthodox continue this practice by wearing a wig or by swathing the head in a scarf. Skirts cover the knee and sleeves the elbow. The Book of Deuteronomy teaches that a woman shall not wear anything that pertains to a man, nor shall a man put on a woman's garment. Thus among the strictly Orthodox any unisex garment is perceived as an abomination. However, non-Orthodox women ignore these customs.

Right A customer tries on a wig at a shop in Israel. Many ultra-Orthodox Jewish women cover their heads once they marry to obey religious modesty edicts.

Above A Jewish father wraps his son's arm in phylacteries at his bar mitzvah at the Western Wall, Jerusalem.

FORBIDDEN CLOTH

The Book of Deuteronomy states it is forbidden to wear a *shatnes*, or mingled stuff, such as wool or linen mixed together. This regulation is one of many laws against mixing. Today modern technology can be employed to determine the precise composition of fabrics, and certify the legality of a particular material. The commandment is understood as forbidding the mingling of linen and wool. Any other combination is permissible. Again, this law is ignored by the non-Orthodox.

MARRIAGE

ACCORDING TO TRADITION, MARRIAGE IS GOD'S PLAN FOR HUMANITY.
IN THE JEWISH FAITH IT IS VIEWED AS A SACRED BOND AS WELL AS A
MEANS TO PERSONAL FULFILMENT.

In Judaism the purpose of marriage is to create a Jewish home, have a Jewish family and thereby perpetuate the Jewish community. Marriage is an institution with cosmic significance, legitimized through divine authority. Initially Jews were permitted to have more than one wife, but this practice was banned in Ashkenazi countries by Rabbenu Gershom (*c*.960–1028CE) in 1000. In modern society all Jewish communities follow this ruling.

ANCIENT JUDAISM
In the Bible, marriages were arranged by fathers. Abraham, for example, sent his servant to find a wife for Isaac, and Judah arranged the marriage of his first-born son. When the proposal of marriage was accepted by the girl's father, the nature and amount of the *mohar*, or

Below A classic image of the relationship of husband and wife in this Dutch painting of The Jewish Bride *by Rembrandt, 1667.*

'payment by the groom', was agreed. By Second Temple times, there was a degree of choice in the selection of a bride: on 15th of Av and the Day of Atonement, young men could select their brides from among the girls dancing in the vineyards.

According to tradition, a period of engagement preceded marriage itself. The ceremony was a seven-day occasion for celebration during which love songs were sung in praise of the bride.

In the talmudic period, a major development occurred concerning the mohar. Since it could be used by the father of the bride, a wife could become penniless if her husband divorced or predeceased her. As a consequence, the mohar evolved into the *ketubah*, or 'marriage document', which gave protection to the bride. In addition, the act of marriage changed from being a personal civil procedure to a public religious ceremony, which required the presence of a *minyan*, or 'quorum', and the recitation of prayers.

Above A Jewish couple share in a Passover Seder meal. From a 15th-century illuminated manuscript.

MARRIAGE PROCEDURES
In biblical and rabbinic times marriage was divided into two stages – betrothal and marriage.

Betrothal involved the commitment of a couple to marry and the terms of financial obligations, and also a ceremony establishing a nuptial relationship independent of the wedding ceremony. In the Bible, the betrothal or nuptial ceremony takes place prior to the wedding and is referred to as *erusin*; in the rabbinic period the sages called it *kiddushin* to indicate the bride was forbidden to all men except her husband. According to the Mishnah, the bride could be acquired in marriage in three ways: by money, deed or intercourse. Traditionally, the method involved placing a ring on the bride's finger. At this stage the groom declared: 'Behold, you are consecrated unto me with this ring according to the law of Moses and Israel.' Then the blessing over wine was recited.

After this ceremony the bride remained in her father's house until the *nissuin*, or 'marriage ceremony'. During the second stage of this procedure the *sheva berakhot*, or 'seven blessings', are recited.

THE WEDDING

From the Middle Ages it became customary for Jewish communities to postpone the betrothal ceremony until just before the nissuin wedding ceremony. Prior to the wedding itself, the bride immerses herself in a mikveh, or 'ritual bath', usually on the evening before the ceremony. To facilitate this the wedding date is determined so that it does not occur during her time of menstruation, or the following week. In some Ashkenazi circles the bride when reaching the *huppah*, or 'marriage canopy', is led around the groom seven times. The wedding ceremony can be held anywhere, but from the Middle Ages, the synagogue or synagogue courtyard was commonly used. In modern times, the Orthodox wedding ceremony normally follows a uniform pattern based on traditional law.

Normally the groom signs the ketubah. He is then led to the bride and covers her face with her veil; the couple are next led to the marriage canopy with their parents walking with the groom and the bride. According to custom, those leading the couple carry lighted candles.

Below Marc Chagall painted The Wedding *in 1918, three years after his marriage. The fiddler and house symbolize their wedded state and a baby is drawn on the cheek of the bride.*

When the participants are under the canopy, the rabbi recites the blessing over wine. Then the bride and groom drink from the cup. The groom then recites the traditional formula: 'Behold you are consecrated unto me according to the law of Moses and of Israel.' He then puts the ring on the bride's right index finger. To demonstrate that the act of marriage consists of two ceremonies, the ketubah is read prior to the nissuin ceremony. The seven blessings are

Above Indian–Jewish wedding in Mumbai. Tradition says the Bene Israel were shipwrecked while fleeing persecution in Galilee and reached India some 2,100 years ago.

then recited over a second cup of wine. The ceremony concludes with the groom stepping on a glass and breaking it. Within Conservative and Reform Judaism the wedding service follows the traditional pattern with varying alterations.

THE *SHEVA BERAKHOT* OR SEVEN BLESSINGS

Blessed are you, O Lord Our God, King of the Universe, who creates the fruit of the vine,
• Who has created all things to your glory.
• Creator of man.
• Who has made man in your image, after your likeness ...
• Made she who was barren (Zion) be glad and exult when her children are gathered within her in joy. Blessed are you, O Lord, who makes Zion joyful through her children.
• O make these loved companions greatly to rejoice, even as of old you did gladden your creatures in the Garden of Eden. Blessed are you, O Lord, who makes bridegroom and bride to rejoice.
• Who has created joy and gladness, bridegroom and bride, mirth and exultation, pleasure and delight, love, brotherhood, peace and fellowship. Soon may there be heard in the cities of Judah and in the streets of Jerusalem, the voice of joy and gladness, the voice of the bridegroom and the voice of the bride, the happy sound of bridegrooms from their canopies, and of youths from their feasts of song.
• Blessed are you, O Lord, who makes the bridegroom to rejoice with the bride.

DIVORCE

MARRIAGE IS REGARDED AS AN IDEAL IN JUDAISM, BUT RELATION-
SHIPS BETWEEN MEN AND WOMEN DO BREAK DOWN. JEWS RECOGNIZE
THIS, AND THE BIBLE SPECIFIES A PROCEDURE FOR DIVORCE.

'When a man takes a wife and marries her, if then she finds no favour in his eyes because he has found some indecency in her, he writes her a bill of divorce and puts it in her hand and sends her out of his house' (Deuteronomy 24:1).

BIBLICAL AND RABBINIC LAW
This verse in Deuteronomy stipulates that the power of divorce rests with the husband, and the act of divorce must be in the form of a legal document. Among early rabbinic sages there was disagreement as to the meaning of the term 'indecency'. The School of Shammai interpreted it as referring to unchastity, whereas the School of Hillel understood the term more widely. It was not permitted for divorce to take place in two instances: if a man claimed that his

Below The Bet Din *grants a divorce. From* Jüdisches Ceremoniell *(1717) published by Paul Christian Kirchner, following his conversion to Judaism.*

wife was not a virgin and his charge was disproved; or if he raped a virgin whom he later married. Conversely, a person was not allowed to remarry his divorced wife if she had married someone else and had not been divorced or widowed. Nor could a priest marry a divorced woman.

THE TALMUDIC PERIOD
During the talmudic period, the law of divorce underwent considerable change, including the elaboration of various situations under which a court could compel a husband to divorce his wife. This applied if she remained barren over a period of ten years, if the husband contracted a loathsome disease, if he refused to support her or was not in a position to do so, if he denied his wife her conjugal rights, or if he beat her despite the court's warnings. In these cases the Talmud states that the husband is coerced by the court only to the extent that he would in fact want to divorce his wife.

Above A 1906 edition of the Gittin tractate of the Talmud, which deals with the concepts of divorce.

DIVORCE PROCEDURE
The procedure for a divorce is based on the Code of Jewish Law. The officiating rabbi asks the husband if he gives the get or bill of divorce of his own free will. After receiving the writing materials from a scribe, he

---

THE BILL OF DIVORCE
A get, or 'bill of divorce', is to be drawn up by a scribe following a formula based on mishnaic law. This document is to be written almost entirely in Aramaic on parchment. Once it has been given to the wife, it is retained by the rabbi, who cuts it in a criss-cross fashion so that it cannot be used a second time. The husband then gives the wife a document that affirms that he has been divorced, and may remarry. The wife is permitted to remarry only after 90 days, so as to determine whether she was pregnant at the stage of divorce. This document must be witnessed by two males over the age of 13 who are not related to each other or to the divorcing husband and wife.

Above Marriage breakdown. An estranged couple sit at opposite ends of a sofa, deliberately avoiding each other.

Left A bet din *(rabbinical court)* in Jerusalem granting a divorce for a woman whose husband has left her.

instructs the scribe to write a get. The get is written, and the witnesses should be present during this process. They then make a distinguishing mark on the get. When it is completed, the witnesses read the get. Eventually the rabbi asks the husband if the get was freely given. The wife is then asked if she freely accepts the get.

The rabbi then tells the wife to remove all jewellery from her hands and holds her hands together with open palms upward to receive the bill of divorce. The scribe holds the get and gives it to the rabbi. The rabbi then gives the get to her husband; he holds it in both hands and drops it into the palms of the wife. When the wife receives the bill of divorce, she walks with it a short distance and returns. She gives the get to the rabbi who reads it again. The four corners of the get are cut, and it is placed in the rabbi's files. The husband and wife then receive written statements certifying that their marriage has been dissolved in accordance with Jewish law.

DIVORCE PROCEEDINGS

It is customary for the husband and wife to be present during the divorce proceedings. If this is not possible, Jewish law stipulates an agent can take the place of either party. The husband may appoint an agent to deliver the

get to his wife. If this agent is unable to complete this task, he has the right to appoint another one, and the second agent yet another. The wife can also appoint an agent to receive the get. Thus it is possible for the entire procedure to take place without the husband or wife seeing one another.

NON-ORTHODOX JUDAISM

Since it is the husband who must give the bill of divorce to his wife, if he cannot be located, this presents an insurmountable obstacle. Similarly, in the Diaspora rabbinic scholars have the status of a woman who is an *agunah*, or 'chained person', who is not

able to remarry according to traditional Jewish law. To vitiate this the Conservative movement has called for the insertion of a clause in the marriage contract whereby both groom and bride in grave circumstances agree to abide by the decision of the *bet din*, or 'religious court'. Within Reform Judaism the traditional practice of granting a bill of divorce has been largely abandoned. Instead civil divorce is regarded as valid.

Below At these divorce proceedings in Amsterdam, Netherlands, the Ashkenazi Jew passes a writ of divorce into the hands of a surrogate for his wife.

DEATH AND MOURNING

THE JEWISH RELIGION SPECIFIES A DETAILED PROCEDURE FOR DEALING
WITH THE DEAD. BURIAL SHOULD TAKE PLACE AS SOON AS POSSIBLE AFTER
THE MEMBERS OF THE BURIAL SOCIETY HAVE TAKEN CARE OF THE BODY.

Above At a Jewish cemetery in Budapest, Hungary. The rabbi chants prayers as family members use a shovel to put dirt on the casket in the open grave.

According to Scripture, human beings will return to the dust of the earth (Genesis 3:19). The Bible teaches that burial – especially in the family tomb – was the normal procedure for dealing with the deceased. Such a practice has been superseded by burial in the earth, preceded by a number of procedures. This is followed by a period of mourning for the dead.

THE ONSET OF DEATH
The rabbis of the Talmud decreed that death takes place when respiration has ceased. However, with the development of modern medical technology, this concept has been changed. It is now possible to resuscitate those who previously would have been viewed as dead. For this reason the Orthodox scholar Moshe Sofer (1762–1839) stated that death is considered to have occurred when

there has been respiratory and cardiac arrest. Mosheh Feinstein (1895–1986) ruled that a person is considered to have died with the death of his brain stem. Despite such disagreements, it is generally accepted that a critically ill person who hovers between life and death is alive. It is forbidden to hasten the death of such a person by any positive action. However, it is permitted to remove an external obstacle, which may be preventing death.

DEALING WITH THE DEAD
Once death has been determined, the eyes and mouth of the person are to be closed, and if necessary the mouth is tied shut. The body is then put on the floor, covered with a sheet, and a lighted candle is placed close to the head. Mirrors are covered in the home of the deceased, and any standing water is poured out. A dead body is not to be left unattended, and it is considered a good deed to sit with the person who has died and recite psalms.

BURIAL
The burial of the body should occur as soon as possible. No burial is allowed to take place on the Sabbath or on Yom Kippur, the Day of Atonement, and in contemporary practice it is considered unacceptable for it to take place on the first and last days of a pilgrim festival.

After the members of the burial society have taken care of the body, they prepare it for burial. It is washed and dressed in a white linen shroud. The corpse is then placed in a coffin. Traditional Jews only permit the use of plain wooden coffins. The deceased is then borne to the grave face upwards. Adult males are buried wearing their prayer shawl. A marker should be placed on a newly filled grave, and a tombstone should be erected and unveiled as soon as possible.

Among Reform Jews, burial practice differs from that of the Orthodox. Embalming and cremation are usually permitted and Reform rabbis often officiate at crematoria. Burial may be delayed for several days, and the person who has died is usually buried in normal clothing. No special places are reserved for priests, nor is any separate arrangement made for someone who has committed suicide or married out of the faith.

Below The Acafoth, or seven turns around the coffin. A 1723 French engraving by Bernard Picart.

Right An Orthodox Jew gestures while praying as he stands in a Jewish cemetery on the Mount of Olives in Jerusalem.

BURIAL SERVICE

Despite the differences between Ashkenazi and Sephardi Jews, there are a number of common features of the burial service. In both rites, mourners rend their garments and liturgical verses are chanted by the rabbi as he leads the funeral procession to the cemetery. Often a eulogy is given either in the funeral chapel or as the mourners help to fill the earth. Memorial prayers and a special mourners' kaddish are recited. Mourners present words of comfort to the bereaved, and all wash their hands before leaving the cemetery.

SHIVAH

The mourning period is known as *shivah*, 'seven', and lasts for seven days beginning with the day of burial. During this time mourners sit on the floor or on low cushions or benches and are forbidden to shave, bathe, go to work, study the Torah, engage in sexual relations, wear leather shoes,

Below A mother mourns at the grave of her son in the military section of Mount Herzl cemetery, Jerusalem.

greet others, cut their hair or wear laundered clothing. Through these seven days, it is customary to visit mourners. Those comforting mourners are not to greet them but rather offer words of consolation.

SHELOSHIM

Shivah concludes on the morning of the seventh day and is followed by mourning of a lesser intensity for 30 days known as *sheloshim*, or 'thirty'. At this time mourners are not permitted to cut their hair, shave,

wear new clothes or attend festivities. Those who mourn are not permitted to attend public celebrations or parties. Mourners are to recite kaddish daily throughout the period of mourning. In the case of those whose mourning continues for a year, it is at times customary to recite kaddish till one month or a week before the first anniversary of death.

Below Four sons saying Kaddish over the coffin of their father in the Gaza Strip settlement of Ganei Tal, Israel.

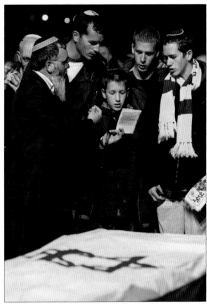

INDEX

Below Challah loaf for the Sabbath.

Above Havdalah lights, wine and spices.

Below Unleavened matzah breads.

ACKNOWLEDGEMENTS

The publisher would like to thank the following for allowing their images to be reproduced in this book.

akg-images: 2, 19t, 24b, 33t, 43t, 48t, 52b, 64, 68t, 70t, 71t, 87, 88t, 106bl, 127tl, 136bl, 140t&b; © Sotheby's 26t, 128b; Bible Land Pictures 101b, 113b; Bildarchiv Pisarek 61tl, 125b; British Library 30t, 35bl, 42bl, 48bl, 49tr, 54b, 70b; Cameraphoto 31t; Erich Lessing 10, 13bl, 30b, 36t, 45b, 48br, 58b, 67t, 86t, 95b; Horizons 130b; IAM 149bl; Israel Images 3, 9, 35br, 53t, 56b, 60t, 63t, 79b, 91bl, 100b, 102, 119b, 128t, 129t, 131t&br, 135b, 141tl, 145t&b, 146b, 148t, 151t, 155bl; Joseph Martin 66t; Jürgen Raible 117b; Laurent Lecat 62b; Rabatti – Dominige 65; RIA Nowosti 105b; Suzanne Held 15tl; ullstein – Archiv Gerstenberg 41b; ullstein bild 27t, 80b, 91t, 109b; World History Archive/IAM 40b.

Alamy: © 19th era 2 131bl; © ASAP 92b; © Eddie Gerald 59br; © Eden Akavia 152t; © Eitan Simanor 108b; © Frances Roberts 53b; © Israel images 55t, 114b; © Lebrecht Music and Arts Photo Library 77b, 152b; © moris kushelevitch 15b; © Nathan Benn 85t, 91br, 107t, 153b; © ohad reinhartz 50t; © Ruby 153tl; © Stefano Paterna 21tr; © The Print Collector 73b.

The Art Archive: 77t, 89tl, 118t; Anagni Cathedral Italy / Collection Dagli Orti 109t; Basilica Aquileia Italy / Collection Dagli Orti 66br; Biblioteca Nacional Lisbon / Gianni Dagli Orti 111bl; Biblioteca Nazionale Marciana Venice / Gianni Dagli Orti 14b; Bibliothèque de l'Arsenal Paris 96bl; Bibliothèque Mazarine Paris / CCI, 22b; Bibliothèque Municipale Amiens / Kharbine-Tapabor / Coll. J.Vigne 119t; Bibliothèque Municipale Moulins / Gianni Dagli Orti 12t; Bibliothèque Municipale Valenciennes / Gianni Dagli Orti 98br;

Below Seder plate of traditional foods eaten at Passover – horseradish, lamb, parsley, bitter herb, haroset and an egg.

Bibliothèque Nationale Paris 42t; Bibliothèque Universitaire de Médecine, Montpellier / Gianni Dagli Orti 89b; Bodleian Library Oxford 25t, /Arch Selden A 5 folio2v, 50b, / Canon Or 62 folio 1r 36b, / Canon or 79 folio 2v 147t, / Laud Or 321 folio127v 99b, / Mich 619 folio 130r 126b, / MS. Reggio 1 fol. 159v 104br, / Opp 776 folio 20v 45t; British Library 4r, 25b, 28, 34br, 83, 96bm, 97bl, 120, 133b, 135t; CCI 44b, 105t, 123t; Collection Antonovich / Gianni Dagli Orti 66bl; Collection Dagli Orti 38b; DeA Picture Library / G. Nimatallah 68b; Fondation Thiers Paris / Gianni Dagli Orti 32b, 55b, 90t, 104bl, 122b, 154b; Gemaldegalerie Dresden 39t; Gianni Dagli Orti 29, 39b, 158; Art Archive, Hermitage Museum Saint Petersburg / SuperStock 94t; Horniman Museum / Eileen Tweedy 75t; Imperial War Museum 116b; Israel Museum Jerusalem / Gianni Dagli Orti 51b; Jewish Museum, New York / SuperStock 18b, 20br, 38t, 41t, 72b, 74t, 93t; Kunsthistorisches Museum Vienna / SuperStock 108t; Library of Congress 49b; Minneapolis Institute of Fine Art / SuperStock 75b; Moldovita Monastery Romania / Collection Dagli Orti 62t; Museo del Bargello Florence / Gianni Dagli Orti 73t; Museo del Prado Madrid 137t; Museum der Stadt Wien / Collection Dagli Orti 90b; Museum of Anatolian Civilisations Ankara / Gianni Dagli Orti 13br; Museum of London 34t, 59bl, 144br; Art Archive, National Gallery London / Eileen Tweedy 76t; Palazzo Comunale Rovigo Italy / Collection Dagli Orti 79t; Palazzo Pitti Florence / Collection Dagli Orti 110b; Private Collection / Gianni Dagli Orti 94b, 95t, 103, 113t; Private Collection Istanbul / Gianni Dagli Orti 134t; Rijksmuseum Amsterdam / SuperStock 139, 150b; Sistine Chapel Vatican / SuperStock 11; St. Peter's Basilica, The Vatican / SuperStock 134b; Steve Raymer / NGS Image Collection, 35t; SuperStock 7t, 46; University Library Istanbul / Gianni Dagli Orti 32t, 47, 98bl, 146t;Victoria and Albert Museum London / V&A Images 69t.

Bridgeman Images: 1, 12b, 34bl, 37t, 42br, 44t, 61b, 72t, 74b, 78t, 101tl, 123bl, 138; Gift of James A. de Rothschild, London 24t; Photo © Bonhams, London, UK 5l; © National Gallery of Scotland, Edinburgh, Scotland 14t; Alinari 37b; Archives Charmet 54t, 69b, 71b, 132b; DaTo Images 43b; Gift of James A. de Rothschild, London 142b; Museo Diocesano de Solsona, Lleida, Spain 26b; Photo © AISA 8–9; Photo © Christie's

Images 126t; Photo © Zev Radovan 5m, 23b, 49tl, 67b, 111br, 112b; The Stieglitz Collection and donated with contribution from Erica & Ludwig Jesselson 142t.

Corbis: © ABIR SULTAN / epa 133tl; © Alfredo Dagli Orti / The Art Archive 60b, 150t; © Andrew Aitchison / In Pictures 33b; © Andrew Holbrooke 144t; © Austrian Archives 63b; © Bettmann 81t, 92t, 117t, 124b; © Chris Hellier 106t; © Christie's Images 6bl, 78b; © Courtesy of Museum of Maritimo (Barcelona), Ramon Manent 31b; © DANIELE LA MONACA / X01660 / Reuters 130t; © Dave Bartruff 112t; © David H. Wells 136br, 147b; © David Rubinger 132t; © Eldad Rafaeli 58t; © ELIANA APONTE / Reuters 149br; © Envision 96t; © Eyal Ofer 141b; © Frans Lanting 40t; © The Gallery Collection 13t; © Gene & Karen Rhoden / Visuals Unlimited 20t; © Gideon Mendel 97t; © Godong / Robert Harding World Imagery 59t; © Hanan Isachar 114t, 125t, 127tr, 136t; © Herbert Spichtinger 17b; © Historical Picture Archive 110t, 118b; © Hulton-Deutsch Collection 80t; IMAGE © Hanan Isachar 82–3, 101tr; © Jim Zuckerman 21b; © John Bryson / Sygma 133tr; © Karen Kasmauski 141tr; © Lalage Snow 81b; © Leland Bobbé 93bl, 111t, 129b; © Luca Tettoni 23t; © Mark Peterson 5r, 143b; © Mark Weiss 106br; © Michael St. Maur Sheil 27b; © NASA 16t, 22t; © Nathan Benn 7b; © Nathan Benn / Ottochrome 56t, 124t, 149t, 154t; © Nik Wheeler 86b; © Nir Alon / Demotix / Demotix / Demotix 107b; © NIR ELIAS / Reuters 155br; © P. Deliss / Godong 144bl; © Pauline St. Denis 99t; © Peter Turnley 51t; © Philadelphia Museum of Art 17t; © Philippe Lissac / Godong 122t; © Richard T. Nowitz 76b, 84, 88b, 93br, 98t, 115; © Robert Mulder / Godong 143t; © Roger Hutchings / In Pictures 19b; © Ron Dahlquist 21tl; © Roy Morsch 123br; © Scott Speakes 104t; © Shai Ginott 61tr; © Sonntag / beyond 153tr; © Steve Raymer 100t; © Sung-Il Kim 18t; © Ted Spiegel 89tr, 121; © Tetra Images / Tetra Images 97br; © Tony Savino / Sygma 116t; © William Whitehurst 20bl.

Photo12: 16b, 57; Eye Ubiquitous 52t; Oronoz 6t.

Rex Features: Alinari 148b, 151b; Europress Photo Agency 137b; Sipa Press 155t.

Shutterstock: Front and back cover – top middle right; Fat Jackey / Shutterstock.com top far left; Felix Lipov / Shutterstock.com top middle left.